Isaiah

Prophet of Righteousness and Justice

מגיד

MAGGID

Yoel Bin-Nun
and
Binyamin Lau

ISAIAH

PROPHET OF RIGHTEOUSNESS
AND JUSTICE

Translated by Sara Daniel

Maggid Books

Isaiah
Prophet of Righteousness and Justice

First English Edition, 2019

Maggid Books
An imprint of Koren Publishers Jerusalem *Ltd.*

POB 8531, New Milford, CT 06776-8531, USA
& POB 4044, Jerusalem 91040, Israel
www.maggidbooks.com

Original Hebrew Edition © Binyamin Lau and Yoel Bin-Nun, 2013
English translation © Koren Publishers Jerusalem, 2019

Cover image: Alex Levin, © Art Levin Studio, Inc. www.artlevin.com

The publication of this book was made possible
through the generous support of *The Jewish Book Trust.*

ISBN 978-1-59264-376-9, *hardcover*

A CIP catalogue record for this title is
available from the British Library

Printed and bound in the United States

This book is dedicated
in memory of
HaRav Yehuda Amital, *zt"l*
איש אשר רוח בו
"A man of spirit" (Num. 27:18)

Contents

Preface.   xi

Introduction: Isaiah the Prophet – a Poet on
the Streets of Jerusalem, by Binyamin Lau   xv

Introduction: Isaiah – an Encounter with
Biblical Innovation, by Yoel Bin-Nun   xxvii

PART ONE: THE DAYS OF UZZIAH

Isaiah Prophesies in Jerusalem (750 BCE)   3

Isaiah 2–4: A Vision of the End of Days –
the Beginning of Isaiah's Prophecy   9

Isaiah 5: The Parable of the Vineyard   19

Isaiah 6: Uzziah's Leprosy and Assyria's Ascent (738 BCE)   31

Jotham Son of Uzziah   47

PART TWO: THE DAYS OF AHAZ

Isaiah 7–8: Isaiah before King Ahaz of Judah
(734–732 BCE)   55

Israel is Conquered and Judah Surrenders (732 BCE)   81

The Kingdoms of Israel and Judah under
Assyrian Rule (731–727 BCE) 93

Isaiah 9:7–10:4: Isaiah's Prophecy of Israel's Shame 97

Ahaz's Final Days: Israel and Judah under Assyrian Rule 103

PART THREE: THE DAYS OF HEZEKIAH

Hezekiah's Revolution: A Return to Former
Glory (727–715 BCE) 111

The Days of Hosea Son of Elah: Samaria's Impending
Destruction (727–722 BCE) 119

Sargon Continues his Military Campaign (717 BCE) 127

Hezekiah's New Vision: A United Kingdom (716–715 BCE) 133

Isaiah 38: Hezekiah Falls Ill 145

Isaiah 39: The Delegation from Babylon 151

The Conquest of Babylonia and the Death
of Sargon (710–705 BCE) 157

The Rise of Sennacherib:
Preparations for Rebellion in Jerusalem (705 BCE) 163

Micah vs. Isaiah: For and Against the Rebellion 167

Sennacherib's Campaign (701 BCE) 183

Isaiah's Prophetic Revolution: From Reproach to Reassurance ... 195

Hezekiah Failed to Sing 201

Isaiah 1: An Overview 205

PART FOUR: THE DAYS OF MANASSEH
BY YOEL BIN-NUN

Isaiah 40–52: Isaiah and His Disciples 213

Isaiah 50–59: Chapters of Persecution – "Innocent Blood"
and Reproach 229

Isaiah 54–58: The Redemption – in Righteousness
and Justice 237

Isaiah 60–64: Complete Redemption and
Devastating Destruction – Vision vs. Reality (III)............... 241

Isaiah 65–66: The Struggle Against
Foreign Worship (II) 247

The Prophetic "Songs of Songs"............................... 253

APPENDICES

Appendix 1: Hezekiah Failed to Sing – the Open
and Closed *Mem* 259

Appendix 2: A Comparison of Isaiah's and
Micah the Morasthite's Visions of Redemption 263

Timeline According to the Commonly Accepted
Chronology... 281

Preface

This book seeks to enrich the encounter between the contemporary Jewish reader and his or her ancient heritage, which is rooted in the Bible.

This encounter is critical for the formation of our Zionist identity with a foundation of sufficient depth and breadth. Zionist society crystallized as a result of the meeting between the Jew and the ancient biblical soil. The State of Israel sprung up out of this consciousness. During the years that followed the establishment of the State, however, society became estranged from its heritage and from the Bible in particular. On the religious front, many perceived Bible studies as a "secular" pursuit, mainly due to the assumptions made in academic circles about the human authorship of the Torah, and the focus on identifying apparent historical discrepancies in the Bible. On the secular front, many feared that the Bible had been "conquered" by the religious world, and was no longer relevant to the lifestyle of the new Israeli.

Recent years have seen an important shift in this paradigm, as the stalwart walls of alienation have begun to crack. The fissures in these walls have created an opportunity for new literary dialogue, which has the power to admit all who wish to enter.

The book you hold in your hand is the product of a dialogue between two very different people, an unlikely partnership. One of us is rooted in the world of exegesis, while the other is drawn to the world of literature. Nonetheless, the storyteller is fond of exegesis, while our exegete craves a good story. Bearing in mind that the whole is greater than the sum of its parts, this encounter motivated the creation of a joint work. Competing discourses gave way to a new language of collaboration and joined hands. The creation of this book demanded that we internalize the principle of "less is more." As we worked, we learned how to conduct even the fiercest of arguments with respect, even love. We pray that this book truly reflects this joining of forces, and that our toil and efforts will indeed blossom and bear the fruit we prayed for.

One of the figures who helped shape our worldviews was Rabbi Yehuda Amital, of blessed memory. For both of us, he was a model of love for Israel, love for Torah, and deep responsibility towards the State of Israel and its institutions. Rabbi Amital was the person who, when founding Yeshivat Har Etzion, made sure that the Bible was given pride of place in the study hall, without apologies. Under his instruction, Bible study became a requisite, integral part of the yeshiva curriculum, and of the worldview of the Torah Jew. He is deeply missed. It is with great love and respect that we dedicate this collaboration to his memory, and wish his entire family a long and fruitful life.

The first three parts of this book focus upon the prophecies that are closely and directly related to events of Isaiah's own time. The first thirty-nine chapters of the book fit this definition. Chapter Forty and onward are referred to as Chapters of Consolation, and transport the reader to prophetic heights far beyond Isaiah's lifetime, toward the distant future of the people's redemption in the Land.

We would like to thank the translator, Sara Daniel, and the team at Maggid Books – Matthew Miller, Reuven Ziegler, Ita Olesker, Shira Finson, Oritt Sinclair, and Carolyn Budow Ben-David – for their hard work in producing the English edition of this book.

The Hebrew edition of this book was originally published in the days leading up to Yom HaAtzma'ut. The Declaration of Independence reads thus:

The State of Israel will be open for Jewish immigration and for the Ingathering of the Exiles; it will foster the development of the country for the benefit of all its inhabitants; it will be based on freedom, justice and peace as envisaged by the prophets of Israel.

There is no doubt that the prophet Isaiah and his visions were one of the leading motivators behind this statement, and behind the characterization of a State that gathers in its exiles and strives for freedom, justice and peace.

We consider this our modest offering to the State of Israel on its birthday. May our reflections upon the history of our people and the words of its prophets be fruitful and meaningful, and may the ship of independence drop anchor and arrive at its harbor upon the shores of peace.

Yoel Bin-Nun   Binyamin Lau

Introduction

Isaiah the Prophet – a Poet on the Streets of Jerusalem

Binyamin Lau

Poetry, Spirit, is the nature of Israel's thought.
Prophecy is poetry, and the entire Torah is called poetry, spirit,
divine inspiration.
In the exile, our poetry was yearning, we hung our harps,
How can we sing the song of God on foreign soil?
And divine inspiration was lost.
In its place came scholarly research, dialectic analysis,
structured study…
Back, back to poetry, to spirit, to divine inspiration
This is the way to revive the days of yore

– Rabbi David HaCohen, the Nazirite, 1923[1]

---

1. Quoted from D. Schwartz, "The Path to the Fountain of Prophecy," in *Prophesy, Son of Man,* ed. O. Zurieli (Jerusalem, 2007), 63 [Hebrew].

A divine poet walked the streets of Jerusalem. His words rose up over the heads of the people who lived in the Golden City. It was the heyday of King Uzziah, the most praiseworthy and promising of the kings of Judah since the days of Solomon. The city grew and prospered with bustling complacency, and only Isaiah etched out the words that he felt in his heart. By day, he gazed up at the spiraling towers of the city; by night, heavenly visions spread themselves out before him, and his eyes constantly darted between the two. As the urban skyline spread out around him, his spiritual turmoil intensified within, until it could no longer be contained.

That was when prophecy burst out.

Isaiah was a poet, a man of the book. He was active in scholarly circles, and his melodious words rang out loftier than everyday speech. People who heard his prophecies mocked these lyrical words: "For with stammering lips and foreign tongue he will speak to this people" (Is. 28:11). Each chapter is a magnificent aesthetic arrangement, a work of art so formidable that many fear to approach it. His words are as marvelous and as daunting as an artifact in a museum. The noise, sights, and smells of the bustling marketplace shatter the reverent silence of Isaiah's ivory tower. Yet Isaiah does not shrink from appearing in public. Sometimes he casts himself in the role of a street-theater actor in order to win the attention of passersby, particularly those with power. He even enlists his own children as props for his prophecies. He is a real person, a family man, a citizen of Judah. He is a character who almost always swims against the tide.

ISAIAH, A PROPHET OF PEACE

Many consider the prophet Isaiah as the prophet of world peace, a utopist who transcends the boundaries of political reality and floats in a vacuum of ideal cosmic harmony. Cast in this role, he becomes the archetype of all prophets of Israel. Thus, for example, Aryeh "Lova" Eliav, an instrumental founder of the State of Israel and of the peace process, wrote:

> Out of all the prophets, the ultimate prophecy is Isaiah's vision of future national and universal peace…the message is simple: peace, peace for all and peace forever. Thus, over two and a half millennia ago, in a small country surrounded by enemies and

consumed with conflict and corruption, a new, tantalizing vision of world peace is conjured up for the first time. Fifteen Hebrew words depict this image: "And they shall beat their swords into plowshares, and their spears into pruning hooks, nation shall not lift sword against nation, nor shall they train for war anymore" (Is. 2:4). These words have been the motto of all those who strive for peace since the days of Isaiah's vision. They have been carved upon stone and inscribed upon parchment, painted, drawn and sung, uttered by politicians and screamed by battle-weary soldiers… How proud I am of the prophets of Israel who stand upon the pinnacle of human hope – the hope for peace."[2]

This vision was a guiding light to Rabbi Abraham Isaac Kook, who viewed World War I as a divine harbinger of the imminent arrival of world peace. The Balfour Declaration and the beginnings of Jewish return to Zion stirred Rabbi Kook to write a messianic vision of world peace in the spirit of Isaiah. In his vision, Israel was to achieve its political goal without violence or war:

> The unwillingness with which we left world politics concealed an element of willingness; [we left] until a happier time, when it will be possible to govern the kingdom without force or barbarity. This is the time we hope for…our souls shudder from the terrible sins that must be committed when governing the kingdom during an evil time. For the time is coming, very soon, when the world will become sweeter and we will be able to prepare ourselves, for we will be able to run our kingdom based upon good, wisdom, virtue and clear divine illumination…It is not worthwhile for Jacob to deal with government during a time of blood, during a time which requires a talent for evil…therefore we were rejected from government, scattered among the nations, and planted deep in the earth, until the time of the pruning will arrive and the voice of the turtledove will be heard in our land.[3]

2. A. Eliav, *Twins of the Gazelle* (Tel Aviv, 2005), 36–37 [Hebrew].
3. Rabbi A. I. Kook, *Orot*, "War," ch.3, 15 [Hebrew].

Rabbi Kook's students were also drawn to this vision of world peace. The complexity of Rabbi Kook's perception of war and peace and its development by his students is beyond the scope of this book; however, I note here two significant examples.[4] During World War II, one of his close disciples, Rabbi David, HaCohen, known as "the Nazirite," wrote in his diary:

> War is a leprous plague upon humanity in our generation and in every generation in history, universal mass murder. Myriads of souls are slaughtered, magnificent buildings and institutions of art and literature are destroyed – Devastation. And whoever manages to kill and destroy and devastate the most is deemed the winner, the reveled victor. We must call out, appeal to the nations, to the people in their masses and the leaders among them, writing articles and books to awaken the movement of peace, to take a firm stance against mass murder – against war.[5]

After World War I, another student of Rabbi Kook's, Moshe Ephraim Ephrati of Ness Ziona, devoted over ten years to the establishment of a world peace organization based on Rabbi Kook's philosophy.[6] Considering the State of Israel's current political reality, this vision of world peace, captured in a sculpture at the United Nations Headquarters in New York City (of a man beating his sword into a plowshare), is a utopian dream that seems far beyond the reach of anyone who lives in the Middle East today.

ISAIAH, A PROPHET OF CONSOLATION

Rather than a figure who calls for peace, many prefer to emphasize Isaiah's role as the national figure of consolation, the one who kindles hope for return and prosperity in the bitter soul of a broken nation. The talmudic sages perceived the Book of Isaiah as a book that deals chiefly

---

4. E. Holzer devoted an entire book to this topic: *A Double Edged Sword* (Jerusalem, 2009) [Hebrew].
5. From the chapter by the Nazirite's son, Rabbi She'ar-Yashuv HaCohen, in *The Book of Harel* [Hebrew], 242.
6. See an article written about him: M. Nachmani, "Peace upon many nations," *Makor Rishon*, February 1, 2013, Shabbat supplement [Hebrew].

with consolation. The Talmud (Bava Batra 14b) presents the books of the prophets in this order: Jeremiah, Ezekiel, and Isaiah. When addressing why Isaiah is presented last even though he preceded the other two chronologically, the Talmud answers:

> Because the Book of Kings ends in destruction, Jeremiah is entirely destruction, Ezekiel begins with destruction and ends in consolation, and Isaiah is entirely consolation. Destruction is placed next to destruction, and consolation is placed next to consolation.

The perception of Isaiah as a book that "is entirely consolation" is reinforced by the *haftara* readings of the seven weeks that follow Tisha B'Av, seven passages of consolation taken from the Book of Isaiah. These seven weeks mark the transition period between the days of mourning and the Days of Awe, weeks that echo with Isaiah's cries of, "Comfort, comfort My people."

ISAIAH AT A POLITICAL CROSSROADS

There is yet another dimension to Isaiah. For decades, he hovered around the royal palace in Jerusalem, a political thinker who sought to undermine what he perceived as problematic governmental inclinations. The image of the future that Isaiah drew is directly related to how he saw the world around him, and how he operated within it.[7]

The main objective of this book is to illuminate this dimension of the prophet's world. This dimension expresses, more than anything else, his call to us today from 2,700 years ago. The events of that period and the prophet's struggles during that time connect his prophecies to our generation as we struggle to fashion Jewish society upon the land of our forefathers. Prophecies pertaining to the political reality can be

---

7. Someone who took particular notice of Isaiah's course of action within society and its politics is Rabbi Yosef Zvi Carlebach, who was murdered in the Holocaust. He wrote a book about the prophets of Israel that was published in German in 1932 and translated into Hebrew in 2012 by Rabbi Zvi Jacobson (and edited by Miriam Gillis Carlebach), *The Three Greatest Prophets: Isaiah, Jeremiah, Ezekiel.*

found in the first thirty-nine chapters of Isaiah. In this clearly marked unit, his words are rousing, tumultuous, daring and explicit, exhibiting no fear or restraint towards the government or the wealthy sectors of society. In its historical context, the prophetic call penetrates deeply, conveying the depth and complexity of the reality that faced the rulers who were being challenged by the prophet. Once these dilemmas are understood, and the protests and warnings of the prophet are heard, there is no escaping the subsequent questions that arise in our own world in the twenty-first century. Our purpose is to transform the reading of the Bible into a living, relevant foundation for living, relevant dialogue.

A BRIEF HISTORY OF JUDAH AND THE WORLD DURING ISAIAH'S TIME

Isaiah's life can be divided into three parts, corresponding to the reigns of three kings of Judah.

Isaiah began his prophetic career in the heyday of King Uzziah of Judah (in the mid-eighth century BCE). Jerusalem boasted a strong, stable army that defeated its enemies to the east (Ammon and Moab) and west (the Philistines); a government that extended the borders of the kingdom (to the south); and diplomatic relations that secured peace and tranquility for the citizens of Judah. To all appearances, the picture was perfect. Yet the prophet still spoke out, penetrating the tranquil veneer and reaching far into the depths behind it. Beneath the prosperous façade, he sensed poverty and pain. He set his sights on the future and saw an exploitative, hedonistic society growing fat and greedy on its own wealth and trampling everything in its wake. In this early chapter of his life, Isaiah can be compared to the prophet Amos, who is mainly concerned with society's segmentation and corruption.

The middle years of Isaiah's career occurred during the rise of the Assyrian Empire, the fall of Samaria (the Kingdom of Israel), and King Ahaz's submission (around 840–830 BCE). During this time, Isaiah addressed issues of political diplomacy, security, and international relations. In Ahaz's time, King Rezin of Aram and King Pekah of Israel fought against Judah. From the text, it seems that there were two competing political factions in Judah at that time; one demanded negotiations with Rezin and Pekah in order to form an alliance and join them in their political aspirations, and the other, with King Ahaz at their head, sought military aid from Assyria in order to fight against Rezin and Pekah. Isaiah's prophecies rejected both of these approaches; he did not wish for Judah to lose their independence to Assyria, and was equally opposed to forming an alliance with Aram and Israel, who in his eyes were unstable empires: "Two smoking stubs of firebrand" (Is. 7:4). This is the stance of one who fights his way upstream, against the spirit of the times. While two political parties wrestled for power, a lone visionary opposed them both. It is no small wonder that he met with bitter disappointment throughout this stage of his career; no one would heed his voice. After Ahaz's submission to Assyria, Isaiah withdrew, defeated by failure. For the first time in the prophetic narrative, we hear the prophet himself waiting for God's word: "And I will wait for the Lord."

With Hezekiah's ascension to the throne, the prophet was spurred back into action. He was filled with hope that the path of the new regime would be guided by the light of the words that God placed in his mouth. At first there seemed to be harmony between the prophet and the king, but as Hezekiah's power grew and he began to take steps towards rebellion and independence, a chasm opened between them. Isaiah began to struggle against Hezekiah as he had struggled against Ahaz. He attempted to dissuade him from rebellion, protested against his ties with Egypt, and objected to the fortification of Jerusalem. However, as before, the king would pay no heed to the prophet's words.

The prophet's consistent calls for political passivity from the kings of Judah fell upon deaf ears every time. His prophecies became the subject of ridicule and scorn; he was accused of being detached from the harsh reality of the real world and its problems.

Ultimately, those who ridiculed the prophet were forced to swallow their own mocking words. The final scene between the king and the prophet consists of Hezekiah pleading to Isaiah to pray for Jerusalem's deliverance. Thus begins the third chapter of Isaiah's prophetic career. In this final section, Isaiah became Jerusalem's protector, lifting the spirits of the people, turning their sights heavenward, and promising peace and consolation for Jerusalem. These prophecies are what render Isaiah into the famous figure of consolation.

Throughout his career, even when he sought to shatter the illusion of financial security and peace, Isaiah never ceased to believe in his city and his people. Even the bleakest of his prophecies, those that warn of destruction and decimation, always contain some grain of hope which will one day bring forth new life. Perhaps this perpetual hope is what transformed Isaiah into the most beloved of prophets.

BETWEEN THE HEAVENLY AND EARTHLY KINGDOMS

Isaiah's political approach is difficult for many to comprehend. According to his worldview, the Jewish state must be governed by God, and God alone. One verse neatly encapsulates this perspective:

> For the Lord is our Judge, the Lord is our lawmaker, the Lord is our king – He will save us. (33:22)

Only one authority can be in charge, and He is the king, the lawmaker, and the judge. Readers of the Bible are familiar with this position from the last of the judges and the first of the prophets – Samuel. It is easy to trace Samuel's influence upon Isaiah's position; the hope for divine rule bursts forth from every sentence of both of their stories. This political approach is based equally upon the goodness of the human heart, upon God's grace, and upon people treating all others with equality. It was this model that Martin Buber sought to establish in Israel in the early days of Zionism.[8] This prophetic outlook challenges the need for earthly leadership and social order. However, the Bible itself questions a nation's ability to live according to this model, which is liable to degenerate into anarchy. The concluding verse of Judges: "In those days there was no king in Israel; each man did what was right in his own eyes," cries out at the injustices that occur in the absence of organized monarchy.[9] Earthly leadership is capable of minimizing the harm that

---

8. M. Buber, *The Kingdom of Heaven*, trans. Yehoshua Amir (Jerusalem, 1965) [Hebrew]. The first edition was published in German in 1932, based on the author's lectures in previous years.
9. See M. Halbertal, "God's Kingship," in *The Jewish Political Tradition*, vol. 1: *Authority*, ed. M. Walzer et al. (New Haven, 2000), 128-132.

one person can inflict on another, as long as it conducts itself according to the principles of *tzedaka* and *mishpat*, righteousness and justice. This is not the place to unravel the intricacies of these key principles; however, the combination of righteousness and justice is the governing force behind leadership that operates according to the letter of the law *as well as* in its spirit. Systems of law and order must allow for compassion for the weak, who may need to circumvent the system.[10] This is the key principle that facilitates the full partnership of earthly and heavenly government, well known to prophets since the time of Abraham, who commanded his family and household to "keep the path of the Lord to do righteousness and justice" (Gen. 18:19). This formula is embedded throughout Isaiah's narrative.[11] When society is run according to righteousness and justice, it will endure. However, when justice (*mishpat*) becomes injustice (*mispaḥ*), and righteousness (*tzedaka*) becomes cries of distress (*tze'aka*), society will collapse.

THE MAKING OF THIS BOOK

When I published my book *Jeremiah: The Fate of a Prophet*, one of the first responses I received was from my teacher, Rabbi Yoel Bin Nun. Since my high school years, he has been a mentor who showed me how the Bible connects to every aspect of contemporary life. For over forty years, together with his peers and students, he has led a fascinating revolution in the way that the Bible is studied in Israel. This revolution was born out of original Jewish thought, loving familiarity with the nuances of the Hebrew language, profound insight into the history of the world and our nation, and deep attachment to the Land. The leading mantra behind this revolution is that the Bible ought to govern each person's spiritual world, particularly now that the Jewish people is back in the Land of Israel, where the Bible is set, and where it was born. Rabbi Yoel Bin-Nun congratulated me on the book's success, especially on its rendition of the prophet's life as a story that could be read and told. Over

---

10. Moshe Weinfeld, *Social Justice in Ancient Israel and in the Ancient Near East* (Jerusalem, 1985) [Hebrew].
11. Isaiah uses the phrase, "righteousness and justice" more than ten times, always as a standard for human leadership.

the course of the conversations that followed, we decided to study the Book of Isaiah together in depth, which led to the birth of this book.

One of the gifts that our generation has been granted is the mind-blowing wealth of information that we have at our fingertips. With a few taps of the keyboard, we have access to sources of knowledge that members of the previous generation would never have dreamed of, not to speak of the generation before them. This wealth of information must be put to good use. We can view the Assyrian armies as they have been documented in museums throughout the world, the maps they used, and the written memoirs that world leaders left behind 2,700 years ago. We have access to the cuneiform records written at that time, which help to fill in the information gaps left by the biblical text. (We must, however, keep in mind that these records were written for the purpose of glorifying the leaders who are mentioned in them, in whose honor these records were kept. The inscriptions decorated their palace walls or tombs).[12] These vast resources (chiefly archaeological and historical) offer a greater understanding of the ancient passages of the Bible. Gaining an understanding of the historical context sheds light on the inner workings of the king and his ministers, enabling us to appreciate what the prophet meant in each situation.

This book does not profess to replace traditional or contemporary commentaries on Isaiah. Rather, it presents the story of a prophet, in the context of the events of his time. His prophecies are an expression of his inner world, and through them, he transmits signals that travel thousands of miles through time and space. Most of Isaiah is in chronological order.[13] Our book is an attempt to hear the pulse of history reverberating through the prophet's lofty, lyrical language. We therefore read each chapter together with its corresponding chapters in Kings and Chronicles, bearing in mind its historical setting and the scholarship

---

12. Archaeologists divide these writings into three types: annals, display inscriptions, and chronicles. For a description of these classifications, see M. Cogan, introduction to *Historical Texts from Assyria and Babylonia: Ninth-Sixth Centuries BCE* (Jerusalem, 2004), 2–17 [Hebrew].

13. There are several exceptions (such as chapters 38–39, the events of which took place before chapters 36–37), and we address these in their correct order, in accordance with the biblical commentaries.

regarding that period. The connection between the ephemeral and the eternal, between poetry and history, is designed to bring the Book of Isaiah closer to you, the reader. The books of the Bible – the prophetic writings in particular – often seem untouchable in their sanctity. My hope is that the story concealed within Isaiah will awaken the desire to listen to the voice of the prophet and that his call for the repair of the Jewish community will be heard and internalized.

Binyamin Lau
Jerusalem
Nisan 5779

Introduction

Isaiah – an Encounter with Biblical Innovation

Yoel Bin-Nun

Pore over the Book of the Lord, and read.

– Isaiah 34:16

More than any other prophet in Israel, Isaiah was involved in interpreting the Torah. His words were full of prophetic interpretations long before the existence of rabbinic midrash. These were not intended as commentary; rather they formed a new prophetic entity out of the holy text. This is not an interpretative metaphor on our part; in several places the prophet states explicitly that he is referring to Torah passages.

The destruction of Edom is described in terms that suggest a return to the beginning of Genesis: "He will stretch out a line of chaos, and the plummet of emptiness" (Is. 34:11). In the same chapter, when describing the birds of prey that nest in these ruins, Isaiah explicitly refers to the lists of unclean birds found in "the Book of the Lord" (cf. Lev. 11 and Deut. 14). Jerusalem's redemption and the ingathering of exiles are described in terms of the exodus from Egypt (Is. 11:15–16; 26:20–21; 27:12–13). Isaiah's criticism of the greatest of the Jerusalemite kings, Solomon and Uzziah (Is. 2:6–11), is based on the laws of kings found in Deuteronomy (Deut. 17:14–20). His prophecy about the crisis of Jerusalem's leadership is phrased in the language of Deuteronomy's passages about leadership: "For behold, the Master the Lord … is removing from Jerusalem and Judah … hero and warrior, judge and prophet, diviner and elder" (Is. 3:1–2). Isaiah's description of the beauty of the daughters of Zion, their clothing and jewelry, holds a clear allusion to the passage about the beautiful captive woman in Deuteronomy (Deut. 21:10–14). However, while in Deuteronomy, the captive is a foreigner and the conqueror an Israelite soldier, Isaiah witnesses the daughters of Zion grieving their city and trying to eradicate their shame. The salvation of the last survivors of Jerusalem is likened to the clouds of glory that sheltered the Israelites as they left Egypt (Is. 4:5–6). The end of days at God's mountain (Is. 2:2) becomes a glorious extension of Israel's national court, described in Deuteronomy: "If a matter shall baffle you in judgment, between blood and blood, plea and plea … you shall arise and go up to the place that the Lord has chosen … according to the law they shall inform you and the judgment they shall tell you, you shall do." (Deut. 17:8–13).

ONE ISAIAH – CONTINUED BY HIS STUDENTS

Amos of Tekoa, an early contemporary of Isaiah, whose work is in dialogue with the wisdom of Proverbs ("for three sins … even four," Amos 1–2; Prov. 30), was a shepherd, a farmer of figs, and a solitary prophetic figure. In contrast, Isaiah was a teacher, a man of the book, and a member of Jerusalem's elite scholarly circles. He had memories of being a student ("the Lord God has given me the tongue of a student" 50:4–9), vast experience as a teacher and guide (8:1–2, 16; 28:9–13; 29:11–13; 30:8–9, 20–21, among others), and above all, students who continued in his way, among them several prophets (Mic. 4:1–3; Nahum 2:1; Hab. 2:2–3, 12–13; Zeph. 3:9–10; 3:14–15; 3:20–21, and others). Isaiah created a school of thought – a prophetic study house – like no other. This is the key to understanding chapters 40–66 (as Amos Hacham hints in his commentary on Isaiah in the *Daat Mikra* series), which I expand upon in Part Four of this book.

In addition to parables of prophetic wisdom (the song of the vineyard in chapter 5; the parable of plowing and threshing, 28:23–29; and so on), Isaiah is brimming with verses of poetic song, including passages that resemble entire Psalms (e.g. Is. 12; 38:9–20). Passages of narrative are woven in throughout the book (7; 38–39; 36–37). In short, the Book of Isaiah is an extraordinary biblical composition, assembling a varied spectrum of biblical mediums.

Here we must ask: How did this extraordinary composition come about?

ISAIAH – FACING THE BEGINNING OF DESTRUCTION AND EXILE

Beyond the remarkable personality of Isaiah son of Amoz himself, did his generation differ significantly from any other generation of kings and prophets? The very fact that at least three other prophets appeared during that era – Hosea, Amos, and Micah (who was influenced by Isaiah) – suggests that this turbulent period had a great impact on prophetic inspiration, and on the encounter between Torah interpretation, wisdom literature, and lyrical poetry.

That turbulent period led Judah and Israel into the throes of destruction and the exile of Samaria. Such suffering had been unknown to the Jewish people since the exodus from Egypt. The nation of Israel found itself scattered among the nations for the first time in history. Ever since, exile has been an inextricable part of Israel's reality. Even the wondrous ingathering of the exiles that has taken place over the past few generations has not yet restored the entire nation to its homeland. The nation and its land have been fragmented since Isaiah's time.

ISAIAH – AT THE CROSSROADS OF BIBLICAL HISTORY

From the devastation of the destruction of Jerusalem and the Second Temple, the Mishna and Talmud emerged. From the destruction of the First Temple, the works of Jeremiah and Ezekiel resulted. The crises that led to the destruction of Samaria and the beginning of the exile generated the dramatic appearance of four prophets at once (Pesaḥim 87a), and an electrifying encounter of the entire range of biblical textual mediums.

For three thousand of the four thousand years of its history, the Land of Israel served as a continental bridgehead with no independent status or history. Egypt ruled the land of Canaan and its surrounding areas before the Israelite conquest and the appearance of the Philistine Sea Peoples. Since Isaiah's day, the land has been ruled by Assyria, Babylonia, Persia, Alexander the Great and his heirs, Rome and its various incarnations, numerous Muslim caliphs, the Ottoman Empire, and finally, the British Mandate.

For a mere few hundred years, the biblical nation of Israel bestowed an independent history and prophetic culture upon the Land of Israel and the entire world. Isaiah and Amos were the first to anticipate the rise of the Assyrian Empire, during those fleeting years when the nation of Israel was united with its land, and they sounded the prophetic trumpet of warning with such intensity and power that their words reverberate painfully until this very day. They understood the implications of the end of Israel's independence all too well. Was the legacy of the exodus from Egypt to be uprooted? How would the nation of Israel survive in the shadows of the empires, scattered and dispersed among the nations?

ISAIAH – VISIONARY OF THE REMNANT, REGROWTH, AND REDEMPTION

At the beginning of his prophetic career (at the start of chapter 2 and in chapter 4), Isaiah already presents his vision of the renewed growth and redemption of the remnant of the people: "On that day, the offshoot of the Lord will be beautiful and glorious, and the fruit of the land will be the pride and glory of the remnant of Israel. And those who are left in Zion, and who have stayed in Jerusalem, will be called holy, everyone who is recorded as the living in Jerusalem" (4:2–3). He repeats this message constantly, throughout his life. Amos also expresses this idea in his characteristically short, sharp words (Amos 9:11–15).

After the devastating deportation of the people of Samaria and some cities of Judah by the king of Assyria, Isaiah bursts forth with his messianic vision of the ingathering of exiles (Is. 11:27). How wondrous, how marvelous for us, to witness this prophecy's fulfillment in the Land of Israel before our very eyes, considering how these ancient visions played such a crucial role in shaping the nation's conceptualization of redemption. Isaiah's words have sustained us and perpetuated Jewish hope for generations, throughout persecution, oppression, and suffering. His prophetic bearing on history has far exceeded the scope of his influence during his lifetime.

WHY IS ISAIAH'S STORY SO FRAGMENTED?

Of all the creative threads that form the tapestry of Isaiah, the narrative thread is the one that is broken up. In chapter 7 we find the beginning of a story (parallel to II Kings 16:5), which trails off in the middle. Several stories are clustered together in chapters 36–37 and in 38–39 (which occurred earlier). These stories also appear, with slight variations, in II Kings (18:13–20:21). But there is no complete story before us, and most chapters of Isaiah remain a mystery. Even if we tease open all its poetic riddles and interpret all its parables, deciphering its lofty, lyrical language, can we be sure which prophecies were uttered in the days of Uzziah? Aside from chapter 7, what other prophecies are from the days of Ahaz? Why does Isaiah walk naked and barefoot for three years (20:2)? How did Isaiah and Hezekiah relate to each other at the start of his reign, and what changed with Sennacherib's invasion? Why is there such tension between the prophet and the king?

Moreover, how are we to understand the discrepancies between the descriptions in Isaiah, Kings and Chronicles, and the profound differences between Isaiah's and Micah's visions of redemption?

In the Torah, the narrative incorporates laws and statutes, commandments and covenants, principles and creeds, poetry, events and crises. The Torah is not merely a legal document, nor an extended covenant, and certainly not a mere book of poetry and prayer. All of these are folded together into a story. Without this story, it would have been impossible to cultivate the collective mindset that the Torah is the book of life because it is our life story.

The same is true of Joshua, Judges and Samuel, and parts of Kings. However, towards the end of Kings, which describes the life of Isaiah and the prophets of his generation, the story becomes fragmented and broken. The void is filled with poetry and parable, and the storyline can no longer be followed. The fragments of narrative and hints scattered throughout the final chapters only emphasize their vast emptiness. Jeremiah is similarly chaotic, despite the relative proliferation of narrative prophecies (most of which are distributed intermittently in chapters 20–36, and continuously in chapters 37–45). The reader is not presented with a complete story.

Is there any correlation between the devastating events that occurred during the lives of Isaiah and the prophets, events that culminated in destruction and exile, and the deep fissures in the biblical narrative?

THE BOOK OF ISAIAH AS A LIFE STORY – THE CONCEPT AND THE BOOK

For over forty years I have taught Isaiah, but never on its own. I teach it together with the Books of Kings and Chronicles, and the works of the prophets (Hosea, Joel, and Amos, as well as Micah, Nahum, Habakkuk, Zephaniah, and Jeremiah). I approach it from a comprehensive historical and biblical perspective, with the aid of documentation left behind by the Assyrian royalty (discovered in archaeological digs in their capital) as well as evidence found in digs in Israel and its surroundings over the past few generations. Even armed with all these sources, there are countless possible opinions and hypotheses. New evidence may appear at any time, challenging the prevalent view and generating new theories, but the proper approach is to make use of all of the information available at the present time.

I turn not only to the Bible and its land, but also to the sacred narrative, a story that was broken off by exile and destruction. How fitting that this act of healing, of piecing together and restoration, should occur during the generation of the return to Zion. How appropriate for our generation to return to the formative and didactic biblical story.

Yet, at the same time, fear wells up in our throats; are we truly worthy? Do we have the proper tools for so lofty a goal? Perhaps it is too presumptuous an act?

And these fears are immediately countered by the cry; dare we exempt ourselves from this mission by resorting to false modesty? Are we truly worthy of the miracle of the ingathering of exiles, of an independent government and life in the land of the prophets? How can we fail to learn from their words, when we live as a nation and state upon holy soil, faced with all the dilemmas of local and world politics?

We cannot go on interpreting lone verses or difficult words, skimming the chapters of Isaiah and the other prophets without attempting to understand them in their entirety. We have not fulfilled the commandment of Torah study if we fail in this.

It is not a mere coincidence that the archaeological and historical findings of recent generations began to emerge just as the nation of Israel was returning to its land to rebuild its State according to the "visions of the prophets" (in the words of Israel's Declaration of Independence).

The answer to our doubts can be found in the words of R. Tarfon at the end of the second chapter of *Pirkei Avot*, "It is not for you to complete the task, but neither are you free to stand aside from it."

"TWO ARE BETTER THAN ONE" (ECCL. 4:9)

While I was engrossed in exegesis and history, and educating students and teachers, gradually building a general perspective on Isaiah and the prophets within the biblical and historical context, Rabbi Benny Lau appeared on the scene. First, he told us the stories of the sages, sketching out their characters and explaining their words in the cultural and historical context. And then, he fearlessly plunged his hands into the seething cauldron of the Bible, and produced a book about Jeremiah, drawing thousands of readers – young and old, scholars and ordinary folk – into the moving story of the most tragic prophet and his world.

I said to him, "Rather than give you all my comments on *Jeremiah*, perhaps you'd like to work together on Isaiah?" Rabbi Benny agreed enthusiastically, without stopping to consider the difficulties that would be involved; how do two people write one book?

I began by giving him all that I had already written on the subject, which was mainly intended for teachers, as well as the works of some of my distinguished students (Rivka Raviv and Yossi Elitzur). Rabbi Benny devoured them all (as he is wont to do), together with the works of scholars and commentators, both traditional and contemporary. Afterwards, we studied together on a weekly basis, and Rabbi Benny began to prepare weekly lectures on the subject for his many followers at the Ramban Synagogue in Jerusalem, where until recently he served as the rabbi.

As an experienced teacher, I have learned that the first chapter of Isaiah contains within it the essence of the entire book, to the extent that to teachers and students alike, every other chapter seems like a mere duplication or paraphrase of the first. Indeed, this book follows Rashi's interpretation of the first chapter of Isaiah; that it stands alone as a summary of Isaiah's entire prophetic career, spanning from the reign of Uzziah to the reign of Hezekiah. We thus infer (following Rabbi David Kimḥi [Radak] on chapter 6) that the first line of chapter 2, "This is what Isaiah son of Amoz saw concerning Judah and Jerusalem," marks the beginning of Isaiah's prophecies, in the days of Uzziah.

In the next stage, Rabbi Benny made notes and outlined chapters, and I commented on them and made revisions, additions and deletions. We did not agree on every point, and there was no lack of arguments (all conducted lovingly from beginning to end). Many new interpretations unfold within these pages, a few of which stirred up such disagreement between us that we considered presenting two different readings of a single chapter (Hezekiah's second coronation over the remnants of the tribes of Israel who came to celebrate Passover in Jerusalem about six years after the destruction of Samaria). Eventually, Rabbi Benny and I agreed that it is indeed best to tell all sides of the story.

Naturally, there remained a disparity between the commentator-researcher and the talented storyteller. When I would fixate upon interpretative accuracy and conceptual depth, honing and unfolding each idea, Rabbi Benny would turn to me and say, "Rav Yoel, this isn't a commentary, it's a story, and a story has to flow."

Yet we managed to achieve our goal; both because I love stories, and see how crucial they are for this generation and generations to come, and because Rabbi Benny loves scholarly research and interpretative nuances, even though some of these did not make it into the book. Others were condensed into footnotes, many of which outline comprehensive studies.

Thus this book was born, like a child, not quite typical of either of its parents, but with its own individual style. It elucidates the structure of the lyrical chapters of Isaiah within their context, and contains new readings and interpretations, historical and scholarly, based on textual and extra-textual findings. All this is presented within a flowing story, which strives to understand the prophet in his own time on the one hand, and on the other, to be applicable to our generation, that of the ingathering of the exiles.

May it be God's will that our words be willingly received in the hearts of readers and students; that they will awaken discussion and dialogue, and inspire new readings and interpretations. And may we merit to bring the words of the prophets, as the word of God, closer and more beloved to our generation and future generations.

Yoel Bin-Nun
Alon Shvut
Nisan 5779

Part One
The Days of Uzziah

Of all the political figures in the Bible, no one came closer to the spirit of our time than Uzziah, king of Judah. He understood the importance of strengthening his military and developing its proficiency and weaponry. But this wise and heroic king was not content with military conquest. He understood that he must develop the land, expand its borders, and make the wilderness bloom. Together with military reinforcement, the expansion of settlement, and conquest of the southern shore, came unprecedented spiritual and cultural blossoming. In Uzziah's time the prophets of the great books arose: Amos, Hosea, and Isaiah, who bequeathed a Torah of justice, kindness and human solidarity, and a vision of the final redemption, to the Jewish nation and to humanity, as no one in Israel or the nations had ever done before.

– David Ben-Gurion, from a lecture on "The Significance of the Negev"
Sde Boker, January 17, 1955

Isaiah Prophesies in Jerusalem (750 BCE)

I saiah son of Amoz stood in the courtyard of his study house in Jerusalem. He stared up at the new towers that broke the northern skyline of the city. Immaculate soldiers in crisp Judahite uniforms stood in the nearby square. They bore shiny weapons, the likes of which had not been seen in Jerusalem for decades. This was the new Royal Guard, the keepers of the new towers and of King Uzziah's palace. The young soldiers, like the students who thronged to his study house, could not remember the bleak darkness that had once engulfed the city. Isaiah himself could only remember the great excitement that had followed that period. He and his cousin Uzziah were born in the midst of the revolution.[1]

MEMORIES OF DAYS OF DEVASTATION

Fifty years earlier, at the turn of the eighth century BCE, no one referred to Judah as a "kingdom." Residents of the south were vulnerable to Amalekite and Edomite attacks, and to being kidnapped and sold as slaves along the eastern trade routes. Arameans threatened the northern front,

---

1. Isaiah's personal background and his blood relation to Uzziah is based on Sota 10b, "Amoz and Amaziah were brothers." It is evident that out of all the prophets, Isaiah was the closest to the throne.

oppressing the residents of the Galilee and Gilead. Judah's northern neighboring state, Israel, hovered at the brink of destruction. The Arameans overwhelmed their land with merciless chariots, and there seemed to be little hope of overcoming their tyranny. Everyone could sense that the end was near, and no neighboring state volunteered to help Israel. The ears of the oldest citizens still rang with the prophet Elisha's harsh warnings that described what King Hazael of Aram would do to Israel:

> Because I know what harm you will do to the Israelite people: you will set their fortresses on fire, put their young men to the sword, dash their little ones in pieces, and rip open their pregnant women. (II Kings 8:12)

The Aramean army soon crushed the Israelite army, leaving only fifty riders and ten chariots intact (II Kings 13:7). The Kingdom of Israel was on the verge of collapse. Judah witnessed the destruction of its sister-state, Samaria, and knew that its end was also imminent. King Hazael of Aram had already conquered Gath, the neighboring Philistine city, and was headed towards Jerusalem.

THE REJECTION OF JEHOASH AND THE ASCENSION OF AMAZIAH, THE FATHER OF UZZIAH

Then, suddenly, everything changed. The Aramean army left the area, and its soldiers marched to a new, unexpected front. The Assyrian Empire had encroached upon Aram's northern border, threatening its very existence. The border between Aram and Israel was suddenly abandoned in Aram's fight for survival. Assyria's attack had saved Israel and Judah, and the echoes of war faded from the Jerusalem streets. All was quiet; the land was saved.

The ensuing days were wrought with confusion, as panic followed the momentary relief. The Judahite officers who had stood on the coastal frontline returned to the city, and spread the report of their frustration at the king's weak military conduct. In Jerusalem, in the Temple itself, a prophet-priest was murdered for condemning the king's departure from the path of the Torah. Rebellion led to Jehoash of Judah's assassination by his own servants. Isaiah's earliest memories were of his uncle Amaziah sitting on the royal throne in Jerusalem, with his son Uzziah by his side.

He remembered well the atmosphere in his home, everyone talking the military lingo of conflict and conquest. Amaziah strove to restore peace to the southern border and reopen the trade routes to the east, and the army began to prepare for largescale war. The political and intellectual figures bickered among themselves; should they form an alliance with their northern neighbors, the Kingdom of Israel? Isaiah was old enough to remember these debates well. The news that Edom had been conquered and its prisoners killed reached Jerusalem, and the city began to celebrate. At this point, Uncle Amaziah, heady with victory, challenged the Israelite king, Jehoash, who had also just been freed from the threat of the Aramean sword. Jehoash was not interested in war, but when Amaziah persevered, the two met in battle in Beit Shemesh, in Judah. Amaziah was captured by the Israelites, who brought him to Jerusalem as a prisoner of war. The humiliated Jerusalemites opened the royal and Temple treasuries to the Israelite victors. Thus, loaded with spoils and the triumph of victory, King Jehoash of Israel returned to Samaria. At this point, antipathy towards Amaziah gradually grew until he fled to Lachish, where he met his death. For the last fifteen years of Amaziah's life, his son Uzziah effectively ruled in his place.

Isaiah kept to his studies. There, in the study house next to the palace, physically close and yet far removed from politics, a holy fire began to burn within him. His nights were filled with visions and fiery revelations. In his dreams he saw the prophet Samuel turning Israel's hearts back towards their Father in heaven. By day, he would gather students to his classroom and fill their ears with the words of God.

THE WAVE OF CONSTRUCTION AND THE FORTIFICATION OF JERUSALEM

Until the age of thirty, Uzziah governed the royal household. His father had been cast out, driven to the fortified city of Lachish, while Uzziah's power grew. After his father's death, he decided to build up the defeated people of whom he was now the ruler, to transform them into an exalted nation. His vision created a new golden age for the once proud city. A frenzy of building lifted the nation from gloom to euphoria. Judah's military doubled in size and glory; the defense industry had never known better days. The people, encouraged, found new land to cultivate. Blue skies shone over the bustling kingdom.

During those early years, Isaiah was ensconced in his study house, although he did not fail to take delight in his cousin Uzziah's efforts to restore Judah's former glory. Sometimes, for his young students, he would attempt to conjure up a picture of Jerusalem in the old days; its gloom and shame. The new generation could not imagine the poverty. They were born into a generation of financial stability, of open, peaceful borders, and of prosperity and free trade. The kingdom spread out in all directions. Uzziah's construction exceeded that of all his predecessors. In addition to Jerusalem's fortification, Uzziah saw to the development of industry, to the construction of towers and strongholds in the desert, and to the paving of the roads leading to the new harbor in Etzion Geber, near Eilat. Only Solomon's kingdom could have competed with the power and might of Uzziah's realm.

The neighboring kingdom, Israel, also grew beyond recognition. Freed from Aramean oppression, it flourished and achieved a level of prosperity that it had not known for many years. This transformation was begun by King Jehoash and maintained by his son Jeroboam II, who ruled for over forty years, the longest of any king in Israel.[2]

Uzziah and Jeroboam maintained an unwritten agreement regarding the distribution of conquered territories. Judah sprawled all the way to the south of Edom and to the west of the Philistine lands. Israel conquered Aramean territory as far as Damascus and Hamat, and also spread into its Ammonite and Moabite borders. Both kingdoms felt invulnerable on every front.

DRUNK ON POWER

The years passed, with Uzziah and Jeroboam growing ever more powerful. By the mid-eighth century BCE, the two kings had become convinced of their invincibility. Gradually, drunk on their power, they began to lose proportion, their arrogance spiraling like the haughty towers of the city. The kingdom's glorious majesty descended into decadence;

---

2. For a description of Jerusalem's might and power in the days of Uzziah, see H. Raviv, *Society in the Kingdoms of Israel and Judea* (Jerusalem, 1993), 164–66 [Hebrew]. For a description of King Jeroboam II's reign, see M. Haran, "The Rise and Fall of the Kingdom of Jeroboam Son of Jehoash," *Zion* 31 (1966): 33–38 [Hebrew].

corruption infiltrated the city's power systems, as those with means and power began to lord over those without. Underneath Jerusalem's golden veneer, rot had begun to set in. Those who held key economic positions developed close relations with those who had influence in the government, creating a tight, impenetrable inner circle that had the power to crush everyone beneath them. This circle was tight enough to conceal its violence and corruption from the eyes of the king, who sat upon his throne, reveling in the magnificence of his kingdom.

Jeroboam's arrogance is addressed in the Book of Amos, the Judean prophet, who paid a swiftly truncated visit to Samaria. Amos' prophecies, uttered during a time of tranquil prosperity, were met with indignant fury by the priests of Beit El and the Israelite government, and the prophet was ousted from Israelite borders: "Away with you, visionary!" (Amos 7:12).

At the same time, Isaiah also began to sense danger in the intoxicating power that had seized Uzziah and the citizens of Jerusalem. Uzziah ruled over his entire kingdom with a mighty hand, and all were in awe of him. Even the intellectuals and spiritual leaders of that generation, the prophets and their disciples, saw the kingdom's political and military power as the fulfillment of the divine will.

At this point, in the mid-eighth century BCE, decades after Uzziah's first victories and achievements, Isaiah first stood up in his well-established study house opposite the palace of the king, and began to prophesy.

7

Isaiah 2–4

A Vision of the End of Days – the Beginning of Isaiah's Prophecy

U zziah's arrogance, as well as the state of the formidable and oppressive kingdom, sparked in Isaiah a vision despairing of earthly government. If the upright and noble Uzziah, one of Judah's greatest kings (comparable to Solomon himself), had become contaminated with the sin of pride, what hope remained for mortal kingship? If the vast conquest that restored Jerusalem to its former glory had resulted in a corrupt generation, then what good had it actually achieved?

Isaiah's new mindset harked back to the days of the prototypical prophet, Samuel. Like Samuel, Isaiah sought to form a modest people, aware of its own transience and limitations, living as courteous guests upon the Land and not as its masters, and striving to prioritize all that is right and just. He began giving a series of lectures expressing his new vision – that God, and only God, is the king. We have no interest in an earthly king, only a heavenly one. Moved by the political reality of an earthly kingdom drunk on power, Isaiah lifted up his eyes and looked to the distant future, to the end of days:

> In the days to come, the mount of the Lord's house shall stand firm
> above the mountains And tower above the hills; and all the nations
> shall gaze on it with joy. And the many peoples shall go and say: Come,
> let us go up to the mount of the Lord, to the house of the God of
> Jacob; that He may instruct us in His ways, and that we may walk in
> His paths. For instruction shall come forth from Zion, the word of
> the Lord from Jerusalem. Thus He will judge among the nations and
> arbitrate for the many peoples, and they shall beat their swords into
> plowshares and their spears into pruning hooks: Nation shall not take
> up sword against nation; they shall never again know war. (Is. 2:1–4)

Isaiah begins his prophecy with a symbolic call. The mountain of the
House of God will be lifted up, its light drawing all nations to it.[1] Isaiah's
vision united the entire world in a utopian dream. Against a harsh historical reality of wars and endless cruel conquests, Isaiah presented the
ultimate vision of world peace.[2]

THE STUDIO OF THE PROPHET-COMMENTATOR

Isaiah was a man of the study house. His methodological approach was
to read the words of the Torah with careful attention, forming prophecies that commented and expounded upon the Torah (preceding rabbinic midrash by a thousand years).[3] His prophecies ring with echoes
of lyrical poetry and wisdom literature.

---

1. As a resident of Jerusalem, Isaiah knew that the Temple Mount was low in relation
   to his surroundings. For the ambiguity of the expression *aḥarit hayamim* – "the end
   of days," see: Y. Peleg, "Two Readings of the Vision of the End of Days," *Shnaton:
   An Annual for Biblical and Ancient Near Eastern Studies* 20 (2010): 45–57 [Hebrew].
2. Y. Kaufmann, *The Religion of Israel: From Its Beginnings to the Babylonian Exile*, vol. 3,
   book 1 (Tel Aviv, 1960), 204–5 [Hebrew]. Kaufmann claims that this is the first universal prophecy of its kind. This prophecy's tremendous impact on the entire world
   is reflected in a sculpture in the United Nations Headquarters Sculpture Garden,
   Let Us Beat Swords into Plowshares. Although the disparity between the vision and
   the current reality seems unbridgeable and painful, the international recognition of
   Isaiah's words promises hope for the future. A comparison of Isaiah's vision and
   Micah's is brought in Appendix 2 of this book.
3. For a development of Isaiah's homiletic approach in chapters 1–4, see: A. HaCohen, "The
   Order of the Prophecies in Chapters 1–4 of Isaiah," *Megadim* 4 (1988): 55–62 [Hebrew].

Deuteronomy contains a blueprint for a moral society:

> If a matter shall baffle you in judgment, between blood and blood, plea and plea ... You shall arise and go up to the place that the Lord has chosen ... According to the law they shall inform you and the judgment they shall tell you, you shall do. (17:8–11)

In chapter 2 of Isaiah, the prophet reformulates this legal passage within a prophetic context.[4] Here, God is presented as a supreme judge who presides over the entire world.

The following verses also express despair at the institution of mortal monarchy, and the longing for heavenly governance:

> O House of Jacob, let us go and walk in the light of the Lord. For you, the House of Jacob, have abandoned your people. They have been influenced by the east, and practice divination like the Philistines, and are fixated with the children of foreigners; and his land is filled with silver and gold, and there is no end to his treasures; and his land is filled with horses, and there is no end to his chariots; and his land is filled with idolatry, they bow down to his own handiwork, to that which his own fingers have crafted. (Is. 2:5–8)

In Deuteronomy, the aforementioned legal passage is immediately followed by the section regarding the king, which opens with "When you come to the land," and contains dire warnings about the dangers of a corrupt king's arrogance:

---

4. The parallel language between the two passages is clear and could not be incidental: "You shall arise and go up" (Deut. 17:8) / "Come, let us go up" (Is. 2:3); "To the place that the Lord has chosen" (Deut. 17:8) / "To the mountain of the Lord" (Is. 2:3); "To the law they shall inform you" (Deut. 17:10) / "He will show us of His ways" (Is. 2:3); "According to the Torah that will be shown to you" (Deut. 17:11) / "The Torah will come from Zion" (Is. 2:3); and others. However, instead of giving a parallel reference to the differentiation between "blood and blood" (Deut. 17:8), Isaiah mentions the transformation of weapons into agricultural tools, and the end of warfare.

Only he must not acquire many horses for himself, so that he will not bring his people to return to Egypt in order to acquire many horses, for the Lord said to you: Do not ever go back again, to return that way anymore, and he must not acquire many wives, so that his heart will not turn astray; and he must not acquire too much silver and gold. (Deut. 17:15–17)

Isaiah read out the verses of Deuteronomy to his students, and simultaneously pointed out the glory of Jerusalem, which grew ever stronger under his cousin Uzziah's rule. Before his very eyes, Isaiah saw how the list of prohibitions was being transgressed, one by one: "And his land is filled with silver and gold … and his land is filled with horses … and his land is filled with idolatry" (Is. 2:7–8). The passage in Deuteronomy ends by defining the purpose behind these warnings: "So that his heart will not be lifted up over his brothers, and not turn astray from the commandment, neither right or left" (Deut. 17:20). Isaiah witnessed how this warning was being tragically fulfilled; how disgrace and corruption were flourishing as a result of arrogance and prosperity: "The lofty look of man shall be humbled, and mortal arrogance shall be bowed down, and the Lord alone shall be lifted up" (Is. 2:10).

Two great and mighty kings are alluded to in this prophecy: Solomon and Uzziah. Isaiah recognized Uzziah's aspirations to restore the glory of Solomon's kingdom to Jerusalem, and also recalled the terrible crisis that followed Solomon's reign, when the kingdom split. He was fearful as this prophecy burst from him, but those around him paid no heed. They had all sunk into a content stupor, drunk on their own victory. Uzziah's kingdom was in its heyday. Assyria had yet to appear on the Judean horizon. Uzziah's military continued its conquests in all directions, and complacency ruled at home. Isaiah's was a lone voice, anxious and apprehensive. He sensed that trouble was stirring. His prophetic seismograph detected a pending earthquake. But no one noticed, and no one cared.

CEASE TO GLORIFY MAN

At this stage, Isaiah's prophecy was concerned with showing how strength and power does not come from man, but rather from God. He pleaded with his listeners to look beneath the surface, and to recognize that one who is powerful today may be persecuted tomorrow: "A man is bowed down and a person is brought down low, do not hold them in esteem" (2:9).

In his vision, Isaiah saw the day of God, a day of fateful upheaval, when the arrogance of humanity will be humbled and "the Lord alone will be lifted up," and the shambles of mortal rule will make way for Heavenly rule. He surveyed all of Uzziah's greatest enterprises and described how they will crumble:

> Go deep into the rock, bury yourselves in the ground, before the terror of the Lord and His dread majesty! Man's haughty look shall be brought low, and the pride of mortals shall be humbled. None but the Lord shall be exalted on that day. For the Lord of Hosts has ready a day against all that is proud and arrogant, against all that is lofty – so that it is brought low: Against all the cedars of Lebanon, tall and stately, and all the oaks of Bashan; against all the high mountains and all the lofty hills; against every soaring tower and every mighty wall; against all the ships of Tarshish and all the gallant barks. Then man's haughtiness shall be humbled and the pride of man brought low. None but the Lord shall be exalted in that day. As for idols, they shall vanish completely. And men shall enter caverns in the rock and hollows in the ground – before the terror of the Lord and His dread majesty, when He comes forth to overawe the earth. On that day, men shall fling away, to the flying foxes and the bats, the idols of silver and the idols of gold which they made for worshiping. And they shall enter the clefts in the rocks and the crevices in the cliffs, before the terror of the Lord and His dread majesty, when He comes forth to overawe the earth. Oh, cease to glorify man, who has but breath in his nostrils! For by what does he merit esteem? (2:10–22)

The prophets dealt extensively with the concept of "the day of the Lord." They contended that there was a fundamental disparity between the popular perception of this day – an eagerly awaited manifestation of God's might and vengeance upon the wicked – and the actual, terrible reality of the day of the Lord, when those who eagerly await it will be crushed by the might of His hand. This was expressed by Amos, who prophesied in Samaria at the same time as Isaiah prophesied in Judah. Amos witnessed people's anticipation of the "day of the Lord," and shattered their fantasies:

> Woe to those who long for the day of the Lord – why do you long for the day of the Lord, for it is darkness and not light; like one fleeing from a lion, only to meet a bear; like one who arrives home and rests his hand on the wall, only to be bitten by a snake; for the day of the Lord is darkness, not light; pitch-black without a glimmer. (Amos 5:18–20)

Like Amos, Isaiah sought to shake the people from their pleasant daydreams, and to make them realize that the path they walked led to a terrible Day of Judgment – the day of the Lord.

CHAPTER 3: DEGRADATION

In chapter 3, Isaiah continues to describe the crisis that will follow this indulgent, decadent era:

> For behold, the Lord, the Lord Almighty, is removing supply and support from Jerusalem and Judah…Hero and warrior, judge and prophet, diviner and elder; the captain of fifty and the man of honor, counselor and artisan and the eloquent orator. (3:1–3)

Isaiah scrutinized the chain of command of his day, and found it to be hopeless. Out of all those who bore the burden of leadership, none would take responsibility. This path would shortly lead to anarchy, where only the fittest survive, and violence rules:

> And I shall give youths as their ministers, and babes shall rule over them. And the people shall oppress each other, man against man, and man against his friend; youth shall be insolent to elder, and the lowly to the honorable; until a man will grab one of his brothers of his father's house –You have clothes, be our leader, take charge of this disaster! (3:4–6)

As subjects of Uzziah, mightiest of the kings of Judah, the prophet's audience found it difficult to relate Isaiah's harsh words to their time. The scene he depicted seemed irrelevant to them. However, it would later become clear that the prophet could see just over the horizon, to a time when Uzziah lost control and the people were left without leadership.

Next, Isaiah began to preach about the evils of slavery:

> The Lord rises to plead, and stands to judge the nations; the Lord comes to trial against the elders of His people and its ministers: It is you who has destroyed my vineyard; the plunder from the poor is in your houses. (3:13–14)

The disparity between the social classes was flagrant. The prophet would walk the streets of Jerusalem and encounter women who were dolled up in extravagant finery, haughty and decadent:

> And the Lord says: Because the daughters of Zion are haughty, walking with outstretched necks and flirtatious eyes, walking along with mincing steps, their legs tinkling. (3:16)

The prophet mocked their proud display by listing dozens of garments, jewels and trinkets. His words jangled with merry extravagance, but they concealed a poisonous sting, for these luxuries were to be replaced with rags. This is Isaiah's way; he is a poet whose weapon is words. He concludes his parody with a tragic prediction:

> Instead of perfume will be a rotten stench; instead of sash, bandage; instead of coiffure, baldness; instead of finery, sackcloth; instead of beauty, blistering. (3:24)

Instead of the fine scents the women used to exude, the daughters of Zion will give off a rotten stench. They will no longer embellish their clothing with decorative belts; rather, they will wrap their wounds with bandages. Bald patches will mottle their once-beautiful heads of hair. Their festive, richly adorned clothes will be replaced with sackcloth, and their clear young skin will be blemished with festering, burning blisters.[5]

Walking the streets of Jerusalem, Isaiah saw only violation and vanity, but the unbearable words of his prophecy transcended the borders of the reality, touching upon a not-too-distant future.

CHAPTER 4: SOLACE IN DIVINE GOVERNMENT

Isaiah's opening prophecy began with a description of the divine hand that governs reality. He continued with a description of the destruction of Uzziah's power-drunk government, and then concluded as he had begun:

> And over the entire site of Mount Zion and all her assemblies, the Lord will create a cloud of smoke by day and a blaze of flaming fire by night, and a canopy shall stretch over all the glory; and it shall be for shelter and shade from the blaze of day, and for refuge and cover from storm and from rain. (4:2–6)

When God restores the Divine Presence to Zion after the humiliating defeat of the earthly government, the clouds of glory will reappear. The pillar of cloud by day, and the pillar of fire by night, will serve as "shelter and shade," just as they did after the exodus from Egypt. Rabbi Akiva refers to this prophecy in his exegesis on the verse: "And they encamped in Sukkot" (Num. 33:5):

> "And they journeyed from Sukkot and encamped in Etam. Etam is a place, just like Sukkot is a place. R. Akiva says: Sukkot is [not a place] but the clouds of glory, as it says, "Over the entire site

---

5. "Instead of beauty, blistering." In Hebrew, *ki taḥat yofi* – Radak explains that *ki* here is derived from the word *kviyya*, burn. "Instead of beauty" recalls the passage in Deuteronomy regarding a beautiful captive woman who must return to Israel without her clothes and jewelry, bewail the loss of her father and mother, and become the wife of the one who captured her. Isaiah's prophecy reinterprets the passage in Deuteronomy, applying it to the situation of the daughters of Zion after the war that he anticipates; they shall return to the land stripped of all their beauty, desperately seeking a man who will cover up their shame.

of Mount Zion…the Lord will create a cloud of smoke by day, and a blaze of flaming fire by night, and a canopy shall stretch over all the glory." (Is. 4:5) This has happened in the past; from where do we learn that it will happen in the future? The verse states: "It shall be for shelter (*vesukka*) and shade by day" (Is. 4:6). (*Mekhilta DeRabbi Yishmael, Beshallaḥ*)

Rabbi Akiva delves into the verse in Isaiah and discovers the prophet's reinterpretation. The "sukka" that sheltered the Children of Israel in the desert was the cloud of glory, an expression of ultimate protection and divine governance. This protection will be restored in the future, when God will return to Israel after it has sunk into a grim reality.[6]

In chapters 2–4, Isaiah anticipated the end of days, which was far-removed from his present reality. Through prophetic exegesis, he expressed his frustration at the institution of earthly government. This frustration would only grow in the years that followed.

---

6. However, in the Talmud, R. Eliezer says that the sukkot were the clouds of glory, while Rabbi Akiva argues that they were huts (Sukka 11b).

Isaiah 5

The Parable of the Vineyard

At this stage, Isaiah saw harsh visions. His thoughts wandered to higher realms, and addressed fundamental questions in relation to God's selection of Israel. He saw the Day of Judgment approaching, stood in his study house, and asked, "How can we be sure that Israel, the chosen people, will still be God's chosen people after the day of the Lord? Is God's choice temporary or eternal? If a king as great as Uzziah has led his kingdom to corruption and degradation, how can there be hope for the people of this land?"

This chapter, which opens with the "parable of the vineyard,"[1] addresses these fundamental questions. Isaiah contended with deep theological issues by way of parables, which encouraged dialogue among his students, as well as engagement with the spiritual realms from within the human world.

---

1. A literary analysis of this chapter can be found in L. Frankel, *Chapters in the Bible* (Jerusalem, 1981), also available at http://mikranet.cet.ac.il/pages/item. asp?item=4650 [Hebrew]. Y. Felix offers a botanical-agricultural reading in *Nature and Land in the Bible* (Jerusalem, 1992), 153–58, also available at http://www.daat. ac.il/daat/tanach/achronim/mishley-2.htm [Hebrew].

The prophet introduces his friend, who planted a vineyard in fertile soil, and did all in his power to cultivate its growth:

> I will sing now of my friend, a song of my beloved's vineyard – my friend had a vineyard on a fertile hillside, and he dug it and cleared it of stones and he planted it with the choicest of vines, and he built a tower within it, and hewed out a winepress within it – and he hoped it would produce good grapes, but it produced bad grapes. (5:1–2)

The prophet described the owner's devotion to his vineyard. Both Isaiah and his listeners were well aware of the labor involved in planting on the Judean hills; its rocky terrain requires particular effort, and there is much work to be done even before beginning to plant. The ground must be dug up to expose the stones, which must be removed or utilized as a fence. The prophet's friend chose the ideal spot for a vineyard – a fertile hillside[2] – and prepared it for planting. First, he dug it up,[3] cultivating it, which enabled the soil to be plowed and smoothed out. Next, he removed the large stones and arranged them into a fence. He planted the choicest, most select of vines in this fertile, soft soil, and he was so sure of its success that he even built a watchtower and a winepress. But despite his efforts, the choice vine, and the fertile soil, he suffered grave disappointment, "he hoped that it would produce good grapes, but it produced bad grapes."

Why did the vineyard produce "bad grapes," and what do these "bad grapes" represent?[4] The song of the vineyard, its opening evocative

---

2. *Keren ben shamen* – A fertile hillside – In the fertile hills where olives are grown (for their oil; *shemen*). In Judah the lower areas, such as Bethlehem and Tekoa, were areas of olive farming, whereas vineyards were usually planted in the higher areas, such as the Hebron Hills.

3. The Hebrew word for "dug it," *vayazzkehu*, is a unique word in the Bible, and is interpreted as "hoed" in rabbinic literature, "and it was found hoed under his olive tree" (Menaḥot 85b).

4. Rashi, among other commentators, explains the word *veasim*, bad grapes, as being derived from the word for "stench". For example, at the end of the plague of frogs the verse states: "and the land stank" (*uteveasim ha'aretz*), (Ex. 8:10), from the dead frogs. This word hints at plague and disease. Others explain that this kind of bad grape is a translucent grape that fills out and ripens too soon, never reaching full ripeness, and is therefore never suitable for wine making.

of the Song of Songs, is transformed from an ode into a lamentation. The "beloved" (owner) then turns to the dwellers of Jerusalem and Judah, asking them to judge him and his vineyard, claiming that he did all in his power to ensure the success of his crop:[5]

> And now, dweller of Jerusalem, person of Judah: Judge between Me and My vineyard. What more could be done for My vineyard that I did not do? Why did I hope for it to produce good grapes, but it produced bad grapes? (5:3–4)

Of course, the question is rhetorical; the prophet provides the answer. After appealing to the dwellers of Jerusalem, the beloved vineyard tender decrees:[6]

> And now, I will tell you what I shall do to my vineyard: Remove its fence, and it will be destroyed. Break down its wall, and it will be trampled. I will leave it as a wasteland, without pruning or weeding and thorn and thistle will grow, and I will command the clouds not to rain down upon it. (5:5–6)

The vineyard tender feels anger towards his vineyard for producing bad fruit, and unleashes his wrath upon it. The fence and the wall, previously unmentioned, further convey how much effort was put into this vineyard.[7] Removing the fence exposes the vineyard to grazing

---

5. This description recalls the description of the neglected vineyard in Proverbs, which chiefly teaches lazy owners about the importance of proper care:

   I went by the field of a lazy man, and by the vineyard of a senseless man; and behold, it was all overgrown with thorns, and thistles had covered it over, and its stone wall was broken down. Then I saw, and considered it well: I looked upon it and learned a lesson. A little sleep, a little dozing, a little arms folded to lie down, and poverty shall come along like a marauder, and lack like an armed man. (Prov. 24:30–34)

6. In contrast to the parable of the poor man's lamb (II Sam. 12:1–6), where the prophet Nathan asks David to judge the case, and after he unknowingly judges his own actions ("The man must die, and pay the lamb's worth four times over!"), Nathan reveals the moral of the parable ("You are the man").

7. To this day, traditional vineyards in Judea and Samaria are surrounded by stone walls that mark their boundaries and prevent the entrance of animals. These walls do

goats, and removing the stone wall allows cattle and sheep to enter and trample the vines.

After the vineyard tender removes the vineyard's protection, he ceases to care for it, "leav[ing] it as a wasteland, without pruning or weeding." No longer will he prune its vines, or even the wild shoots which threaten its fruit. No longer will he turn its soil, leaving it instead to form a hard crust which prevents proper ventilation and water absorption.

Only after this friend has unleashed his frustration upon the rogue vineyard is another secret revealed, "I will command the clouds not to rain down upon it." With this statement, the vineyard tender's true identity is revealed to the prophet's audience. The friend, the vineyard tender, is He who makes the rain fall. The parable's end reveals the identity of the true Master of the vineyard, who is at once its tender, judge, and executioner.[8]

INJUSTICE AND CRIES OF DISTRESS

At this stage, Isaiah plainly states the moral of the story:

> For the vineyard of the Lord of Hosts is the House of Israel, and the people of Judah He planted for His delight, and he hoped for justice (*mishpat*), and behold, there is injustice (*mispaḥ*); for righteousness (*tzedaka*), and behold, cries of distress (*tze'aka*). (5:7)

Uzziah's mighty conquests and intense fortification of the city, which restored Judah's political glory, did not improve society's morality or justice. Isaiah's wordplay – *mishpat-mispaḥ* and *tzedaka-tze'aka* – expresses the corruption of the Kingdom of Judah. Instead of being a source of

---

not, however, prevent nimble goats from entering, so most construct a fence of thorns on top of the wall. The vast damage caused by goats led to a decree in the time of Joshua forbidding the raising of goats in inhabited areas of the Land. Goat herding was permissible only in rural areas, "Let them graze in the woodland" (Bava Kamma 81a).

8. The vineyard constituted a central part of Judah's agriculture, and an inextricable part of their lifestyle, so it is no surprise that this motif was used in the parables of several prophets. Jeremiah also expresses his frustration at Judah thus: "And I had planted you, a choice vine of entirely true seed, and how you turned into a degenerate, alien plant" (Jer. 21).

justice, the judicial system became a system of corruption and contamination. *Tzedaka*, a concept that expresses both righteousness and charity, and signifies the spreading of kindness and mercy beyond the letter of the law, is no more; it has been replaced by *tze'aka* – screams, shouts, and cries of distress.

THE CRIES OF THE OPPRESSED AND THE DESTITUTE IS TEARING THE HEAVENS

The Bible is brimming with the cries of the oppressed. The first cries are heard from the downtrodden of Sodom, who were being crushed by a cruel regime that perceived charity as an offense. Moments before the destruction of Sodom and Gomorrah, God descended to see: "if what they have done is as bad as the cry that has reached Me" (Gen. 18:21).

One of the most memorable cries is that which bursts out from the hearts of Israel, enslaved and oppressed in Egypt:

> And it came to pass during that long period, that the king of Egypt died, and the Children of Israel groaned from the labor and they cried out, and their supplication arose to God out of the labor. (Ex. 2:23)

Pharaoh's death must have given birth to a fleeting hope of relief, but alas, it was quickly snuffed out. Nothing changed when the new Pharaoh ascended the throne, and the Children of Israel could no longer bear the back-breaking labor. God alone hears the cries of lost, rootless and powerless slaves. This cry was the beginning of Israel's redemption from Egypt, and it is mentioned at the burning bush, where God informs Moses of his mission to deliver Israel from the oppressive hands of Egypt:

> And the Lord said: I have surely seen the affliction of my people who are in Egypt, and I have heard their cries before their taskmasters, for I know their pain. (3:7)

The Torah commands us to preserve this cry in our collective memory:

> And you shall not mistreat or oppress a stranger, for you were strangers in the land of Egypt. You shall not exploit the widow or the orphan; for if you exploit them, and if they cry out to Me, I will surely hear their cry, and I shall unleash My wrath against you and smite you by the sword, and your own wives shall become widows, and your own children orphans. (22:20–23)

Israel is supposed to harness the power of the law for the protection of the underbelly of society: "for you were strangers in the land of Egypt." The widow and the orphan are considered vulnerable, and their cries of distress will not go unheard. If society does not answer these cries, then God will hear them.

ISAIAH'S LAMENTATIONS IN UZZIAH'S TIME

When Isaiah stated, "Behold, cries of distress," the reader understands that these cries have reached God's ears, and that consequences will soon follow. The parable of the vineyard piqued his audience's interest and provided a fitting background for the description of the sins of Judahite society. Isaiah then began lamenting the fate of Jerusalem, which had conducted itself like Sodom. Each stanza of this lamentation begins with the cry of "woe," an expression which moved his audience to heart-rending weeping.

THE FIRST LAMENTATION: OVERSTEPPING, COVETOUS PROPRIETORS

> Woe to those who join house to house, that lay field to field until there is no room, and you shall live alone in the land; the Lord of Hosts declared to my ears: Will not these great houses become desolate, spacious and splendid, yet empty of inhabitants; for ten acres of vineyard will produce but a measure of wine, and a field planted with ten measures of seed will produce but a measure of grain. (Is. 5:8–10)

"Those who join house to house" were neighbors who exploited their building rights, building right up to the boundaries of their properties and even surpassing them at times, to the extent that their enormous houses touched one another and there was no public space or public property.[9]

In his lamentation, Isaiah depicted society as a reincarnation of Sodom, a greedy, possessive society obsessed with monetary gain and the acquisition of property. He bewailed the implications of such a reality: "And you shall live alone in the land." Rashi's interpretation further emphasizes this image, extending the estrangement between people to estrangement between the nation and their Father in heaven:

> And you shall live alone in the land – You think that neither the Holy One, blessed be He, nor the poor, have a share in the land. You are stealing His share of the tithes, and the land from the poor, so that you alone will occupy it. (Rashi ad loc.)

God's reaction follows the principle of "measure for measure." The expanded houses will become empty and uninhabited, and the yield of the vast fields will be inversely proportional to their size. Greed and excess will result in the land's desolation.

THE SECOND LAMENTATION: DRUNKEN REVELRY IN JERUSALEM

> Woe to those who arise early in the morning, chasing drink, who stay up late into the night, inflamed with wine; there are harps and lyres, drums and flutes and wine at their feasts, and they regard not the deeds of the Lord, look not to the work of His hands; therefore, my people will be exiled without foreknowledge, and those of honor will die of hunger, and its multitudes

---

9. In ancient times, the space in between houses was intended for the homeless. This was an unwritten social obligation, based on the principle of commensalism, where one benefits and the other suffers no loss. The poor benefited from this space, and the neighboring houses would not have benefited from it anyway. The sages spoke out against the "attributes of Sodom" (Bava Kamma 21b), that is, those of means are required to allow the poor to live on the edges of their property so that the society will not resemble that of Sodom.

will be parched with thirst; therefore, She'ol will widen its throat and open its gaping jaws without measure, into it will descend its nobility and multitudes, its rowdy and its revelers; and humanity will be bowed down, people will be humbled, arrogant eyes will be humbled; and the Lord of Hosts shall be exalted through His judgment, the Holy God made holy in righteousness; and sheep shall graze as if it were their pasture, and the lambs of wandering strangers shall feed among the ruins. (5:11–17)

Isaiah conjured up a portrait of wealthy people who were unable to see what was to come, as from early in the morning until late at night they were involved in hedonistic pursuits, drinking wine and seeking pleasure. The impending exile would come as a shock to them, "without foreknowledge." the underworld would soon open its gaping jaws and swallow the pleasure seekers.[10]

At the same time as Isaiah was prophesying in Judah, Amos prophesied in Israel. He, too, opened his description of sin and punishment with the cry, "woe," and described the proud, complacent atmosphere of Jeroboam's thriving kingdom:

Who lie on ivory beds, and lounge on couches, and dine on choice lambs, and fattened calves; who pluck at the strings of the lyre, fancying themselves like David, who drink wine by the bowlful, and anoint themselves with the finest of oils, who fear not for the ruin of Joseph; therefore they will now be exiled first, turned away from their lounging with cries. (Amos 6:4–7)

---

10. Two years before World War I, which brought about Europe's collapse, the Titanic, a magnificent cruise ship, sunk after hitting an iceberg. As the ship's lower levels began to fill with icy water, the revelers on deck, unaware that many of them were about to be swallowed into the ocean's yawning depths, kept dancing, and the music played on. Reading about the Titanic, and the captain's stubborn refusal to take proper safety measures, adamant about its invincibility, one understands the words of the prophet Isaiah around 2860 years earlier. The prophet perceived the people of Judah and Israel as oblivious passengers, dancing on the deck of a ship that was about to sink into the gaping jaws of the Assyrian Empire (although it is not mentioned by name in this chapter).

The leaders of the kingdom, only recently released from the aggressive Arameans, who had overwhelmed the Gilead region with "iron chariots," suddenly experienced military and economic success the likes of which they had never known. The Arameans retreated to their northern border, leaving their southern region vulnerable to Jeroboam II's invasion. Samarian society gorged themselves on their newfound prosperity, as wealth replaced good values. Members of the ruling class lounged on beds inlaid with ivory, feasting, completely unaware of the exile and disaster that loomed around the corner.

Chapter 5 of Isaiah describes the Kingdom of Judah in Uzziah's day, which was much like the corrupt, decadent scene playing out in Samaria. Isaiah's despair of the kingship of Judah resurfaced, and he warned that when there is no justice or righteousness in the land, only God will remain, "And humanity will be bowed down, people will be humbled...the Lord of Hosts shall be exalted through His judgment, the Holy God made holy in righteousness."

THE THIRD LAMENTATION: GOD'S WRATH

Woe to those who draw iniquity along with ropes of deceit, and sin as with cart ropes, who say, let Him make haste, and quickly do His deeds, so that we may see, let the decree of the Holy One of Israel draw near and come, so that we may know it;

Woe to those who deem evil good, and good evil, who claim darkness is light and light is darkness, who claim bitter is sweet and sweet is bitter;

Woe to those who are wise in their own eyes, who see themselves as prudent;

Woe to those who mightily drink wine, who valiantly pour strong drink; who acquit the guilty for a bribe, and deny justice to the innocent; therefore, as a tongue of flame consumes straw, and as dry grass disintegrates in fire, their roots shall become rotten and their flowers will blow away like dust; for they have rejected the

27

> Torah of the Lord of Hosts, and spurned the word of the Holy
> One of Israel; therefore, the Lord's wrath shall burn against His
> people, and He shall raise His hand against them and strike them,
> and the mountains will quake, and their corpses shall lie like
> refuse in the streets, yet for all this, His anger is not yet abated,
> and His hand is still stretched out. (Is. 5:18–25)

In this lamentation, the prophet repeated (three times) themes which he had expressed in his previous lamentations; he bewailed the blindness that renders darkness into light and bitter into sweet, and he again described drunkenness and the perversion of justice through bribery. This stanza opens with a unique metaphor: "Woe to those who draw iniquity along with ropes of deceit, and sin as with cart ropes." Just as a strong rope is woven of many strands, heavy sin is composed of many minor corruptions.[11]

The metaphor used by the prophet described the nation calling for a hastening of the end; they wanted to force the wagon forward by pulling on its ropes: "Let Him make haste, and quickly do His deeds, so that we may see." These words may be read in a cynical tone, mocking the prophet's prediction of disaster: "Let the decree of the Holy One of Israel draw near and come, so that we may know it." Another possible reading of the nation's words is that they truly were eagerly anticipating the day of the Lord, sure of their own salvation (similarly to Amos' prophecy, mentioned earlier). The prophet responded by describing the figurative fire that the Lord will ignite in Judah, which will spread like "a tongue of flame consumes straw, and as dry grass disintegrates in fire." This fire will consume the people of Judah, whose corpses will lie rotting in the streets. Moreover, the prophet warned, there is more to come: "Yet for all this, His anger is not yet abated, and His hand is still stretched out." This is not consolation, but harsh reproach, as we shall see in chapter 9. God was warning that the blows will continue to escalate until the Assyrian invasion.

---

11. The sages extended this metaphor by likening the thin, almost invisible threads that gradually form a thick, powerful rope, to the subtle methods that the evil inclination employs to tempt us to sin: "What are cart ropes? R. Asi said: The evil inclination; at first it is as thin as a thread, and eventually resembles a thick cart rope" (Sanhedrin 99b).

THE FOURTH LAMENTATION: ENEMY
TROOPS WILL DARKEN THE LAND

There is a classic device found in biblical poetry, referred to as "the three-four sequence." This pattern is discussed by Yair Zakovitch:

> The subject of this work is a biblical literary device, the three-four sequence, a literary unit made up of four tiers. The first three repeat each other, and do not usually progress or develop from component to component. The fourth component, however, contains a dramatic turn, whose change is the main objective, the climax, of the literary unit in question.[12]

This model can be applied to Isaiah's "lamentations" in chapter 5. In the first three stanzas, the prophet describes Jerusalem's corruption and punishment. Now, in the fourth lamentation, the prophecy takes a dramatic turn. Suddenly, the destruction takes on a palpable shape and form. The final stanza presents a vivid description of the enemy who will descend upon the land:

> He lifts up a banner for the distant nations, and whistles for them from the ends of the earth, and behold, they are coming, swiftly and lightly, no one is tired or weary, no one is slumbering or sleeping, not a girdle has loosened, and not a shoelace has broken; he whose arrows are sharp, and all his bows are at the ready. Their horses' hooves seem like flint, and their wheels like a storm; their roar is like a lion's, they roar and growl like a young lion, they will seize their prey and carry it off, and there is no savior; and they will roar upon it on that day like the roar of the sea, and looking to the land, there is only stifling darkness, and the light has darkened in the heavens. (5:26–30)

Isaiah described the bold figure of the enemy who will come from afar, in a reinterpretation of the words of reproach in Deuteronomy:

---

12. Y. Zakovitch, introduction to "The Pattern of the Numerical Sequence Three-Four in the Bible" (PhD diss., Hebrew University of Jerusalem, 1979) [Hebrew].

> The Lord will bring a nation upon you from afar, from the ends
> of the earth, as the eagle soars, a nation whose tongue you have
> never heard, a brazen nation without respect for the old or pity
> for the young. (Deut. 28:49–50)

Isaiah did not mention this enemy's name, but it would have been
impossible not to recognize that he was referring to the Assyrian army.[13]
The fierce cavalry and storming chariots decided the greatest conquests
of the Assyrian military, which included the armies of its subordinate
nations ("the distant nations"). Although the Assyrian army had not
yet reached the region of Judah in Uzziah's time, Isaiah described them
with startling accuracy.[14] Moreover, the enemy's anonymity may serve
to emphasize the fact that it was really an extension of the One who
sent it. As Isaiah explicitly says later on, "Woe to Assyria, rod of My
wrath" (10:5).

This prophecy, which began with the parable of the vineyard,
concludes with Isaiah lifting his eyes, not to heaven, but to the all too
real threat of the enemy sharpening its swords just over the northern
horizon. The enemy had yet to arrive, but Isaiah heard the clash of its
weapons and the pounding of hoofbeats, and knew that it was only a
matter of time before darkness fell upon the already slumbering Kingdom of Judah.

---

13. Some claim that at this stage, Isaiah was not yet familiar with the Assyrian army, and
thus imagined the mighty army about to sweep through the land: a swift, organized,
alert, well-equipped force with sharp arrows and chariots at the ready. However, only
those familiar with the Assyrian army could have described it so accurately. The king
of Assyria, Ashurnasirpal II (883–859 BCE), established his fierce cavalry in order to
scatter the ambushes that lay in wait for his chariots. Since the time of Tiglath-Pileser,
the Assyrian forces secured victory after victory, to the point that Isaiah quotes him
as having said, "Like one who gathers stray eggs, I gathered all the land, with nary a
wing flap or a single chirp" (10:14).

14. Some commentators explain the omission of Assyria's name in this chapter as a way
of retaining this prophecy's relevance for generations to come, however it may have
been calculated to increase the impact of the prophecy; a more obscure description
of the enemy creates a more threatening prophecy. See A. Hacham, *Isaiah* (*Daat
Mikra*), 64 [Hebrew].

Isaiah 6

Uzziah's Leprosy and Assyria's Ascent (738 BCE)

POLITICAL CONTEXT: 745 BCE – TIGLATH-PILESER III'S ASCENT TO THE THRONE

The year 745 BCE saw a rebellion in the Assyrian capital, Kalhu, which is referred to today as Nimrud.[1] The citizens of Assyria had known glory in the days of Shalmaneser III, nearly a century before, when Assyria was the most powerful empire in Mesopotamia. In the decades that followed, however, the empire had been weakened by internal political struggles and rebellions. Assyria was still strong enough to threaten the Kingdom of Aram, but its internal crises and shaky security shook the people's faith in their government, who were eventually overthrown.

The throne was seized by Tiglath-Pileser III, a man of the military, who may (or may not) have been of royal blood. He opened a new chapter in Assyrian history, successfully implementing major changes in its political and military action, as well as a sophisticated administrative system, including empire-wide postal and information services. These revolutionary changes reignited the Assyrian dream of conquering the world.

---

1. Assyria was situated in today's northern Iraq, next to Mosul, in the Nineveh Province.

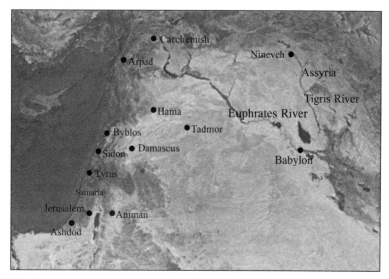

Map of Assyria

In 740 BCE, after a few years of military victories in the east and the north, Tiglath-Pileser ventured west, fighting against Arpad and Hama in northern Syria, and then south, to Damascus and Israel. An Assyrian display inscription dated 738 BCE describes a local rebellion against Tiglath-Pileser.[2] This inscription does not mention how the rebellion broke out, but from a careful comparison to biblical verses and the list of kings who paid tribute to Assyria,[3] it is possible to learn who participated: The kings of the Lebanon Mountain, the Hermon, the coastal towns, Byblos, Tyrus, Hama, Arpad and Carchemish, King Rezin of Damascus and King Menahem of Samaria (see below). According to the inscription, one of the leaders of the rebellion was "Azariah". A characteristic Israelite or Judahite name, scholars have identified it with King Uzziah of Judah, who is referred to in the Bible as both "Uzziah" and "Azariah."[4]

---

2. This display inscription, which contains the word "Azariah" is catalogued in Cogan, *Historical Texts*, 34–36.
3. A. Damsky, *A Guide to External Sources of Israel's History in Biblical Times* (Ramat Gan, 1982), 43–44 [Hebrew].
4. One hundred fifty years ago, there was an attempt to join together two broken inscriptions. One contained the name "Azariah," and the other *"Ya'uda,"*

However, no king, nor any such alliance, was able to stand up to Tiglath-Pileser, who conquered the surrounding nations like "one who gathers stray eggs" (Is. 10:14). The local rulers' recognition of Assyria's supremacy is reflected in the list of kings who paid taxes to Tiglath-Pileser in 738 BCE.

The Assyrian ruler began to work his way towards Egypt, seeking dominion over Aram and Israel along the way. In his third conquest, in 734–732 BCE, he conquered Damascus and defeated Samaria, and that entire region became part of the Assyrian commonwealth.

KING MENAHEM OF ISRAEL'S SURRENDER (738 BCE)

After the death of Jeroboam II, the Kingdom of Israel rapidly fell into decline. The Bible documents fierce struggles over who was to inherit his kingdom (II Kings 15:8–26). Jeroboam's son, Zechariah, ruled for six months before Shallum son of Jabesh conspired against him and ruled in his place. Barely a month passed before he was assassinated by Menahem son of Gadi, who then took the throne.

This stormy period shook the Kingdom of Israel, and eventually led to Samaria's destruction and the exile of most of the tribes of Israel. It is possible to identify various forces that weakened the Kingdom of Israel from the inside, leading to its collapse. The tribes who lived in the Transjordan undermined the kingdom's central government in Samaria, which was controlled by the tribes of Joseph. This power struggle was the underlying cause of the revolutions that weakened Israel's entire infrastructure. Isaiah, who witnessed this decline from his vantage point in Judah, described it thus:

---

the Assyrian word for Judah. However, this was challenged and rejected, and N. Na'aman's study, "The Assyrian Missions to Judea in Light of New Assyrian Evidence," *Shnaton: An Annual for Biblical and Ancient Near Eastern Studies* 2 (1977): 164–80 [Hebrew], proved that the second piece belonged to a tablet from Hezekiah's time. Regardless, the connection between Azariah/Uzziah and Tiglath-Pileser remains feasible. This led H. Tadmor to conclude that Uzziah still reigned as a king of international acclaim in the year 738 BCE (before he became ill), see, "King Azariah of Judah in Assyrian inscriptions," in B. Mazer, ed., *In the Days of the First Temple* (Jerusalem, 1962), 158–93 [Hebrew].

> Through the wrath of God, the land is scorched, and the
> people shall be kindling for its fire, and no one shall spare his
> brother; on the right, they will devour, and still hunger, on
> the left they will consume, and not be satisfied, people will
> consume the flesh of their own arm; Manasseh will feed on
> Ephraim, and Ephraim on Manasseh, together, they will be
> against Judah. (9:18–20)

The first two verses describe the conflict between "the right" and "the left,"
that is, the south and north of Israel. The third verse moves on to the
struggle between the Israelite tribes of Ephraim and Manasseh, and how
they will eventually unite against a common enemy, Judah. The prophet
Hosea's description of the battle-scene completes the terrible picture:

> Gilead is a city of evildoers, stained with bloody footprints, as
> marauders lie in ambush, so do its bands of priests, they murder
> on the road to Shechem, committing treachery. (Hosea 6:8–9)

Soon after Zechariah son of Jeroboam ascended the throne, the kingdom began to collapse. After about a century of stability – the four generations of Jehu's dynasty – an eastern wind blew in from the Gilead,
claiming the crown for itself. This was no underground rebellion, but
an open act of defiance, committed "before the people" (II Kings 15:10),
for all to see. However, the reign of Shallum son of Jabesh lasted for just
a month before he was murdered by Menahem son of Gadi of Tirzah,
in Samaria. His cruel despotism enabled his survival for a full decade:

> Then Menahem smote Tiphsah and everyone in it, and its bor-
> ders from Tirzah, for they would not open to him, so he smote
> it, and he slashed open all its pregnant women. (II Kings 15:16)

Many have found this verse difficult to understand.[5] Most modern
scholars hold that Tiphsah was an important city in the Kingdom of

---

5. Haran, "Rise and Fall," 29–33, proposes that Tiphsah is the city of Thapsacus, situated along the western banks of the Euphrates, which had been at the edge of King

Samaria.[6] According to this reading, this verse depicts the governmental deterioration that had occurred since Jeroboam's death. Menahem first conquered Tirzah and then made his way up to Samaria, where he seized government of the kingdom. He then continued until he got to the borders of Ephraim and Manasseh (perhaps in Tapuah), where he completed his cruel campaign. His brutality culminated with the murder of the city's pregnant women. This act was common among foreign conquerors, such as Ammon and Aram (II Kings 8:12; Amos 1:13), and possibly Assyria (Hosea 14:1). Menahem seems to have been influenced by Israel's violent neighbors.

Menahem reigned for ten years, but times were still turbulent. His son Pekahiah was assassinated by Pekah son of Remaliah, with the help of fifty men from Gilead (II Kings 15:25). The tribes of the Gilead may have been autonomous during that decade. Towards the end of his life, Menahem became subordinate to Tiglath-Pileser, as the Book of Kings testifies:

> King Pulu of Assyria came to the Land, and Menahem gave a thousand talents of silver to Pulu to join in alliance with him, to retain his own kingdom, and Menahem exacted the silver from Israel and all its warriors, to pay the king of Assyria, fifty shekels of silver per person, and the king of Assyria returned and did not stay in the Land. (II Kings 15:19–20)

Pulu is Tiglath-Pileser's Babylonian name, a mark of honor for the Assyrian king, who also ruled over the venerable ancient Babylon.[7]

Solomon's glorified empire (I Kings 5:4). Nevertheless, it is difficult to believe that Menahem's kingdom reached that far.

6. *Encyclopedia Biblica*, s.v. "Menahem." (Jerusalem, 1978), 31 [Hebrew].

7. Ibid., 32. This name, however, has only been found in later Babylonian records, and therefore there is some doubt regarding the identification of Pulu as Tiglath-Pileser. The Book of Chronicles appears to refer to two different kings, "And the God of Israel stirred up the spirit of Pul king of Assyria, **and** the spirit of Tiglath-Pileser king of Assyria, who took the Reubenites, the Gadites, and half of Manasseh into exile" (I Chr. 5:26). The word for "took into exile" is in the singular form, however. Yehiel Bin-Nun, in his book *The Land of Moriah: Bible and Language Studies* (Alon Shvut, 2006), 196–206 [Hebrew], notes many instances, including this verse, where

The Assyrian records mention Menahem's surrender thus: "I have received tribute from ... Rezin of Damascus, and Menahem from the city of Samaria."[8]

According to these sources, the crumbling Kingdom of Israel began to look to the Assyrian ruler for support, in the hope that their alliance would strengthen Menahem's royal house.

About one hundred years ago, excavations in Samaria yielded more than sixty clay fragments engraved with Hebrew script.[9] There are various opinions concerning the dating and significance of these fragments. Most scholars, based on the inscription "in the year 17" found on several of the fragments, attribute these artifacts to the period of Jehu's dynasty (until the death of Jeroboam II). However, based on his discovery of tax records that list payments of wine and oil to the king, Yigal Yadin suggests that these are payments that Menahem exacted from his soldiers in order to pay the Assyrian tribute.[10] According to Yadin, the numbers engraved on most of the fragments refer to the final year of Menahem's reign, 738 BCE. The list of taxpayers is consistent with the biblical verses. This was the beginning of Menahem's collapse. The heavy taxation that he instituted certainly contributed to the kingdom's deterioration and his heir's loss of control in a bloody Gileadite rebellion.

According to the Book of Kings, Menahem paid "a thousand talents of silver to Pulu to join in alliance with him, to retain his own kingdom" (II Kings 15:19). Commentators have calculated that this sum is roughly equivalent to three million silver shekels (one talent = 3000

---

the conjunctive letter *vav* functions as an explanatory word. According to this, the verse means, "Pul, **that is**, Tiglath-Pileser." See also G. Galil, ed., II Kings (*World of the Bible*) (Tel Aviv, 1999), 120 [Hebrew].

8. H. Tadmor, "The Annals of Tiglath-Pileser III, King of Assyria," (Jerusalem, Israeli National Academy for Sciences: 1967), lines 150–57 [Hebrew]; Damsky, *Guide*, 43.

9. These fragments were discovered in the royal vaults of Tel Shomron, and they included names of places, names of dynasties of the tribes of Manasseh (including those of some of Tzlofhad's daughters), and taxes of oil and wine. The family lists seem to follow the property distribution according to Joshua 17:2–6.

10. For a complete description of the Samarian fragments, see S. Ahituv, *Writing and Inscription* (Jerusalem, 2005) [Hebrew], 246–300; Y. Yadin, "Ancient Judaean Weights and the Date of the Samaria Ostraca," *Scripta Hierosolymitana* 8 (1960): 1–17.

shekels; Ex. 15:19). This sum was exacted from the "warriors," fifty silver shekels from each, which means that there were around sixty thousand taxpayers.

PEKAH SON OF REMALIAH'S REBELLION

Towards the end of Menahem's reign, when a heavy tax was imposed upon all Israelite and Samarian landowners, anti-Assyrian factions began to form, looking for the right moment to strike out against Menahem. Once Tiglath-Pileser had come to power in the region, Menahem's authority had dwindled. When Menahem's son Pekahiah succeeded the throne, Pekah son of Remaliah, aided by fifty Gileadite men (from the eastern side of the Jordan) swiftly seized power. There is considerable support for the theory that Pekah had been running a shadow government, presumably in Gilead, which remained undetected due to the widening chasm between Gilead and Samaria.

Pekah and his Gileadite supporters endeavored to stabilize the position of the Transjordan through an alliance with Aram-Damascus. It may be that because of this alliance, Israel was forced to take an anti-Assyrian position, despite the clear threat of Tiglath-Pileser's encroaching army.[11]

It is also likely that Pekah had been appointed as an official in Pekahiah son of Menahem's government, as part of an attempt to repair Samarian relations with the Gileadites, but he exploited this opportunity and usurped the throne. The first step Pekah took was to form an alliance with King Rezin of Aram, in a last stand against Assyrian domination.

More information about the harsh civil war that crushed the Kingdom of Israel from within, and also damaged the Kingdom of Judah, can be found in Hosea's prophecy:

> Sound a horn at Gibeah, a trumpet at Ramah, raise the alarm in Beit Aven; after you, Benjamin! Ephraim is stricken with horror on a day of chastisement. Against the tribes of Israel I proclaim certainties: The officers of Judah have acted like shifters of field boundaries; on them I will pour out My wrath like water. (Hos. 5:8–10)

---

11. Raviv, *Society,* 132.

This is a description of Judah and Benjamin's attack on Ephraim, which began with the recruitment of soldiers on the Benjamin hill (in Gibeah), continued at Ramah (referred to today as El Ram, north of Jerusalem), and ended with an attack on Ephraim in the Beit El region (Beit Avon). This attack, which is not mentioned in the Book of Kings, appears to have taken place when Israel was particularly vulnerable, during Menahem son of Gadi's reign, after the Assyrian army had arrived and extorted a heavy fine (II Kings 15:19–20). Indeed, Hosea described Ephraim's desperate appeal to Assyria, which went unanswered. Judah's cruel exploitation of Israel's weakness is what may have led to Pekah son of Remaliah's vendetta against Judah, described in Isaiah 7 and 9.

KING UZZIAH'S LEPROSY

Tiglath-Pileser's arrival certainly affected Uzziah's kingdom as well. We have no records of Assyria's conduct towards Judah during Tiglath-Pileser's first conquest in 738 BCE. A few places in the Bible and the midrash mention an earthquake (referred to as *hara'ash*, which literally means "the noise") that shook Judah, leprosy that plagued King Uzziah, and the Assyrian Empire's arrival in the region. Rashi notes an ancient tradition that all three events occurred on a single day:

> For on the day of the earthquake, the day that Uzziah became afflicted with leprosy, it was said, "And I heard the voice of the Lord" (Is. 6:8). (Rashi on Is. 6:4)

This tradition is based on the opening of Amos ("two years before the earthquake," Amos 1:1), and on a verse from Zechariah that describes the terrible earthquake that took place in the days of Uzziah:

> And you shall flee as you fled before the earthquake in the days of King Uzziah of Judah. (Zechariah 14:5)

According to the midrashic tradition, the two calamities – Uzziah's leprosy and the earthquake – were connected, although Isaiah's agitation seems to be more concerned with the earthquake.[12] The nation of Israel's exile from its land, a process that began with the earthquake-like Assyrian invasion, continues to this day.

According to biblical tradition, the fall of Uzziah was caused by his arrogance (hinted to in Isaiah chapter 2), and to his unwarranted interference in the Temple (II Chr. 26). The author of Chronicles notes that Uzziah's arrogance is what caused his leprosy, although this is not mentioned in Kings:

> But in his strength, his arrogance led to corruption, and he violated the Lord his God, and he came to the Lord's Sanctuary to offer incense on the incense altar; and the priest Azariah went in after him, eighty valiant priests of the Lord with him, and they stood against King Uzziah and said to him: It is not for you, Uzziah, to offer incense to the Lord, for the priests, sons of Aaron, are consecrated to offer incense, leave the Temple you have violated, and the honor is not yours from the Lord God; and Uzziah became angry, and in his hand was a pan for offering incense, and in his anger at the priests, leprosy burst out on his forehead before the priests in the House of the Lord above the incense altar; and the High Priest Azariah and all the priests turned to him and behold, he had leprosy on his forehead, and they rushed him out from there, and he himself hurried out, for the Lord had struck him; and King Uzziah was a leper until the day of his death, and he dwelled in the leper house, leprous, banned from the House of the Lord, with his son Jotham over the royal house, judging the people of the Land. (II Chr. 26:16–21)

---

12. See M. Weiss, *Scriptures in their Own Light: Collected Essays* (Jerusalem, 1988), 80–86 [Hebrew], who rejects all traditional and modern interpretations that attempt to identify an actual earthquake in Isaiah and Amos' time. This opinion is shared by Maimonides (*Guide of the Perplexed*, II:29) who argues that Isaiah's descriptions are a metaphor for political and historical turbulence. However, the verse in Zechariah refers to an actual earthquake, and in this context, it is more difficult to read his words metaphorically. The prophets may have used their traumatic experiences of actual earthquakes as a metaphor for the Assyrian conquest. This would appear to be the case in Isaiah 24, where the earthquake seems to refer to Sennacherib's conquest (see below).

Military success, the expansion of his empire, and economic prosperity did not suffice for the greatest of the kings of Judah. One realm was out of his hands – the Temple. God's house was under priestly charge, but Uzziah sought control there too. He entered the Inner Sanctuary to offer incense, an exclusive privilege of the High Priest. At the moment of this forbidden act, Uzziah's exalted kingship was instantly cut short. The leprosy that erupted on his forehead caused him to be rushed out of the Temple, away from the palace and into the leper house, where he remained until the day of his death. This is how the Book of Chronicles explained the king's disappearance from the narrative when Tiglath-Pileser had begun to march towards the region.

CHAPTER 6: WHEN WAS THIS PROPHECY SPOKEN?

Many commentators see chapter 6 as Isaiah's inaugural prophecy, basing their view on the verse where Isaiah volunteers for the mission: "Here I am, send me" (6:8). The sages address this statement in the *Midrash Tannaim*: "In the year of King Uzziah's death – this was the beginning of the book, and why was it written here? Because there is no order in the Torah" (*Mekhilta, Beshallaḥ* 7). Rashi takes a similar view.

This reading, however, raises several difficulties, two of which are related to the dating of the prophecy and its content.

Chapter 1 opens with the statement that Isaiah prophesied during the reigns of four kings, beginning with Uzziah. Chapter 6 takes place during the year of Uzziah's death, and if it were Isaiah's inaugural prophecy, then he would not have been characterized as one who prophesied in Uzziah's time, but rather after it. Radak was the first to note this problem, and commented that "[In the year of King Uzziah's death] must be explained as his actual death, and according to this, [the chapter] is not the beginning of [Isaiah's] prophecy." Abarbanel interprets chapter 6 as Isaiah's consenting to take on a particular prophetic mission, which concludes his prophecy during Uzziah's time. A modern scholar, Yehezkel Kaufmann, supports this approach by arguing that inaugural prophecies are usually characterized by the motif of refusal to take on the prophetic mission (cf. Moses in Ex. 3; Jeremiah in Jer. 1), while here the prophet readily volunteered: "I am here, send me."[13] Kaufmann also reads the chapter as the final prophecy of the series of prophecies uttered in Uzziah's time (spanning from chapters 2–6). These prophecies criticized the arrogant glory of a complacently prosperous kingdom, and were less relevant after Uzziah's reign.

The *Targum Yonatan's* comment on the first verse of the chapter equates leprosy with death: "In the year that King Uzziah was struck with leprosy, the prophet said…" This is cited in the midrash on the verse: "And the king of Egypt died" (Ex. 2:23); "He was afflicted with leprosy, for the leper is likened to one who has died, as it says, 'Please do not let her be like a dead person' (Num. 12:11), and it says, 'In the year of King Uzziah's death' (Is. 6:1)". (Exodus Rabba, 1:34).

The description of King Uzziah as a dead person is also hinted to in Chronicles, as his son replaced him as king at that time.

It therefore appears that chapter 6 dates to the year that King Uzziah was afflicted with leprosy, around the same time that Tiglath-Pileser entered the region (738 BCE). It is possible to directly compare Amos' prophecies in the Kingdom of Israel during the glory of Jeroboam II's reign, "two years before the earthquake"; and Isaiah's prophecies in the golden days of Uzziah, until the year of his "death," that is, the year he stepped down from the historical stage. The parallel themes between Amos and Isaiah are evident from the language of their concluding prophecies:

Amos 9	Isaiah 6
(1) *I saw the Lord* Standing by the Altar, and He said: Strike the tops of the pillars, *so that the thresholds shake*, and break them over everyone's head, and those left I will kill with the sword, not one will escape, and not one will flee…	(1) In the year of King Uzziah's death *I saw the Lord* Sitting tall and lofty on a throne, the train of his garment filling the Sanctuary…

---

13. Kaufmann, *The Religion of Israel*, vol. 3, 207.

Amos 9	Isaiah 6
(7) Are you any different than Cushites to me, Children of Israel, says the Lord, For didn't I raise Israel up from the Land of Egypt, and the Philistines from Kaftor and Aram from Kir;	(4) At the calling voice the doorposts and *the thresholds shook*, and the house filled with smoke…
(8) Behold, the Lord God's eyes are upon the sinful kingdom, and I shall wipe it off of the face of the earth, But I will surely not destroy the House of Jacob, says the Lord;	(9) And He said, Go, and say to this people: You will surely hear, but you will never understand, You will surely see, but you will never know;
(9) For I will give the command, And I will shake the House of Israel among all the nations as a sieve is shaken, and not a pebble will fall to the ground.	(10) Let the hearts of this people grow fat And stiffen their ears, and cement their eyes closed, Lest they see with their eyes, and listen with their ears, and understand with their hearts, and repent and be healed;
(10) By the sword all the sinners of my people shall fall, Those who say: evil will not befall or overtake us,	(11) And I said, Until when, O Lord? And He said: Until their cities are totally ruined, devoid of inhabitant, And the land is ruined wasteland;
(11) On that day, I will restore the fallen Tabernacle of David, And I will repair its breached fences and restore its ruins, and I shall build it as in days of old.	(12) and the Lord shall exile the people to a distant land, and desolation shall fill the Land;
	(13) Yet a tenth shall remain, and shall be destroyed again and again, Yet like a terebinth, like an oak, whose stump remains when its branches are cut down, The holy seed will be its trunk.

In the Kingdom of Israel, Amos saw God standing by the open altar, and witnessed its destruction. In the same period, in Jerusalem, Isaiah saw God inside the Sanctuary. In both visions, the earthquake shook the "thresholds," and the result was devastation and ruin, but not complete destruction, for the Tabernacle of David will be restored, and the "holy seed" will again blossom from the bare trunk.

JUDGMENT, DECREE, AND RENEWED GROWTH

Isaiah's vision in chapter 6 seems like an inaugural prophecy, but in fact it heralded departure. The significance of the holy vision of God upon His throne is discussed in the final chapter of Isaiah:

> Thus says the Lord: Heaven is My throne, and the earth My footstool, what kind of a house can you build for me, and what kind of resting place can be for My rest? Has not My hand made all of these, and all these come into being through the words of God? Yet towards these I will look fondly: towards the destitute, and the broken-spirited, and those who tremble at My word. (Is. 66:1–2)

If the Temple and the Sanctuary are not worthy of God's Divine Presence, then He will return to His throne in heaven, and the entire earth shall instead become "His footstool." Therefore, it is possible to read the words *ram venissa* (Is. 6:1) – usually translated as "tall and lofty" – not as adjectives describing God, but rather as verbs; God's glory was "rising and lifting," leaving the earthly Sanctuary that was no longer worthy of His presence, and moving upwards towards the heavens.

In his vision, Isaiah heard a voice calling out to him: "Let the hearts of this people grow fat." This appears to mean subduing the people's spirits and distancing them from the voice of God. A prophecy whose sole purpose is to portend death, with no hope of life, is anomalous. For some time, Isaiah had drifted apart from his cousin, the king, whose arrogance had grown along with his kingdom's might. Isaiah had long ceased to be shocked at the sight of the women strutting down the streets, flaunting themselves in their finest attire. Now, he grew even more distant from the world around him. His visions transported him to another world altogether. There, among the heavenly hosts, he heard a voice calling to him, demanding that he let the hearts of the people grow fat, and to make sure that they never stir from their decadent slumber. At that moment, their fate was being sealed. The prophet, their emissary of reproach, played a part in this heavenly court case.

The story of Micaiah son of Imla, in chapter 22 of Kings 1,[14] sheds light on this vision. King Ahab of Israel was urging King Jehoshaphat of Judah to join him in the battle for Ramoth-Gilead. Ahab had four hundred "prophets" at his disposal, who unanimously predicted a victorious outcome. Jehoshaphat did not feel assured by this pandering chorus, and asked to consult another prophet; one who spoke God's word. Micaiah son of Imla, who was feared by Ahab, arrives. After several evasive replies, Micaiah described his heavenly vision:

> I saw the Lord sitting on his throne, and all the heavenly hosts standing around him, at his right and his left; and the Lord said: Who will entice Ahab, so that he may go up, and fall in Ramoth-Gilead, and this one said this, and that one said that; and a spirit came out, and stood before the Lord, and said: I will entice him, and the Lord said to him: With what? And it said: I will go out, and become a deceiving spirit in the mouths of all his prophets, and He said: You will manage to entice him, go out and do so. (I Kings 22: 19–22)

Like in Isaiah chapter 6, this too is a vision of a heavenly court. This trial concerns Ahab's fate. The presiding judge (who is the Judge of the entire world) asked a cruel question, "Who will entice Ahab?" Ahab's sentence had already been passed, and all that remained was its enforcement.

A comparison between the two tales is startling. Isaiah unwittingly volunteered to "fatten" the hearts of Israel, and to "cement their

---

14. For an interpretation of this prophecy, see also M. Tsevat, "Isaiah 6," in *A Tribute in Honor of Zalman Shazar's Eightieth Birthday*, ed. B.Z. Luria (Jerusalem, 1973), 161–72 [Hebrew]. For a slightly different comparison of Isaiah and Micaiah, see M. Breuer, *Studies in Isaiah* (Alon Shvut, 2010), 231–32 [Hebrew].

eyes closed" to any appeal or repentance that could overthrow the decree against them. Read according to the model of the court case in Kings, Isaiah seems to have been given the role of executor of Judah's destruction.

This similarity, however, ends at this point. While the "deceiving spirit" in I Kings 22 hurried off to fulfill its mission, Isaiah cried out in desperation, "Until when, O Lord," expressing pain and love for his people. He merited to hear God's answer:

> And I said, Until when, O Lord? And He said: Until their cities are totally ruined, devoid of inhabitant, and the land is ruined wasteland; and the Lord shall exile the people to a distant land, and desolation shall fill the Land; yet a tenth shall remain, and shall be destroyed again and again, yet like a terebinth, like an oak, whose trunk remains when its branches are cut down, the holy seed will be its trunk. (Is. 6:11–13)

While Isaiah prophesied of a dark era of destruction and desolation, his words contained a shred of hope. Although their branches will be cut down, the roots of the nation will endure. Though the land will be cleared almost entirely of its inhabitants, a tenth will remain, just as the tree trunk still stands upright when its branches are cut down. New shoots will sprout from this trunk.

After Isaiah prostrated himself before the Lord, crying, "Until when," God, appeased, revealed the end of the exile, "The holy seed will be its trunk." This disclosure was a new message for Isaiah. It replaced God's order to "Let the hearts of this people grow fat," with words to stir the people to repentance in order that they be granted continuity, and "repent and be healed."

TAKING LEAVE OF UZZIAH

Isaiah bid farewell to his cousin with a harsh prophecy. Like Micaiah's parting words to Ahab on the eve of his death at Ramoth-Gilead, Isaiah left his cousin on the threshold of the leper house with a prediction of doom. Uzziah stepped down from the historical stage while Jerusalem was still in its heyday. Judah still held full power, and the nation was still content in its drunken stupor. Uzziah's son, Jotham, took his place as Judah slept on.

Isaiah, meanwhile, had visions of higher realms. He heard God's voice echo through the heavenly spheres, bidding him to ensure that the people do not stir from their slumber until their kingdom comes crashing down upon them. Isaiah's pain was tremendous. His cry echoed from deep within his heart, "Until when?" He was no mere messenger, wordlessly carrying out the orders that he received. Rather, he was a prophet who lived among his people and sought what was best for them. Visions of Judah's destruction came to him, and a scream rose up within him. This scream caused the harsh decree to be lightened by the addition of a glimmer of hope: "The holy seed will be its trunk."

Jotham Son of Uzziah

T he prophecy spoken "in the year of Uzziah's death" marked the beginning of the reign of Jotham, Uzziah's heir. Little is known about his reign, for it is mentioned only briefly in the Bible:

> And the Lord afflicted the king, and he became a leper until the day of his death, and he dwelt in the leper house; with the king's son Jotham over the royal house, judging the people of the Land … And Azariah lay with his fathers, and they buried him with his ancestors in the city of David, and Jotham his son ruled in his place. (II Kings 15:5, 7)

Uzziah-Azariah's death is followed by a record of the kings of Israel who reigned in his time. The last few verses of the chapter discuss the years of Jotham's reign:

> In the second year of Pekah son of Remaliah, king of Israel, Jotham son of King Uzziah of Judah reigned; he was twenty-five years old when he reigned, and he reigned for sixteen years in Jerusalem, and his mother's name was Jerusha the daughter of Zadok; and he did what was right in the eyes of the Lord, just as his father Uzziah did; only he did not remove the high places, for the people were still offering sacrifices and incense on the high

places; he built the upper gate of the House of the Lord; and the rest of Jotham's deeds are written in the book of chronicles of the kings of Judah. (II Kings 15:32–36)

We know that Uzziah was the (active) king during Tiglath-Pileser's mission to Aram, Phoenicia and Israel, in 738 BCE, and that Uzziah's grandson, Ahaz, reigned during the Assyrian king's exile of Rezin and Pekah, in 732 BCE. It is difficult to explain how Jotham could have reigned for sixteen years in between these two monarchs.[1] Even if we assume that Uzziah was smitten with leprosy a few years earlier, with these years counting towards Jotham's reign, it is difficult to account for sixteen years of Jotham's reign and sixteen years of Ahaz's reign. One solution is to include the years that Jotham served as crown prince during Uzziah's active reign (from approximately 749 BCE). After Uzziah fell ill, Jotham became the active monarch, with his son Ahaz serving as crown prince. The total years of Jotham's reign seem to include all his years in office, although he was not yet officially appointed during his father's lifetime as Uzziah had been (II Kings 14:21). After Jotham's death (which was soon after Uzziah's death, in 733 BCE), Ahaz became the king. The administrative overlap between the reigns of fathers and sons, which seems to have been the custom in the Kingdom of Judah, helps to reconcile the chronological discrepancies between the information relayed in the Book of Kings and what is known from external sources.[2]

Scholars and commentators do not consider Jotham's reign to have had any significant bearing on Judah's internal or external political affairs, and regard him merely as the link between Uzziah and Ahaz. His character and achievements may have been overshadowed by his

---

1. There are meticulous records, found in archives in ancient Assyrian cities, which record the major events of each year (according to the Eponym dating system), such as new laws, conquests, and wars.
2. See II Kings 15:30, and compare to II Kings 17:1. Jotham's twentieth year appears to coincide with Ahaz's twelfth year; that is, they ruled together for eight years. See also H. Tadmor, "Chronology," in *Encyclopedia Biblica*, vol. 4 (Jerusalem, 1962), 261–62; 282–86 [Hebrew]; S. Yeivin, "Chronological Reflections on the Book of Isaiah," *Bible and Jewish History Studies in the President's House* 1, 21–22 [Hebrew].

father's.[3] In Chronicles, however, an entire (albeit brief) chapter is devoted to Jotham's reign. These verses testify to his righteousness as well as his impressive economic achievements:

> And he did what was right in the eyes of the Lord, just as his father Uzziah had done, only he did not attempt to enter the Sanctuary of the Lord, though the people were still corrupt; he built the upper gate of the House of the Lord, and did extensive work on the Ophel wall; and built cities on the Judean Hill, and in the woodlands, he built fortresses and towers; and he fought against the king of the Ammonites and he prevailed over them; and in that year, the Ammonites gave him a hundred talents of silver, and ten thousand cors of wheat, and ten thousand of barley, the Ammonites repeated this in the second year and the third year; and Jotham grew strong, for his paths were straight before the Lord his God; and the rest of Jotham's deeds and all his words and ways have been written in the book of kings of Israel and Judah; he was twenty-five years when he began to reign, and he ruled in Jerusalem for sixteen years. (II Chr. 27:2–8)

This chapter accredits Jotham with all the good his father Uzziah did, without ascribing to him Uzziah's sin of "attempt[ing] to enter the Sanctuary of the Lord." Rashi's commentary on Chronicles notes that all the kings of Judah sinned, with the exception of Jotham:

> Concerning David it is written: "Only concerning the matter of Uriah the Hittite." Concerning Solomon it is written: "His wives turned his heart away." Rehoboam forsook the Lord's Torah. Abijah "Went in all his father's sins." Asa took silver and gold from the treasuries of the House of the Lord and put the prophet in prison. Jehoshaphat associated with a wicked man (Ahab and his

---

3. A striking example of this can be found in Herzog College's *Training Manual for Teachers: II Kings* (Alon Shvut, 2005) [Hebrew], which describes in full the history of the kings of Judah, complete with illustrations, but noticeably skips directly from Uzziah to Ahaz without even mentioning Jotham's name.

son Ahaziah). Joram killed his brother. Ahaziah's mother advised
him to sin. Joash killed Zechariah and later became a ritual pros-
titute.[4] Amaziah prostrated himself before the graven images of
Seir. Uzziah entered the Temple to burn incense. Ahaz went in the
ways of the kings of Israel and also made monuments to foreign
gods. Hezekiah became haughty and there was anger upon him,
and the sages did not concur with him regarding three things that
he did. Manasseh did evil in the eyes of the Lord. Josiah did not
heed the words of the prophecy of God. Zedekiah did evil in the
eyes of the Lord and did not humble himself before Jeremiah. In
Jotham, however, no trace of sin was found (R. Eliezer b. Moshe
told me this). (Rashi on II Chr. 27:2)

Jotham, who was righteous and followed God's path, became a unique,
almost legendary figure in rabbinic literature:

Hezekiah said in the name of R. Jeremiah, who said it in the name
of R. Shimon b. Yoḥai: I am able to exempt the whole world from
judgment from the day that I was born until now, and if only
Eliezer, my son, were with me, [we could exempt it] from the
day of the creation of the world to the present time, and if only
Jotham son of Uzziah, were with us, [we could exempt it] from
the creation of the world to its final end. (Sukka 45b)

Rashi, in his commentary on the Talmud, notes that Jotham's righteousness was expressed in the honor that he showed his father:

He was righteous and more humble than the rest of the kings,
and he was credited with honoring his father, and regarding
him it is said: "A son will honor his father" (Mal. 1:6). For all
the time his father had leprosy, he judged the people of the
land, as it is written (II Kings 15:5): "With his son Jotham
over the royal house, judging the people of the land," though
he did not claim the royal crown during his lifetime, and he

---

4. See II Chr. 24:17, and Radak's quotation of the Midrash ad loc.

would state all the cases he would judge in the name of his father. (Rashi ad loc.)

Jotham's glory days began, it may therefore be said, during Uzziah's great industrial revolution, when he served as his father's top executive. Once his father took ill and Tiglath-Pileser advanced in the region, the kingdoms of Judah and Israel began to decline. The verse that concludes the description of Jotham's reign can be attributed to this period (the mid-730s BCE):

> In those days, the Lord began to send King Rezin of Aram and Pekah son of Remaliah against Judah. (II Kings 15:37)

This is the first hint of the escalating tension between Judah and the Aram-Israel alliance that had formed against Assyria. As we have no record of any steps that Jotham took in relation to Assyria or Israel, we can conclude that Jotham managed to avoid any direct confrontation with the rising empire, thus maintaining his father Uzziah's policy.

Surprisingly, from the time of Uzziah's death (or his affliction with leprosy) until the beginning of Ahaz's reign, not a word is heard from the prophet Isaiah. It appears that after a few years of reproach and harsh warnings of impending punishment, followed by a difficult mission ("Fatten the hearts of the people"), the prophet fell silent. He saw how Jotham governed the people with a just, righteous hand. Scanning the streets of Jerusalem, Isaiah may have nurtured the hope that the decree of destruction had been annulled by the just, godly path of King Jotham.

Part Two
The Days of Ahaz

A man lived in Jerusalem in the days of Ahaz son of Judah, and his name was Jehoram son of Aviezer, a general in Judah, with a company of a thousand men, and he had fields and vineyards in the Carmel and Samaria, and flocks of sheep and herds of cattle in Bethlehem of Judah. And he had silver and gold, and palaces of ivory and all delightful treasures ... A friend had Jehoram, more beloved and closer than a brother, and his name was Jedidiah the Generous, of royal Judahite stock, and the minister of the king's property, a pleasant man of tender years, a rich man and a shield for the sons of prophets who studied God's Torah, for he loved their pleasant teachings, and stretched out his ear to hear them, and he supported them with the generosity of his hand; therefore he was called Jedidiah the Generous.

Jehoram and Jedidiah shone like two precious stones in a generation of turmoil, the generation of Ahaz, for they were both faithful to their God and their holy people, and they followed God's teachings, bound with the instructions that the son of Amoz had sealed with them.

– Abraham Mapu, opening paragraph of *The Love of Zion*
[Hebrew] 1853

Isaiah 7–8

Isaiah before King Ahaz of Judah (734–732 BCE)

I t was winter in Jerusalem. People were huddled inside. Rumors from the edge of the kingdom slowly seeped into the capital, rumors that whispered of thousands slain. Some told of a straggling convoy of prisoners led away to exile, of women and girls dragged to the Samarian marketplaces. These rumors stirred King Ahaz to leave his warm palace and venture out into the cold winds to the post that looked out towards the north, opposite the aqueduct of the Upper Pool. Duty required that he approach the border between the kingdoms of Judah and Israel to see it with his own eyes. The past year had been a difficult one for Judah. Ahaz had inherited a mighty kingdom, the Kingdom of Uzziah the Great. But Judah had been struck from every side, and had lost its wealth and power all at once.

ISRAEL'S WAR AGAINST JUDAH

Five years previously, Judah had led a regional alliance of kings against Assyria, which met with disaster against Tiglath-Pileser's sword. Despite the crushing defeat, some nations continued to struggle against the rising Assyrian Empire. In a surprising political maneuver, an alliance formed between two armies who had long been hated enemies: Aram and Israel. King Rezin of Aram and King Pekah son of Remaliah joined forces to stand against the encroaching enemy. Each king had his own military vision.

Rezin of Aram sent out his forces along the eastern bank of the Jordan, all the way down to Eilat, openly declaring his intention to seize control of Ammon, Moab and Edom, and to unite them against Assyria. Domination over the Transjordan would allow him to control its trade routes and give him a path into Egypt, a source of relief in times of crisis. Pekah son of Remaliah also ventured southward, instigating war against the Kingdom of Judah, then under Ahaz's rule. His vision was similar to Rezin's; Pekah wished to seize control of Judah.

The alliance between Aram and Israel shook the land of Judah. The neighboring Edomites and Philistines did not hesitate to join in the attacks against their old enemy in the south and the Shephelah (lowlands). Uzziah's great kingdom came crashing down.

At times, the text intentionally downplays certain events. One of the bloodiest, most gaping wounds in the history of Israelite-Judahite relations is almost completely hidden from the eyes of the reader. The Books of Kings and Isaiah merely relay that Rezin and Pekah went up to Jerusalem but "could not overthrow it" (Is. 7:1; II Kings 16:5). It appears that Jerusalem managed to resist the forces that crushed the surrounding cities. A mass slaughter, barely alluded to in Kings, is however described in detail in Chronicles:

> And the Lord their God gave them into the hand of the king of Aram, and they smote them and took a great many captives, and brought them to Damascus, and they were also given to the hand of the king of Israel, who struck a great blow against them; and Pekah son of Remaliah killed a hundred and twenty thousand in Judah in one day, all valiant men, for they had forsaken the Lord, the God of their forefathers; and Zikhri, a hero of Ephraim, killed Maaseiah, the king's son; and Azrikam, the governor of the palace, and Elkanah, second to the king; and the Israelites captured two hundred thousand women, boys and girls from their brothers, and plundered great spoil from them, and they brought the spoil to Samaria. (II Chr. 28:5–8)

The war began with Rezin and Pekah dealing a heavy blow to Ahaz. The text focuses upon the elimination of Judah's symbols of power (members of the royal family and leaders of state), as well as the capture of 200,000 women and children, and the great plunder carried off to Samaria. In short, a mortal wound was dealt to Judah.

ARAM CONQUERS EILAT

The kings of Aram-Damascus had long nurtured a dream to conquer the Transjordan, cross Gilead, Ammon and Moab, and reach Edom, and the city of Eilat, in order to allow Aram-Damascus (today's Syria) access to the Red Sea and to Egypt. Military and commercial control of this route was the key to wealth and power, as had been proven time and again during the reigns of Solomon, Jehoshaphat and Uzziah, when Judah ruled over Edom and Eilat. Now, in the throes of war against Judah, Pekah of Israel allowed the king of Aram to fulfill this dream. Pekah had established his kingdom with the help of the Gileadites, and now he allowed Rezin to pass through their land in his move southward. This explains the verse in Kings:

> At that time, King Rezin of Aram restored Eilat to Aram, and he drove the Judeans out of Eiloth; and the Arameans (and the Edomites) came to Eilat, and they dwell there until this day. (II Kings 16:5–6)

The Aramean army did not go to Jerusalem. In fact, it did not appear on the western side of the Jordan at all. While Pekah was attacking Jerusalem, Aramean forces passed through the Israelite-ruled Gilead. This token of Israel's alliance allowed Aram to attack Judah from the south, seize control of Edom, and drive the Judeans out of Eilat. Rezin's army defeated the Judahite guard that had been stationed in the Edomite cities and in Eilat since the days of Amaziah and Uzziah (II Kings 14:7; 22), and restored Edomite rule, under Aramean patronage. This is consistent with both the spoken (*Keri*) and written (*Ketiv*) forms of the Masoretic text in verse 6; one states that the Arameans came to Eilat, and the other that the Edomites came. Once the Aramean soldiers left the area, the Edomites were left to themselves, and Judah did not return to the area. King Ahaz was likely gripped with terror at the turn of events. The southern border of his kingdom had reverted back to the northern Negev, cut off his trade routes, and rendered his once mighty kingdom a tiny, weak state.

PHILISTIA'S RELEASE FROM JUDAH'S YOKE

Immediately following Israel's attack on Judah, the Book of Chronicles relates how war broke out in the south and in the west:

> The Edomites had returned, and they smote Judah and took captives; and the Philistines raided the towns of the Shephelah and the south of Judea, and they captured Beit Shemesh and Ayalon and Gederoth, and Sokho and its surrounding villages, and Timna and its surrounding villages, and Gimzo and its surrounding villages, and they dwelt there; for the Lord had defeated Judah because of King Ahaz of Israel, for he had ruined Judah and greatly betrayed the Lord. (II Chr. 28:17–19)

Thus the war against Judah reached its peak, as the surrounding nations fought for independence. Judah came crashing down from the heights that it reached during Uzziah's reign, leaving Ahaz with a small, battered kingdom.

ARAM, ASSYRIA AND ISRAEL: THREE PARALLEL JOURNEYS FROM THE NORTH TO THE SOUTH

During the Aramean and Israelite conquests, Tiglath-Pileser was also marching southward, along the west coast, against Philistia, in the twelfth year of his reign (734 BCE). From Assyrian records, we know that the aim of this mission was to instigate a war against King Hanun of Gaza. The records describe Hanun's escape to Egypt.

Three military missions embarked southward that year. The eastern route was taken by Rezin, the head of the new alliance against Assyria. The central route, from Samaria to Jerusalem, was taken by Pekah, second-in-command to Rezin. And the western route, from the coastal cities of Lebanon, until Philistia, marked the path of destruction wreaked by Tiglath-Pileser as he marched mercilessly through the region.

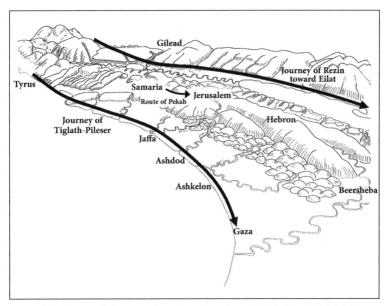

Map of the three parallel missions from the north to the south (relief map by Meir Kahana; conquests marked by Michal Elon)

At that time, it was not at all clear who would triumph, or whether the Aram-Israel coalition stood a chance against the mighty forces of Tiglath-Pileser.

CHAPTER 7: ISAIAH BEFORE AHAZ AT THE BEGINNING OF TIGLATH-PILESER'S MISSION (734 BCE)

While Aram and Israel prepared for their conquests, and Tiglath-Pileser began his southward march, Isaiah ventured out of his study house and stood before the king to warn him against foolish political moves. The next chapters describe the prophet's stand against the king:

> And it was told to the House of David, saying: Aram has joined forces with Ephraim, and his heart and the heart of his people was shaken, as trees of the forest shake from the wind; and the Lord said to Isaiah: Go out now to meet Ahaz, you and She'ar-Yashuv, your son, to the end of the aqueduct of the Upper Pool, on the

path to the Washer's Field[1]; and you shall say to him: Take care
and be silent, and do not fear, and let not your heart weaken at
these two smoking stubs of firebrand, at the wrath of Rezin and
Aram and the son of Remaliah; Aram and Ephraim and the son of
Remaliah have plotted your downfall, saying: Let us go up against
Judah and shatter it, and tear it up for us, and appoint a king within
it, the son of Taval; thus says the Lord: This will not take place,
this will not happen; for the head of Aram is Damascus, and the
head of Damascus is only Rezin, and in sixty-five years Ephraim
shall no longer be a people; and the head of Ephraim is Samaria,
and the head of Samaria is only the son of Remaliah, if you do
not stand firm in your faith, you will not stand at all. (Is. 7:2–9)

It is clear why the king shook with terror at the devastating attacks on the
Judean fronts. His kingdom was trapped between the Assyrian Empire,
charging from the northeast towards the Philistine coast, and the newly
formed alliance, tearing its way from the southernmost border of Judah
towards the capital. All feared utter annihilation.

At that point, the prophet Isaiah once again entered the scene;
that same prophet whose accusative voice had rung out in the chambers
of Ahaz's grandfather, and who had remained silent during the reign of
Ahaz's father. For years, Isaiah had holed himself away in his study house.
His students' ears rang with his warnings of the coming destruction,
together with an unwavering belief in Israel's eternity. Now, as Jerusalem
trembled, trapped between the Aram-Israel alliance and the encroaching Assyrian Empire, Isaiah felt that he had a responsibility to speak to
the king in the name of the Lord.

Isaiah first clarified why Pekah and Rezin set out on their
conquests:

---

1. The Upper Pool collected rainwater from where the Shechem Gate stands today,
   and the aqueduct directed the water to the northern side of the Temple Mount. An
   aqueduct and pool were discovered there during excavations of the Western Wall
   tunnels. Most scholars maintain that these sites date to the Second Temple period,
   but there have been indications that they are from the First Temple. The "path to the
   Washer's Field" is probably the road that led east, to the Lion Gate of today, and was
   referred to thus because of the pools there where people would wash their laundry.

> Let us go up against Judah and shatter it, and tear it up for us, and
> appoint a king within it, the son of Taval. (7:5–6)

Isaiah was not concerned with the war itself at this point, but rather with
its background. The Aramean-Israelite attack was undertaken to uproot
the Davidic dynasty, and to replace the king of Judah with one who was
faithful to the political agenda of the alliance. Isaiah mentioned the
candidate favored by Judah's enemies, "the son of Taval." This mystery
candidate has been identified with various different figures.[2] The most
intriguing interpretation identifies the son of Taval as a member of the
Tobiad family line. The Tobiads were important landowners in the Gilead region.[3] The family is known for being Nehemiah's most vehement
opponents in the days of the return to Zion, but it is possible that one of
their ancestors is alluded to here, centuries before their main appearance.[4]

This is the key to understanding the ties between the Rezin-Pekah
alliance and the son of Taval. The Tobiad's influence in Jerusalem, and
his esteemed position in the Transjordan, cast him as a leading player in
the new coalition's revolution in Jerusalem. The Gileadites, already long-
time opponents of the Assyrians, took on an important role in the anti-
Assyrian union, as well as in the plan to take over Judah and Jerusalem.

---

2. Rashi, for example, suggests several possibilities as to who the son of Taval (*ben
   taval*) might have been:
   (1) Someone good for us (*tov alenu*), according to *Targum Yonatan's* explanation; (2)
   Someone who is not (*al*) good (*tov*) in the eyes of the Lord; (3) Using the *albam*
   cipher (a Hebrew substitution cipher where the alphabet is divided into two equal
   groups of eleven letters. The first letter of the first group, *aleph*, substitutes the first
   letter of the second group, *lamed*. The second letter of the first group, *beit*, substitutes
   the second letter of the second group, *mem*, and so on), the word *tavel* becomes *ramla*.
   The son of Taval may therefore be the son of Ramla, or Remaliah. When Rashi brings
   so many explanations, it is a sign that he is not satisfied with any of them. While the
   third explanation indicates that Pekah son of Remaliah himself intended to preside
   over Jerusalem, a feasible possibility, it seems unlikely according to the plain meaning
   of the text, which states that the two kings wish to appoint a third.
3. Magnificent palaces dating back to the Second Temple period have been found near
   Iraq Al Amir, Jordan, south of the Gilead, with inscriptions. See "Iraq al-Amir," *Virtual
   World Project*, http://moses.creighton.edu/vr/IraqAlAmir/site.html.
4. B. Mazar, *Canaan and Israel* (Jerusalem, 1974), 270–90 [Hebrew].

Isaiah's message to the frightened king was sharp and difficult to obey, "Take care and be silent." Do not interfere; sit still and do nothing. The prophet instructed King Ahaz to ignore the fierce international politics churning around him; to pay no notice to the bared fangs of the neighboring coalition. Although Aram and Israel had inflicted grievous harm upon the Kingdom of Judah, and seemed on the verge of striking again, Isaiah mocked their power, and deemed them, "Two smoking stubs of firebrand," about to be extinguished.

A prophet has no political responsibility. He is a spiritual figure, a moral guide and compass who must protect the government from going astray. Isaiah witnessed the king on the verge of collapse, about to cave in to the demands of the alliance. Judah's gaping wounds, inflicted by the Samarian sword, had convinced the people that the new alliance had the power to defeat the encroaching Assyrians. The echo of Assyrian hoof beats could already be heard thundering towards Philistia and Egypt. In the midst of it all stood Isaiah, a man of the study house, entreating Ahaz to let chaos erupt around him. The Kingdom of Judah has nothing to do with the great clash of alien swords, he said, or with the rise and fall of foreign nations. The prophet's trust in mortal rule was tentative. Judah's strength and resilience depends not on the fortunes of war, but rather on its moral conduct, on values that retain the traditions of Jotham and Uzziah, father and grandfather of the king.

"IF YOU DO NOT STAND FIRM IN YOUR FAITH, YOU WILL NOT STAND AT ALL": AHAZ GRASPS AT FOREIGN SUPPORT

Isaiah stood before the king and sought to raise his spirits, to strengthen his resolve, and to shift his gaze beyond the immediate political horizon. The prophet's eyes looked to the past and future, stretching out before him. Ahaz's eyes, on the other hand, were focused on the brittle present.

Ahaz conjured up a royal memory, a legend of the House of David, which told of how one of its most important kings chose to submit to a distant kingdom in order to defeat a nearby enemy. In the years immediately following the split between the kingdoms of Judah and Israel, King Asa of Judah saw how King Baasha of Israel was intent upon conquering

Judah and Jerusalem for himself. In despair, Asa turned to the king of Aram and asked for aid:

> And King Baasha of Israel went up to Judah, and fortified Rama, so that no one could go in or out to King Asa of Judah; and Asa took all the remaining gold and silver from the treasury of the House of the Lord, and the royal treasury, and he gave them to his servants; and King Asa sent them to Ben Hadad son of Tabrimmon son of Hezion, the king of Aram, who dwelt in Damascus, saying: There is a treaty between me and you, between my father and yours, here I have sent you a gift of silver and gold, go, break your treaty with King Baasha of Israel, so that he will withdraw from me; and Ben Hadad listened to King Asa, and he sent the commanders of his forces up to the cities of Jerusalem, and he smote Ijon and Dan and Abel Beit Maakha, and all of Kinrot, and all of the land of Naphtali. (I Kings 15:18–20)

Ahaz had probably heard this tale many times in the palace where he grew up, sitting on his father's knee, or perhaps his grandfather's. Perhaps they criticized Asa's act, expressing contempt for his plea to a foreign nation, and his inability to subdue the local enemy. According to the Book of Kings, Asa was considered one of the most righteous rulers of the dynasty: "Only Asa's heart was whole with the Lord, for all his days" (II Kings 15:11–14), and the text even compares him to "his father David." However, according to the Book of Chronicles, Asa's act was severely criticized by a prophet of his time:

> And at that time, the seer Hanani came to King Asa of Judah, and he said to him: You relied upon the king of Aram, and you did not rely upon the Lord your God, therefore the army of the king of Aram shall escape your hand; were not the Cushites and the Lubites a great army, of many chariots and riders – and when you relied upon the Lord, they were given into your hand; for the eyes of the Lord roam the entire land, strengthening whoever's heart is true to Him, you have acted foolishly, therefore

from now on you shall have wars; and Asa was angry at the seer and had him thrown in jail, for he was furious with him for this, and Asa dealt harshly with some of the people at that time. (II Chr. 16:7–10)[5]

Isaiah appealed to King Ahaz in the same spirit as the seer Hanani pleaded with King Asa. Turning to another nation for support in a time of crisis reflects a lack of faith, and any king of Judah who does so will not endure upon the throne.

The reign of Ahaz's father Jotham was exactly midway between David's ascent to the throne and the Temple's destruction. The Davidic chain had never yet been broken, but now, the Israelite kingdom's attack on Jerusalem, and their plans to appoint the son of Taval over the city, posed a real threat to the dynasty. Ahaz dreaded that he would forever be remembered as the king who brought about the downfall of the House of David. In the prophet's eyes, if Ahaz would wait for the crisis to pass, the "two smoking stubs of firebrand" would soon burn out, and the Davidic line would be safe. Rezin and Pekah's power was waning; very soon, they would disappear without a trace.

This is expressed in the prophet's conclusion:

For the head of Aram is Damascus, and the head of Damascus is only Rezin, and in sixty-five years Ephraim shall no longer be a people; and the head of Ephraim is Samaria, and the head of Samaria is only the son of Remaliah, if you do not stand firm in your faith, you will not stand at all. (Is. 7:8–9)

The sixty-five years Isaiah mentioned do not appear to have been a precise estimate; rather, the prophet was declaring that before the children of the present day have grown, "The land of the two kings you dread will be abandoned" (7:15). Radak explains that Isaiah was quoting an ancient prophecy, however, it is likely that this number was stated to express

---

5. The Book of Chronicles, as we know it today, was written at the beginning of the Second Temple period, based on earlier sources. It is impossible to precisely determine the Bible's attitude towards Asa's deed, as the two books seemingly differ on this point.

that the two regimes will end in less than a lifetime (cf. "The days of our lives are seventy years," Ps. 90:10). The two kings who threatened the king of Jerusalem would not reign for long. Within a single lifetime, their kingdoms would be no more.[6]

Significantly, Isaiah took great care to emphasize the place of each king, "The head of Aram is Damascus, and the head of Damascus is Rezin…The head of Ephraim is Samaria, and the head of Samaria is the son of Remaliah." Of course, he also stated that these "heads" were in fact "tails," "Two smoking *stubs* of firebrand," that were about to be extinguished.

A similar declaration to "If you do not stand firm in your faith, you will not stand at all," was made by King Jehoshaphat of Judah over a century before Isaiah's time, in a stirring speech to his troops before they went to battle against Ammon and Moab in Ein Gedi:

> And as they departed, Jehoshaphat stood and said: Listen to me, Judah and Jerusalemites, have faith in the Lord your God and stand firm, believe in His prophets and you shall succeed. (II Chr. 20:20)

Jehoshaphat was not calling for blind faith, rather he emphasized the need for national strength. Overcoming the present crisis with faith would achieve peace and security in the future. This explains why Isaiah began this prophecy with: "It was told to the House of David," rather than, "It was told to Ahaz." Ahaz was but a link in the Davidic chain. Isaiah saw generations of kings sitting upon David's throne, recalling God's promise that no one besides his seed would reign in Jerusalem (II Sam. 7:12–13). The prophet enjoined Ahaz to hold the throne with the same faith that his ancestors displayed. Just as "the head of Aram is Damascus," and "the head of Ephraim is Samaria," he emphasized that, "the head of Judah is Jerusalem." God promised the city to David's line, on the condition that the ruler upon the throne is faithful, "If you do not stand firm in your faith, you will not stand at all."

---

6. As A. Hacham proposed in *Daat Mikra*, quoting his father. There are many other possible explanations; however they are not as well-founded.

Isaiah was commanded to take his firstborn son "She'ar-Yashuv" along with him to the king. The boy's special name reflects the events of the day. Rabbi Abraham ibn Ezra wrote that the name "She'ar-Yashuv" means that "the remainder (*she'ar*) of the People of Israel will repent," a promise of consolation after the destruction. Radak maintained that the name signified not only a spiritual but a physical return, "The remainder of Judah will return again after the exile, but not the ten tribes [the Samarian exile]." This relates to the historical context; just a few years after this prediction, the exile of the tribes who lived in the Galilee and the Transjordan began. Thirteen years later, Samaria was destroyed, and thirty-three years after that, Sennacherib exiled tens of thousands of people from the Shephelah.

In bringing She'ar-Yashuv to the king, Isaiah was delivering a strong message; if you do not believe, and if you choose to surrender, then many will be exiled. Your kingdom will fall and the entire nation will be forced out of the land. Only a fraction of the people (*she'ar*) will survive to return when it is over.[7]

THE PROPHET'S SECOND APPEARANCE
BEFORE AHAZ (733 BCE)

In the twelfth year of Tiglath-Pileser's reign (and military campaign), Ahaz was seized with fear in the face of the coalition of Pekah of Israel and Rezin of Aram. Aram flanked Judah from the east, having passed through the Gilead and having seized control of Edom. Pekah assembled reinforcements from the north and was approaching Jerusalem.

Jerusalem resounded with the struggles of that time. Bruised and battered captives returned from Samaria and told the people about the mighty forces they had witnessed there. The coalition between Israel and their once-enemy, Aram, breathed courage into the people of Samaria. Aram's march through Gilead and their capture of Edom signified the alliance's next move – the joining of forces with Egypt to form a barrier against the Assyrian invasion. In Jerusalem, the number of coalition supporters grew. A combination of national pride and

---

7. This is also the interpretation of M. Weiss, "She'ar-Yashuv," *Maayanot HaMikra* 5, http://www.daat.ac.il/daat/tanach/achronim/yashuv.htm [Hebrew].

readiness to join with local forces against the common enemy, Assyria, created a fierce political faction.

In the opposing camp, politicians, public figures, and Ahaz himself watched Assyria and discussed its political goals. The rising empire was marching towards Gaza, conquering everything in its path; Aram was just a stop along the way. They predicted that the Assyrian army would soon march through Israel and Judah and would easily topple the kingdoms. "In order to survive, we must submit to them," they said, "Jerusalem must accept Assyria's patronage."

Amidst these two opposing parties, the prophet Isaiah stood firm. In his view, there was no point in joining Rezin and Pekah's coalition, nor was there any need to surrender to Assyria and to be absorbed into its growing empire. Assyria would not harm Jerusalem, so long as they did not join the coalition against it. Isaiah adjured Ahaz to do nothing; neither join Aram and Israel, nor hand Jerusalem's keys over to Assyria, "Take care and be silent, and do not fear, and let not your heart weaken."

No external sources testify to the events unfolding in Jerusalem at that time, but it can be assumed that Ahaz maintained political contact with Assyria. Diplomatic delegations came and went, and information about important meetings was deliberately leaked to the public. The media worked diligently to shape public opinion.

"ASK FOR A SIGN": ISAIAH ATTEMPTS TO STRENGTHEN AHAZ'S FAITH

In the next stage of the prophecy, Isaiah told Ahaz to ask for a sign from God:

> Ask for a sign from the Lord your God, of the deepest depths or the highest heights; and Ahaz said: I will not ask and I will not test the Lord. (Is. 7:11–12)

The prophet advised Ahaz that if he did not believe the words that he heard, he should request physical confirmation of the truth which he would be able to see with his own eyes. However, this suggestion placed Ahaz in a quandary. A faith that depends on the presence of a visual sign is a lesser faith. However, such signs are infinitely more convincing than mere words.[8]

The prophet proposed that Ahaz demand whatever sign he wished, "Ask for a sign from the Lord your God, of the deepest depths or the highest heights." This description includes an intriguing wordplay on the words for "ask," (*shaal*), and "depths," (*sheol*), implying that the asking may be done in a lowly way. The continuation of the verse, however, reinforces the notion that asking could also have a lofty purpose. The king's answer was manipulative and sanctimonious, "I will not ask, and I will not test the Lord," echoing Deuteronomy 6:16, and implying that asking God for a sign was not a legitimate course of action.

The king's answer, seemingly worthy of a firm believer who had no need for any such sign, earned an indignant response, "And he said: listen now, House of David, is it not enough for you to aggravate people, that you must also aggravate my God?" (Is. 7:13). After all, it was not a human who initiated the request for a sign in this instance, but God, through Isaiah, and Ahaz's refusal rings with false piety. Ahaz was, in fact, in desperate need of a sign, and so were the frightened people of Jerusalem. But he refused to listen to God's word, and turned his back on the prophet, revealing his stubborn resolve to abandon his father's path.

THE BIRTH OF IMMANUEL AS A SIGN OF PEKAH AND REZIN'S DOWNFALL

Despite the response of the stubborn, aloof king, the prophet promises to produce a sign from God himself:

---

8. Since their early days in Egypt and until they entered the land, the Children of Israel witnessed many signs and wonders, however, they also frequently had crises of faith. God tested Israel, and Israel repeatedly tested God (Ex. 16–17). When Moses delivered his parting speech to the nation before they entered the land, he described the testing of God as a sin, "Do not test the Lord your God, as you tested Him at Masa" (Deut. 6:16). There were several instances, after they had entered the land, when a leader asked God for a sign. The most prominent example of this can be found in the story of Gideon, in the Book of Judges. However, it is beyond the scope of this book to examine these examples. See also Y. Zakovitch, *The Concept of the Miracle in the Bible* (Tel Aviv, 1987) [Hebrew].

> Therefore, God will be the one to give you a sign, behold, the maiden will conceive and bear a son, and you shall call his name Immanu-El [God is with us], he shall be eating butter and honey when he is old enough to reject evil and choose good; for before the boy will know to reject evil and choose good, the land of the two kings you dread will be abandoned. (Is. 7:14–16)

Some (including Radak) claim that the maiden he referred to is Ahaz's wife, and that the prophet gave Ahaz a sign within his own household. It is more likely, however, that he spoke of his own young wife, who was soon to bear him a son.[9] Isaiah's oldest son, She'ar-Yashuv, was mentioned when he brought him on his first mission to Ahaz (7:3–9), next to the Upper Pool of the aqueduct. Isaiah's second child, Immanuel, was the sign that God would send to Ahaz to strengthen his resilience and discourage him from taking action and forming alliances. He assured Ahaz that before the child is old enough to distinguish between good and evil, Damascus and Samaria will have been overthrown, and will threaten Judah no more.

The time frame given in the prophecy is consistent with Assyrian records, which document Rezin's rebellion in the twelfth year of Tiglath-Pileser's reign (734 BCE), and his defeat and elimination in 732 BCE.[10] The prophecy was uttered at the beginning of Tiglath-Pileser's mission to Damascus (733 BCE). In his first appearance before Ahaz, Isaiah predicted that Aram and Israel, "two smoking stubs of firebrand," would collapse in less than a lifetime ("in sixty-five years"), but this failed to encourage Ahaz. In his second appearance, the prophet brought the coalition's anticipated destruction forward considerably, stating that within a few years they will be defeated and their land will be deserted. Radak interprets this verse:

---

9. In the Septuagint, the word *alma* was translated as "virgin," resulting in the Christian reading of this passage as a prophecy of a virgin birth. However the literal meaning of *alma* is young woman or maiden.

10. A. Malamat, "Wars of Israel and Assyria," in *The Military History of the Land of Israel in Biblical Times*, ed. J. Liver (Tel Aviv, 1964), 241–60 [Hebrew].

Before this boy will begin to speak, which is the usual time for choosing good and rejecting evil. Within three years, or sooner, the land of Samaria will be abandoned, and Damascus desolate. (Radak on Is. 7:16)

THE PROPHECY OF JUDAH'S DESTRUCTION TOGETHER WITH THE REST OF THE LAND

Isaiah had wanted to console and encourage the king. However, perhaps he caught a look of haughty disbelief on Ahaz's face and became enraged by his contempt, because in verse 17 the tone changes dramatically to one of warning. After describing the downfall of Damascus and Samaria at the hands of Assyria, Isaiah described the downfall of Judah by the same hands. He declared that Ahaz's insistence on submitting to Assyria would eventually result in Judah's defeat:

> The Lord will cause to come upon you and your people and your ancestral house such days as never have come since Ephraim turned away from Judah – the king of Assyria. (Is. 7:17)

PROPHECIES OF "THAT DAY" (7:18–25)[11]

The next prophecy comprises five passages describing Assyria's invasion and the destruction, exile and devastation it will wreak. While destruction was already predicted in chapters 5 and 6, the description here was more imminent and specific, and it explicitly referred to Assyria.

The prophet described the Assyrian invasion using four different metaphors:

1. FLIES FROM EGYPT AND WASPS FROM ASSYRIA

> And it shall come to pass on that day – The Lord shall whistle for the flies at the edge of the Egyptian Nile and for the wasps

---

11. S. Vargon, "Prophecy of Consolation or Prophecy of Doom," *Beit Mikra* 167 (2002): 289–303 [Hebrew]. Vargon notes that classical commentators read these verses as a prophecy of consolation for Hezekiah's time, but argues that it is more appropriate to read them in context of the Assyrian invasion, rather than being saved from it.

in the land of Assyria; and all shall settle in the desolate streams, and in the fissures of the rocks, and among all the brambles and all the briars. (7:18–19)

The first metaphor described swarms of insects infiltrating: "The desolate streams, and in the fissures of the rocks, and among all the brambles and all the briars." They will darken every corner of the kingdom.[12]

Isaiah overturned both of Judah's (and Israel's) political options: forming a coalition with Egypt against Assyria (Rezin and Pekah's aspiration), and submission to Assyria. In the prophet's opinion, both options would lead to total domination by Assyria.

2. THE HIRED RAZOR

On that day, the Lord will use a razor hired from the other side of the river, the king of Assyria, to shave your head and the hair of your legs, and to cut off your beard as well. (7:20)

The second metaphor the prophet used to describe the impending invasion is the shaving of hair. In the ancient world, the Egyptians were clean-shaven, while the Semites took pride in their well-groomed beards. The Book of Samuel describes the severe insult conveyed through the shaving of another's beard; David's delegates to the king of Ammon were accused of spying, and their beards were half-shaven and their genitals mutilated in chastisement. These men were "greatly shamed," and David ordered them to remain in Jericho, "Until your beards grow and then you shall return" (II Sam. 10:4–5). The elaborate beards of the Assyrian

---

12. The wasp was a symbol of Egyptian royalty in ancient times. This suggests interesting interpretations on the verses: "And I shall send the wasp before you…to drive out the Canaanite" (Ex. 23:28), and "the Lord your God will also send the wasp against them" (Deut. 7:20). Towards the end of the Canaanite period in the Land of Israel, Egypt conducted frequent conquests in the Canaanite lowlands. These conquests greatly weakened the Canaanites and increased their dependence on Egypt. Here, Isaiah reverses this symbol. The Egyptians are now the "flies" while the Assyrians are the "wasps," that is, the dominant empire. This hints to Egypt's inability to overcome Assyria; any attempt to rely on Egypt will end in disaster for Israel and Judah.

kings were depicted in statues and tombstones. Thus Isaiah's description represented deep humiliation. God would bring the king of Assyria from the other side of the river as a hired barber who would shave the hair of Judah and Israel as a mark of shame.

3. AN ABUNDANCE OF MILK AND HONEY

> And it will come to pass on that day – Each person will raise a female calf and two sheep, And from surplus of milk, they will eat butter, for butter and honey will be eaten by all those who remain upon the land. (Is. 7:21–22)

The remnant of the people was already mentioned twice in the Book of Isaiah, in the vision of the canopy protecting "those who are left in Zion, and who have stayed in Jerusalem (4:3–6), and at the end of the bleak picture of the desolate land with but "a tenth" of "holy seed" remaining (6:13). Now, for the third time, this remnant is mentioned. It is important to note the irony in the blessing that is described. The vineyards will have grown wild and the fields will be a mass of thorn and thistle, but then, new growth shall spring up. This is the blessing of nature, and it does not depend upon human efforts. It is a blessing inherent to the Land of Israel, the land flowing with milk and honey. The few who survive will enjoy the natural bounty of the land, eating of the abundant milk of the animals and the sweet fruits of the land. This presents an idyllic picture in the aftermath of destruction; the remnant of the people will live off the fat of the land, and not under the thumb of human oppressors.[13]

4. THE DESOLATION OF THE ONCE-POPULATED LAND

> And it will come to pass on that day – Every place that once had a thousand vines, worth a thousand pieces of silver, will have become thorn and thistle, whoever ventures there will take arrow

---

13. B. Oppenheimer, "The Unique Historical Approach of Isaiah," *Bible and Jewish History Studies in the President's House* 1, 8–9 [Hebrew].

and bow, for the entire land shall be thorn and thistle; and all the hills that will be cultivated, which are not overrun with thorn and thistle, shall be overrun by cattle and trampled by sheep. (7:23–25)

This passage seems to contradict the previous two verses, which promised abundance to those who remain. Israel and Judah had transformed the mountainous regions into fertile farming ground covered with vineyards: "A thousand vines worth a thousand pieces of silver" (7:23). However, these were destined to become overgrown and thorny jungles that concealed wild animals, where: "Whoever ventures there will take arrow and bow." Fields will be overrun with wild cattle and "trampled by sheep."

It is unclear whether the four descriptions that begin with the phrase "on that day" refer to the fate of Judah alone, or to that of Israel as well. In the context of the first part of the chapter, it seems that Isaiah's words were directed towards the king of Judah.

CHAPTER 8: THE BIRTH OF MAHER-SHALAL-HASH-BAZ

> And the Lord said to me: Take for yourself a large tablet, and write upon it in clear inscription, *Maher-Shalal-Hash-Baz*; then I called in reliable witnesses, Uriah the priest and Zechariah son of Jeberekhiah, and I was intimate with the prophetess, and she conceived and bore a son, and the Lord said to me: Call his name Maher-Shalal-Hash-Baz, for before the boy will be able to say 'mother' and 'father,' the wealth of Damascus and the spoil of Samaria shall be carried off before the king of Assyria. (8:1–4)

Judahite society had split into two; one party called for joining the local coalition against Assyria, while the other pressed for requesting aid and protection from Assyria against the coalition. Stubbornly campaigning against both, Isaiah demanded that Judah stay out of international politics.

The first encounter between Isaiah and King Ahaz took place north of the Temple Mount, by the aqueduct of the Upper Pool. There, the prophet stood with his son She'ar-Yashuv, urging the king to stand firm against the coalition, and stay out of international politics in general. He demanded that Ahaz remain faithful: "If you do not stand firm in your faith, you will not stand at all."

By their second encounter, the regional coalition had grown in power and strength, and Jerusalem was fearful. The pressure to join the coalition was mounting, as was the temptation to surrender to the Assyrian Empire before Tiglath-Pileser set out to attack Rezin (which occurred in 733 BCE). Isaiah attempted to reassure Ahaz that the end of the two local kings was nigh, "Before the boy will know to reject evil and choose good." Isaiah warned that that the Assyrian army would not only destroy the kingdoms of Aram and Israel, but that they would "shave" the entire region, leaving it a wasteland.

In preparation for their third meeting, Isaiah was commanded to inscribe the words, "*Maher-Shalal-Hash-Baz*," (Quick to plunder, swift to spoil) in clear letters on a large tablet, before witnesses.[14] These words were to be the name of his third son. The visual aid raised the prophecy to a new level. Words which are only heard are quickly forgotten, but once they are seen by the eye, they do not fade from the memory so soon.

The inscription lent authority to the previous prophecy. God's word promising the fall of Aram and Israel was soon to be fulfilled. Before Tiglath-Pileser had even embarked on his journey, the prophet predicted that the spoils would soon be divided. Isaiah then told of how he was intimate with his wife, "the prophetess," who conceived and bore a third son. At God's command, this child bore as his name the prophecy that was inscribed upon the tablet. Its meaning is clear: "Before the boy will be able to say mother and father," that is, in less than a year, the Kingdom of Damascus will fall to the king of Assyria.[15]

---

14. Rashi comments: "In script which any man can skim through quickly, even a very common man, even if he is not intelligent." Based on this interpretation, we can understand the word *enosh*, which is used in the verse to describe the "clear inscription," and which literally means "human," as an expression of human weakness, not strength.

15. Rashi comments that as they were born in the same year, Immanuel and Maher-Shalal-Hash-Baz must be two names for the same child. Radak, however, explains that the "maiden" who bore Immanuel was the wife of Ahaz, and Maher-Shalal-Hash-Baz was Isaiah's son who was born in the same year.

According to the plain meaning of the passage – three prophecies to the king corresponding to three sons born to the prophet – the two brothers, Immanuel and Maher-Shalal-Hash-Baz would have been born one year apart. Immanuel would not have reached the age of two, and Maher-Shalal-Hash-Baz would not yet be a year old, when Tiglath-Pileser destroyed Aram and its leader (in the fourteenth year of his reign, 732 BCE). At that time, Pekah was assassinated and replaced with Hosea son of Elah, who was appointed by the Assyrian Empire.[16]

The prophet fulfilled God's word before two "reliable" witnesses – the priest Uriah, and Zechariah son of Jeberekhiah. It appears that Uriah was the High Priest in Ahaz's time (II Kings 16:10–11). Zechariah son of Jeberekhiah shares a name with the prophet of redemption from the early days of the Second Temple, and is possibly his ancestor. A link is thus made between Isaiah's ominous prophecy (quick to plunder, swift to spoil), and the redemption of the Second Temple era.[17]

REPROACH AGAINST THOSE WHO SPURN THE SLOW-FLOWING WATERS OF THE SILOAM (SHILOAH)

Isaiah turned his attention to the party that rejected the idea of joining the anti-Assyrian coalition, and thus attacked both sides simultaneously:

---

16. The assassination of Pekah is mentioned in II Kings 15, immediately following the exile of the Gilead and the Galilee by Tiglath-Pileser. It is also documented in Assyrian records, where Tiglath-Pileser describes this exile and adds, "their King Pekah was eliminated, and I appointed Hosea as king." See H. Tadmor, "The Conquest of the Galilee by Tiglath-Pileser III," in *The Entire Land of Naphtali*, ed. H.Z. Hirschberg and Y. Aviram (Jerusalem, 1968), 62–67 [Hebrew]; Damsky, *Guide*, 45.

17. In Tractate Makkot (24b), Rabbi Akiva connects the witnesses to their namesakes in other time periods, namely Uriah son of Shemaiah from Kiriath-jearim (Jeremiah 26:20–23), who was killed by Joachim, and Zechariah the prophet, a contemporary of Zerubbabel and Joshua the priest. Uriah son of Shemaiah prophesied the destruction before Jeremiah did. Rabbi Akiva claims that these two prophets were juxtaposed here to show that just as Uriah's prediction of destruction was fulfilled, so would Zechariah's prophecy of redemption be. The connection between destruction and redemption can be found in the simple meaning of the text of Isaiah. In every prediction of destruction, Isaiah includes a trace of redemption, the tidings of "She'ar-Yashuv," the remnant who will return.

> And the Lord spoke to me again, saying: Because this people
> has spurned the slow-flowing waters of Shiloah, and delighted
> in Rezin and the son of Remaliah. (Is. 8:5–6)

These words may have been calculated to ease the public pressure on
Ahaz to join the coalition. The prophet pleaded with the party heads,
asking them to slow down like the gentle waters of the Shiloah. This
expression is similar in meaning to Isaiah's first appeal to Ahaz: "Take
care and be silent, and do not fear, and let not your heart weaken." The
prophet argued against the anti-Assyrian rebels, who were placing
their trust in Rezin and Pekah, rather than focusing on gathering inner
strength. This inner strength was symbolized by the gently flowing
waters of the Shiloah.[18]

The sages noted the word *le'at*, slow, and compared it to Jacob's
evasive words to Esau when he excused himself from accompanying
him to Mount Seir:

> Let my lord go on ahead of his servant, while I travel *slowly*, at
> the pace of the cattle before me and at the pace of the children,
> until I come to my lord in Seir. (Gen. 33:10)

Rashi (based on Genesis Rabba, 78:17) comments: "Slowly, at my pace,
like the slow-flowing waters of the Shiloah." The midrash teaches that like
each different body of water, each person moves at their own unique pace.
Trying to change to the pace of a different body of water will only "drain"
a person. Before Ahaz surrendered to Tiglath-Pileser, Isaiah wished to
impart to him the importance of pooling one's inner resources, and of
building strength and resilience through them.

---

18. This probably refers to the irrigation system of the Kidron Valley through the Upper Pool
aqueduct; the waters of Shiloah are the waters of the Gihon Spring, which irrigated the
Kidron Valley. This changed once Hezekiah's tunnel redirected the waters to the Pool
of Siloam, and the upper aqueduct dried up. Hezekiah's tunnel was built for Jerusalem's
defense against the Assyrian siege, and in preparation of the rebellion against Assyria. It
is no wonder that Isaiah was opposed to the rechanneling of the waters, just as he was
opposed to the preparations for the rebellion (22:11). See Yoel Bin-Nun, "He Shall Not
Shoot an Arrow at it: The Pool and the Aqueduct," *Al Atar* 11 (2003): 29–43 [Hebrew].

The prophet's response to those who spurned the waters of the Shiloah was harsh and biting:

> Therefore, My Lord will bring up against them the mighty, many waters of the river, the king of Assyria and all his glory, it shall rise above all its channels, and flow over all its beds, and swirl through Judah like a flash flood reaching up to the neck. Its outspread wings will cover the breadth of your land, Immanuel. (Is. 8:7–8)

The rebels would be washed away with a mighty rush of water from Assyria's River Tigris, a metaphor for the Assyrian army, who passed through enemy lands like a devastating flood. The waters would rise to Judah's neck.

Isaiah used the image of a massive bird of prey, whose broad wings would cast a shadow over the long, narrow borders of the Land of Israel. This was a reinterpretation of a verse from the Torah. A passage of reproach in Deuteronomy describes the enemy's attack upon the Land:

> The Lord will bring a nation upon you from afar, from the ends of the earth, as the eagle soars, a nation whose tongue you have never heard, a brazen nation without respect for the old or pity for the young. (Deut. 28:49–50)

PLOT A PLOT – IT SHALL BE FOILED: MOCKING THE COALITION AGAINST ASSYRIA

After describing the approaching Assyrian army's strength and might, the prophet devoted a few verses to the arrogance of those who plan to bring its invasion to a halt:

> Sound the war cry, O peoples – you shall be broken! Hear this, you remotest parts of the earth: Gird yourselves – you shall be broken; gird yourselves – you shall be broken! Plot a plot – it shall be foiled; make a plan – it shall not succeed. For with us is God! (Is. 8:9–10)

These verses mocked the nations preparing for battle: "Gird yourselves," don your battle-clothes, but "You shall be broken." The prophet watched the preparations for war: the rush to enlist, the sharpening of swords, and the adrenaline rising, and he knew that it was all in vain. As the nations around him prepared for battle, the prophet called out, "Plot a plot – it shall be foiled; make a plan – it shall not succeed, for with us is God."

This phrase is often used to express the expectation of victory over enemies who wish us harm; we shall overcome, because "God is with us." In the prophet's time, those preparing for battle may have felt that God was on their side too. However, "God is with us" does not mean that Israel is always on the winning side. When God has decided that Assyria (or Babylonia, Persia, Greece or Rome) will dominate, no joining of forces will be able to stop them. These words are not directed against Ahaz, but against the party that supported the anti-Assyrian coalition.

THE ARGUMENT AGAINST BOTH PARTIES IN JUDAH

> For this is what the Lord said to me, when He took me by the hand and charged me not to walk in the path of that people: You must not call conspiracy all that this people calls conspiracy, do not revere what it reveres, nor hold it in awe. None but the Lord of Hosts shall you sanctify; give reverence to Him alone, hold Him alone in awe. (8:11–13)

In his final words to Ahaz (who was about to surrender to the Assyrians), Isaiah described how the Lord held his hand and demanded that the prophet express His words. He encouraged him not to be tempted into rebellion, nor to surrender, but rather to constantly adhere to the path of God, like the "slow-flowing waters of the Shiloah."

Next, the prophet turned to the two political factions that had developed. First, to the pro-rebellion party, he said, "You must not call conspiracy, all that this people calls conspiracy." He declared that the Aram-Israel alliance was not a substantial threat, and that it would not endure. Second, to the appeasers who wished to surrender to Assyria, with Ahaz at their head, God's message was, "Do not revere what it reveres, nor hold it in awe."

The message continued, "None but the Lord of Hosts shall you sanctify, give reverence to Him alone, and hold Him alone in awe." Ahaz and his government, who were not prepared to rely on God and trust in Him, would fall, but so would those who thought that God was on the side of the coalition against Assyria. Here, the prophet presents a surprising prophetic reinterpretation of a Torah idea:

> He shall be for a sanctuary, a stone people strike against: A rock people stumble over for the two houses of Israel, and a trap and a snare for those who dwell in Jerusalem. The masses shall trip over these and shall fall and be injured, shall be snared and be caught. (8:14–15)

The Torah warns of the dangers of overstepping boundaries and approaching sacred areas. At Mount Sinai, God warned that those who come too close to the mountain will "surely be stoned or shot through, whether man or beast, he shall not live" (Ex. 19:12–13). Nadab and Abihu entered the forbidden area of the Sanctuary and died (Lev. 10:1–3). And when the Ark was brought to Jerusalem, whoever touched it was punished with death (II Sam. 6:6–8). The sacred requires proper respect, as Moses is commanded by the burning bush: "Remove your shoes from your feet" (Ex. 3:5).

This is what the prophet expressed to those rushing into war against Assyria. Those who declared that "the Lord is with us" in fact brandished a double edged sword, and would be cut down by their own weapons. They hoped to harness the sacred to advance their own ends, but they would soon be struck down for daring to do so.

Israel is Conquered and Judah Surrenders (732 BCE)

T he Book of Kings, which does not describe the Assyrian conquest of Philistia, does mention some details about the campaign of Damascus (733 BCE). Tiglath-Pileser made his way through the cities of the northern Jordan Valley, and then conquered the Upper Galilee and the Gilead (the Israelite territory of the Transjordan). In his third military campaign (732 BCE), Tiglath-Pileser conquered Damascus, making it into yet another Assyrian province.

The success of the Assyrian military campaigns reflects Tiglath-Pileser's brilliance as a strategist. In his twelfth year as king, 734 BCE, he conquered the Phoenician coast, all the way to Philistine and Egypt in the south. In 733 BCE, he conquered vast areas of the Kingdom of Aram, the Galilee, and the Gilead, leaving Damascus, the capital of Aram, isolated and vulnerable, and in 732 BCE, he conquered the city itself.

The campaigns against Damascus are described at length in six different Assyrian inscriptions. In Kings, the beginning of the Israelite exile is recorded thus:

> In the days of King Pekah of Israel, came Tiglath-Pileser, king
> of Assyria, and he took Ijon and Abel Beit Maakha and Janoah,
> And Kedesh and Hazor, and the Gilead and the Galilee, All
> the land of Naphtali, and he exiled them to Assyria. (II Kings
> 15:29)

The information gleaned from the various sources allows us to sketch out
a map of the Assyrian campaign.[1] The formidable army left the Lebanon
Valley and set out south towards Ijon (today's Marjayoun), Abel Beit
Maakha and Kedesh, and then, it seems, headed towards today's Beit
Netofa and the coast, to "The Way of the Sea" (Isaiah 8:23).

At the same time, part of the army continued southwards in the
Jordan Valley, towards Hazor and the Sea of Galilee, and from there they
crossed to the eastern side of the Jordan and conquered the Gilead. The
conquest of the Gilead was one of Assyria's decisive victories, as this
area was a local bastion of resistance against them. The eastern tribes'
capture is documented in the Book of Chronicles:

> The sons of Reuben, the firstborn of Israel: Enoch, Pallu, Hezron,
> and Carmi. The sons of Joel: his son Shemaiah, his son Gog, his
> son Shimei, his son Micah, his son Reaiah, his son Baal, his son
> Be'era – whom King Tiglath-Pileser of Assyria exiled – was chief-
> tain of the Reubenites. (I Chr. 5:3–6)

The deportation of Be'era, chieftain of the Reubenites, is the biblical
reference to Tiglath-Pileser's infiltration of the Transjordan.

Tiglath-Pileser III was the first Assyrian king to enter Israelite territory, and he immediately began to implement a policy of exile upon
the conquered population.[2] The Israelite exile began with the conquest
of the Gilead and the Galilee. According to Assyrian documentation,
more than thirteen thousand people were exiled from these regions, and

---

1. For a comprehensive description of the campaign, see Y. Aharoni, *The Land of Israel
   in Biblical Times* (Jerusalem, 1988), 283 ff. [Hebrew].
2. For a detailed description of the Assyrian exile, see N. Na'aman, "Population Changes in
   the Land of Israel following the Assyrian Exiles," *Cathedra* 54 (1990): 43–62 [Hebrew].

it is clear that many others fled around that time. The Assyrian records make no mention of a population exchange, which was practiced in other conquered territories, and was implemented later following Sargon's campaign to Samaria (725 BCE). Tiglath-Pileser may have chosen not to resettle the Galilee as he did not ascribe any particular importance to this area. In his eyes, the most important routes led from Damascus towards the sea (Tyre), and from there, to Philistia and Egypt.[3] Archaeological evidence indicates that the Lower Galilee was destroyed and not rebuilt for a very long time.[4]

The reduced Kingdom of Israel, confined solely to the Mount Ephraim region, was surrounded by three new Assyrian provinces. In the Assyrian records, these provinces are referred to by the names of their capitals; Megiddo (which included the northern valleys and the Galilee), Dor (from the Sharon until Philistia), and Gilead (Israelite Transjordan). Mount Ephraim was allowed to exist as an independent region only because Israel surrendered to Assyria. Pekah was assassinated and replaced with Hosea son of Elah, who had the approval of the Assyrian government:

> And Hosea son of Elah conspired against Pekah son of Remaliah, and he smote him and had him executed, and he ruled in his place in the twentieth year of Jotham son of Uzziah. (II Kings 15:30)

AHAZ SURRENDERS TO ASSYRIA:
"I AM YOUR SERVANT AND SON"

Since the onset of Rezin and Pekah's rebellion, Isaiah had tried to prevent political decline with all his might. He struggled to stop both the widespread Judahite desire to join the coalition, and the king's desire to submit to Assyria. He declared that Judah should allow the Assyrian chariots to march through the land as they came from Damascus and Israel and headed towards Philistia and Egypt, for Judah was not an Assyrian target.

---

3. Tadmor, "The Conquest of the Galilee by Tiglath-Pileser III," 62–67.
4. Z. Gal, "The Lower Galilee during the Iron Age" (PhD diss., Tel Aviv University, 1983), 118 [Hebrew].

Eventually, Ahaz succumbed to his political insecurity and chose to surrender.

The delegation he sent to the Assyrians brought no usual message of surrender. Ahaz not only presented himself as the servant of the Assyrian King, but he also emphasized his utter devotion to the Empire:

> And Ahaz sent messengers to King Tiglath-Pileser of Assyria, saying: I am your servant and son, go up and save me from the hand of the king of Aram and the hand of the king of Israel, who have risen up against me; and Ahaz took the silver and gold from the Temple and the royal treasuries, and sent a gift to the king of Assyria; and the king of Assyria listened to him, and the king of Assyria went up to Damascus and seized it and exiled it to Kir, and executed Rezin. (II Kings 16:7–9)

Ahaz appealed to the king of Assyria, describing himself as: "Your servant and son." Assyrian records of surrender usually contain the formulation "your servant." On occasion, the phrase "your son," is used as an expression of closeness and the seeking of patronage. The formula, "your servant and son," is unique and suggests that Ahaz did not merely turn to Assyria as a servant to his master, but as a son embracing his father.[5]

The biblical description of the great Assyrian king galloping to Ahaz's aid is hyperbolical, for he was already on his way to the area, and had targeted the two kingdoms long before Ahaz's request. At most, Tiglath-Pileser's reaction to Ahaz's plea might have been to boast at how favorable the Assyrian Empire was in the eyes of the local kings. The biblical text may be a reflection of the Judahite perspective; Ahaz had "secured" Judah's safety, and no one could challenge his policies any longer.

Judah surrendered, and Israel crumbled; Isaiah's great struggle had borne no fruit at that time.

---

5. M. Cogan and H. Tadmor, "Ahaz and Tiglath-Pileser in the Book of Kings," *Eretz Yisrael* 14 (1978): 59–61 [Hebrew].

JUDAH AFTER SURRENDER: ABANDONING GOD'S
PATH AND ADOPTING ASSYRIAN CULTURE

Despite the loss of independence and power, Ahaz's surrender brought peace to Judah. The surrender was not only political; it rendered Judah an Assyrian province from a cultural and religious perspective as well. Changes of this nature were implemented by Ahaz; the Assyrian government made no such demands.

In the eyes of many Judeans, Ahaz became a national hero. In contrast to most of the surrounding nations, he had managed to save Jerusalem from the Assyrian sword. While their neighbors wallowed in their own blood (Gaza, Ashkelon, and Ashdod were conquered and looted; Damascus was destroyed; Israel fell), Judah remained untouched, politically and economically. The security situation improved immeasurably, for Aram, Israel, and Philistia no longer posed any threat. Under Ahaz's guidance, traditional Judahite culture made way for Assyrian customs and rituals; Jerusalem modeled itself on Assyria. Ahaz's participation in Tiglath-Pileser's victory parade through Damascus is recorded in the Book of Kings:

> And King Ahaz went towards King Tiglath-Pileser of Assyria in Damascus, and he saw the altar in Damascus; and King Ahaz sent an image of the altar to Uriah the priest, and detailed sketches for its construction. (II Kings 16:10)

Going to Damascus to congratulate the head of the empire was a reasonable diplomatic step,[6] but when Ahaz caught sight of the Assyrian victory altar, he made a fateful decision; Jerusalem would now serve Assyria's gods. Ahaz had submitted to Assyria as "your servant and son," and so he decided to worship the gods of his new "father." Assyrian kings did not force their religion upon the nations they conquered, allowing religious freedom throughout the empire, and occasionally even adopting the local gods in order to rule the province with a firmer hand. Ahaz, however, did not only submit to Assyrian rule; he

---

6. Assyrian records show that other kings also came to show their allegiance to Tiglath-Pileser.

changed the official religion of his kingdom to adopt Assyrian ritual and worship.[7]

The detailed instructions of the altar's design were sent to the priest Uriah, one of Isaiah's "reliable witnesses," to be reproduced in the Temple in Jerusalem. This led to the renewal of idol worship in Jerusalem:

> The priest Uriah built the altar, just as King Ahaz had instructed him from Damascus; so the priest Uriah did, by the King Ahaz's arrival from Damascus; when the king arrived from Damascus, and when the king saw the altar, the king drew near the altar, ascended it, and offered his burnt offering and meal offering; he poured his libation, and he dashed the blood of his offering of well-being against the altar. As for the bronze altar which had been before the Lord, he moved it from its place in front of the Temple, between the altar and the House of the Lord, and placed it on the north side of the altar; and King Ahaz commanded the priest Uriah, saying: On the great altar you shall offer the morning burnt offering and the evening meal offering and the king's burnt offering and his meal offering, with the burnt offerings of all the people of the land, their meal offerings and their libations ... The priest Uriah did just as King Ahaz commanded; King Ahaz cut off the insets – the laver stands – and removed the lavers from them. He also removed the tank from the bronze oxen that supported it and set it on a stone pavement; he also extended to the House of the Lord the sabbath passage that had been built in the palace and the king's outer entrance, on account of the king of Assyria. (II Kings 16:11–18)

Josephus interpreted Ahaz's deed thus:

> It seemed that he preferred to honor all the gods, than the God of his forefathers, and he reached such disrespect and profligacy

---

7. In one of Tiglath-Pileser's records, the name "Jehoahaz king of Judah" is mentioned in a list of kings who paid taxes (see Damsky, *Guide*, 46). While the prefix "Jeho" was typical among the kings of Judah, it appears that the Bible removed God's name from the king who removed God's name from Jerusalem and the Temple.

that he eventually closed the Temple and forbade the sacrifice of the accepted offerings, and he robbed it of its holy gifts. (Josephus, *Antiquities* IX, 12:3)

II Chronicles (28:24) describes the closing of the Temple and the cessation of the offerings, and Josephus explains the disparity between Kings and Chronicles as two different stages of Ahaz's actions. First, Ahaz brought idolatry into the Temple, and this led to the closing of the Sanctuary. Substitute altars were placed: "At every corner in Jerusalem." Ahaz removed parts of the Temple courtyard that had been placed there by Solomon (I Kings 7:25–37; cf. II Kings 16:17), thereby declaring that the Temple will serve as God's house no more, for God had abandoned His people. This declaration enabled – and even encouraged – the worship of the prominent gods of that time, the gods of Assyria.

One of Ahaz's gravest sins was to bring the worship of Moloch into Jerusalem:

> And he walked in the paths of the kings of Israel, and he passed his son through the fire, like the abominations of the nations, who the Lord had dispossessed before the Israelites. (II Kings 16:3)

Among the prophets of Israel, the ritual sacrifice of children to the god Moloch was considered the most abhorrent of sins, and Ahaz was the first king to bring such practice into Jerusalem.

The sages extend Ahaz's treachery, explaining that he committed sins regarding Torah study in addition to expressing contempt for the Temple:

> R. Honya said in the name of R. Lazar: Why was he named Ahaz? Because he sent his hands (*aḥaz*) against synagogues and study houses. What can Ahaz be compared to? To a king who sent his son to a tutor, and wished to kill him; he said, if I kill him, I will receive the death penalty, but if I take his nurse away, he will die by himself; Thus said Ahaz: If there are no kids, there are no goats; if there are no goats, there are no sheep; if there are no sheep, there is no shepherd; if there is no shepherd, there is no world ... Thus

he felt sure of saying that if there are no children – there are no adults; if there are no adults – there are no wise people; if there are no wise people, there are no prophets; if there are no prophets, there is no divine inspiration; if there is no divine inspiration, there are no synagogues or study houses, for it is as if the Holy One is not placing His spirit upon Israel; R. Yaakov b. Abaye, in the name of R. Aha, brings this description from the verse in Isaiah 8:17, in his prophecies from the days of Ahaz: "And I will wait for the Lord, who is concealing His face from the House of Jacob, and I will hope for Him." (Y. Sanhedrin 51a)

THE PROPHET SECLUDES HIMSELF AMONG HIS STUDENTS

After Ahaz's decision, the prophet withdrew into his study house with his children and students, and reflected upon the impending darkness; upon the failure of the rebels who believed that God was on their side, and the failure of the desperate heretics who did not. The only action he could take was to educate the leaders of the next generation:

> Bind up the message, seal the instruction with my students and I will wait for the Lord, who is concealing His face from the House of Jacob, and I will hope for Him. Here am I and the children the Lord has given me as signs and wonders in Israel, from the Lord of Hosts, who dwells on Mount Zion. (Is. 8:16–18)

The Talmud Yerushalmi offers a general perspective about the divine concealment of Ahaz's reign:

> R. Yaakov b. Abaye in the name of R. Aha learns from here: "And I will wait for the Lord, who is concealing His face from the House of Jacob, and I will hope for Him." There was no harder hour in the world than that same hour when God said to Moses, "I will surely conceal My face from you on that day." From that hour, "I will hope for Him," as He said to him at Sinai, "for you shall not be forgotten in the mouth of My seed." And what helps in a time of divine concealment? "Here am I and the children the Lord has

given me." Were they his children – weren't they his students? This teaches us that they were beloved unto him, and he would refer to them as "my children." (Y. Sanhedrin 51a)

Isaiah understood that a time of divine concealment had come, and he began to redefine the purpose of prophecy. Until now, he had tried to convince the king to halt the political avalanche. Once that failed, he adopted the refrain of, "I will wait for the Lord…I will hope for Him." This message became a beacon of hope for Israel, lighting up its darkest hours. It was a prophetic prototype for those who came after Isaiah. Several generations later, during the dark era of the rise of Babylonia, the prophet Habakkuk also received divine instructions to write upon a tablet:

> And the Lord answered me, and He said: Write the prophecy down, inscribe it clearly on tablets, so that it can be read easily. For there is yet a prophecy for a set term, a truthful witness for a time that will come. Even if it tarries, wait for it still; for it will surely come, without delay. (Hab. 2:2–3)

This hope became an integral part of the Jewish doctrine: "And even though he may tarry, I still await him, every day" (Maimonides, *Thirteen Principles of Faith*).

THE PEOPLE SEEK REDEMPTION THROUGH NECROMANCERS AND ORACLES

The Torah forbids consulting with necromancers or oracles:

> Let no one be found among you who consigns his son or daughter to the fire, or who is an augur, a soothsayer, a diviner, a sorcerer, one who casts spells; or necromancers or oracles, or one who inquires of the dead. For anyone who does such things is abhorrent to the Lord, and it is because of these abhorrent things that the Lord your God is dispossessing them before you; you must be wholehearted with the Lord your God. Those nations that you are about to dispossess do indeed resort to soothsayers and augurs; to you, however, the Lord your God has not

assigned the like. The Lord your God will raise up for you a prophet from among your own people, like myself; Him you shall obey. (Deut. 18:10–15)

At the beginning of his reign, King Saul took care to abolish all necromancy and sorcery from the land (I Sam. 28:3). On the eve of his last battle in the Jezreel Valley and the Gilboa, however, desperate and alone, he turned to a necromancer and asked her to raise up the spirit of the prophet Samuel (I Sam. 28:7–25). He resorted to this forbidden act only after God had turned away from him:

> And Saul inquired of the Lord, but the Lord did not answer him, neither in dreams, nor through the Urim, nor through prophets. (I Sam. 28:6)

Isaiah witnessed how the surrender to Assyria had affected the people. They had become embittered through hunger and suffering, and they turned to necromancers and oracles for answers, but found no rest:

> And if should people say to you: Inquire of the ghosts and familiar spirits that chirp and moan; for a people may inquire of its gods, of the dead on behalf of the living, for instruction and message, for one who speaks thus there shall be no dawn; and he shall go about in it wretched and hungry; and when he is hungry, he shall rage and revolt, cursing his king and his gods, turning his face upward, and he may look to the land, beholding distress and desolation, fearful gloom, and utter darkness. (Is. 8:19–22)

DOES ISAIAH BRING THE WAR OF ASA AND BAASHA BACK TO THE NATION'S CONSCIOUSNESS?

> For there is to be no weariness for those that distress her, the first dealt lightly with the land of Zebulun and the land of Naphtali, and the last dealt harshly – With the Way of the Sea, the other side of the Jordan, and the Galilee of the nations. (8:23)

While this verse clearly refers to the devastating effects of Tiglath-Pileser's campaign, it has nonetheless been subjected to various interpretations. The main debate centers upon the meaning of "first" and "last." Rashi takes these words out of the immediate historical context and interprets them in relation to the Assyrian conquest in general, and the destruction of Samaria. He reads "the first" as Tiglath-Pileser's exile of the Transjordanian tribes (in the twelfth year of Ahaz's reign), and "the last" as the exile of Samaria, following its complete destruction. Rashi interprets the word *hikhbid*, "dealt harshly," in connection with the "last," as: "He swept everything away, like one who sweeps a house," leaving nothing behind.[8] According to Rashi, Isaiah knew what would befall the Kingdom of Samaria in the future. The main problem with this interpretation, however, is that the verse's context is Jerusalem, and the fear that seized the inhabitants of Judah in the wake of the submission to Assyria.

Hanan Eshel proposes a reading of the words "first" and "last" within a wider biblical-historical context.[9] This was not the first time that a king of Judah had sought assistance from a foreign empire. As mentioned earlier, Asa sent a gift to a foreign king to request military aid, and this may have been on Ahaz's mind when he considered surrendering to Tiglath-Pileser. In this passage, Isaiah may have been reacting to this national memory. Long ago, Asa asked for the aid of Aram, who stepped in and easily defeated the northern Kingdom of Israel:

> And Ben Hadad listened to King Asa, and he sent the commanders of his forces up to the cities of Jerusalem, and he smote Ijon and Dan and Abel Beit Maakha, and all of Kinrot, and all of the land of Naphtali. (I Kings 15:20)

This was more than enough of a warning for King Baasha, who rapidly retreated from Judah. Now, however, the situation was different. Isaiah told Ahaz that, "The first [that is, Ben Hadad of Aram] dealt lightly," but

---

8. See also Rashi on II Kings 17:1.
9. H. Eshel, "A Reference to the War between Asa and Baasha in Isaiah's Prophecy to Ahaz," *Shnaton: An Annual for Biblical and Ancient Near Eastern Studies* 7–8 (1983–1984): 250–53 [Hebrew].

"The last [Tiglath-Pileser] dealt severely," for the Assyrian king would trample the entire Israelite kingdom in his march through "the Way of the Sea, the other side of the Jordan, the Galilee of the nations." This was a description of Tiglath-Pileser's next campaign; aside from the Upper Galilee, the Assyrian king would conquer the Gilead and the Lower Galilee, and would penetrate the very heart of the Kingdom of Israel.

Regardless of the meaning behind these words, the concluding verse of this dark prophecy foretells of a vicious enemy who will trample everything in its path, leaving only destruction in its wake.

The Kingdoms of Israel and Judah under Assyrian Rule (731–727 BCE)

Tiglath-Pileser did not physically enter the Samarian Hills, but under his direction, Hosea son of Elah seized control in Samaria, assassinating Pekah and submitting to Assyrian authority. From Assyrian records, it is evident that in Samaria, Tiglath-Pileser set the rules:

> I conquered the entire land of the house of Omri... I brought their possessions to the land of Assyria. They removed their king, Pekah, and I appointed Hosea as a king over them... ten talents of gold, and one hundred talents of silver, I forcibly exacted from their land, and brought it to Assyria.[1]

The Book of Kings relates little information about the first years of King Hosea's reign. It is possible to glean some details from the words of the *prophet* Hosea, who prophesied while the Kingdom of Israel still stood.

---

1. Cogan, *Historical Texts*, 44–46. This shows the Assyrian approval of Hosea as a vassal of the empire.

King Hosea son of Elah paid tribute to Tiglath-Pileser in the year 731 BCE, while the Assyrian army was fighting against Babylonia. After this, there is a record of a tax payment to Shalmaneser V: "And they became his servant, and gave him a gift" (II Kings 17:3). At one stage, perhaps succumbing to internal pressure, Hosea attempted to rebel against Shalmaneser by contacting King So of Egypt:[2] "And no tax was paid to the king of Assyria, as in previous years" (II Kings 17:4).

Until Hosea son of Elah's rebellion, both Israel and Judah were small, weakened kingdoms under Assyrian rule. Ahaz made major political, religious and cultural changes in order to become part of the Assyrian Empire, and presumably Hosea did the same, particularly as it was his Assyrian propensities that awarded him the throne. The new-found similarities between Israel and Judah may have led to certain level of reconciliation between the two kingdoms. In the Talmud, this idea was suggested in the name of Ula, who explains why the fifteenth of Av became a festival:[3]

> Ula said: This was the day that Hosea son of Elah removed the barriers that Jeroboam son of Nebat had placed upon the roads in order to prevent Israel from making pilgrimage [to Jerusalem], and said: they may go wherever they want. (Taanit 30b)

The sages discuss the verse regarding Hosea son of Elah: "And he did what was evil in the eyes of the Lord, only not as much as the kings of Israel who were before him" (II Kings 17:2):

> R. Kahana and R. Asi said to Rav, It says that Hosea son of Elah "did what was evil in the eyes of the Lord, only not as much as the kings of Israel [who were before him]," and it is written, "And Shalmaneser marched against him" (II Kings 17:3)? He said to

---

2. The name So is probably derived from Sais, the capital of Lower Egypt. The king of Egypt at the time was Tefnakht, founder of the twenty fourth Egyptian dynasty. See I. Ephal, *The History of the Land of Israel: Israel and Judah in the Biblical Period*, (Jerusalem, 1998), 155 [Hebrew].

3. Ula's words come after other possible explanations of the source for this festival, which is mentioned in the Mishna (Taanit 4:8) as a day of celebration.

them: The barriers placed on the roads by Jeroboam to prevent Israel from making pilgrimage [to Jerusalem, according to I Kings 12:26–29], were removed by Hosea, and even so, Israel did not make pilgrimage, so God said: For all the years that Israel did not make pilgrimage, they will spend in exile. (Gittin 88a)

A similar idea is expressed by Rav in the Talmud Yerushalmi:

R. Ḥiya b. Ashi said in the name of Rav: Why the fifteenth of Av? …On that day, Hosea son of Elah removed the barriers that Jeroboam son of Nebat placed on the roads. [Rabbi] Kahana asked Rav: All this good was done by Hosea son of Elah, yet it is written, "And Shalmaneser marched against him"? He said to him: Because he removed the collar from his own neck, and placed it around the public neck – he did not say, all the people should go up, but whoever wants to can go up. (Y. Taanit 26a)

Hosea indeed removed the barriers that Jeroboam son of Nebat had placed on the roads to Jerusalem, the barriers between Israel and Judah. Yet the sages claim that through this act, he removed: "The collar from his own neck," that is, his behavior showed a lack of leadership. Both Judah and Israel were subject to Tiglath-Pileser's authority, and there was little significance to what transpired at their common borders. The removal of the barriers did not symbolize reunion, however, because Hosea's passive act failed to reunite the two kingdoms around Jerusalem as the epicenter of holiness. Ahaz, too, was incapable of doing this, and by the time Hezekiah took the throne, the Kingdom of Israel was no more. Hosea technically enabled Israel's pilgrimage to Jerusalem, but he did not call upon the people to make the journey. Instead, he removed the responsibility for Israel's spiritual redemption from his own shoulders, and thus Samaria's last chance for redemption was lost. Following Samaria's destruction and exile, Hezekiah would raise Jerusalem's banner alone.

Isaiah 9:7–10:4

Isaiah's Prophecy of Israel's Shame

Whaiah saw the diminished Kingdom of Israel, he broke out in a prophecy that spoke of the arrogance of the coalition with Aram. This prophecy comprises four stanzas, each ending with the refrain: "Yet for all this, His anger is not yet abated, and His hand is still stretched out."

STANZA 1: ISRAELITE ARROGANCE AND THE BEGINNING OF POLITICAL COLLAPSE

The Lord sent word against Jacob, and it fell upon Israel. And all the people noted – Ephraim and the inhabitants of Samaria – In arrogance and haughtiness: Bricks have fallen – We'll rebuild with hewn stone; sycamores have been felled – We'll grow cedars instead. So the Lord let the enemies of Rezin triumph over it, and stirred up its foes – Aram from the east and Philistia from behind And they consumed Israel with gaping mouths Yet for all this, His anger is not abated, and His hand is still stretched out. (9:7–11)

These verses paint a picture of an arrogant society's reaction to its own collapse. Though its houses were crumbling and its trees were being felled (symbolizing the fall of Jehu's dynasty and all its achievements), its reaction was haughty: "Bricks have fallen, we'll rebuild with hewn stone; sycamores have been felled – we'll grow cedars instead."

Archaeological evidence shows that houses in the First Temple period were built upon foundations of rough stone, with brick walls. Hewn stones were used for the foundations of more important buildings, such as city walls, palaces, and temples.

Sycamore timber was used for building due to its strong, easily carved, easily replenished wood: "For a tree has hope, if it is cut down yet regrows" (Job 14:7). For larger buildings, however, the short sycamore trunks did not suffice, and the lofty trunks of cedars were used. Unlike the sycamore, cedar trunks do not grow back once cut down, thus the verse: "Sycamores have been felled – we'll grow cedars instead" rings with certain irony. So it was in Samaria; earlier, more modest generations had endured crises and regained their strength, while the last, proud generation was cut off, and Israel was no more.

This description is related to the consciousness of the people of Samaria. The "bricks" and "sycamores" that were felled symbolized Samaria and its kings before the era of Pekah, while the hewn foundations and cedar walls they dreamt of building represented the victory they hoped to achieve over Assyria through the coalition with Rezin of Aram. This was severe ridicule on the prophet's part, as since Ahab's day, Samaria had boasted cedar palaces with foundations of hewn stone, and Ahab's dynasty, like the dynasty of Jehu, was infinitely more powerful than Pekah son of Remaliah's, and had the resilience of the local sycamore.

Next, Isaiah described the rise of Assyria; God strengthened, or "stirred up" Rezin's enemies. The description of Aram on the eastern side and Philistia on the west illustrates Judah's alarming situation in the face of the Aram-Israel coalition.[1] This means that in verse 11: "And

---

1. It is interesting to see how biblical translations differ according to the translators' political reality. In the Hellenistic era, this verse was amended to "*Syria* from the east and the *Greeks* from behind." See H. Rabin, ed., *Biblical Translations* (Jerusalem, 1984), 79 [Hebrew].

they consumed Israel with gaping mouths," "Israel" was actually referring to Judah. The Aram-Israel coalition bred arrogance in Samaria, where people believed that their alliance would halt the rising Assyrian Empire and wipe out Judah.

A short while later, God brought "Rezin's enemies" upon him, as is related in Kings: "And the king of Assyria went up to Damascus and seized it and exiled it to Kir, and executed Rezin" (II Kings 16:9). This simultaneously fulfilled the prophecies of Isaiah (who predicted the crushing of Samaria's pride) and Amos: "Thus says the Lord: For three sins of Damascus, even four, I will not revoke it...the people of Aram shall be exiled to Kir, so says the Lord" (Amos 1:3-5).

The refrain, "Yet for all this, His anger is not abated, and His hand is still stretched out," echoes a verse in chapter 5, "Therefore, the Lord's wrath shall burn against His people...yet for all this, His anger is not abated, and His hand is still stretched out" (5:25). There, too, this phrase preceded a description of Assyria's attack on the region.

STANZA 2: MISLEADING LEADERS

> For the people has not turned back to He that struck the blow, and has not sought the Lord of Hosts; So the Lord will cut off from Israel head and tail, palm branch and reed, in a single day – Elders and magnates are the head; prophets who give false instruction are the tail. The people's leaders have been misleaders, and they have been led to confusion; that is why the Lord will not rejoice over its youths, nor show compassion to its orphans and widows; for all are ungodly and wicked, and every mouth speaks impiety. Yet for all this, His anger is not abated, and His hand is still stretched out. (Is. 9:12-17)

The second stanza described how the people had been misled by their leaders. The first stanza referred to external political affairs, while the second discussed internal corruption and deceit. God, Isaiah warned, would wipe out these leaders.

Isaiah described the "head and tail" of society using nature imagery; he saw the lofty palm tree towering over a flowing spring, alongside the slender tails of bulrushes.[2] The palm tree is a well-known metaphor for an important leader, as well as a righteous person: "A righteous person shall flourish like a palm tree" (Ps. 92:13). However, like the cedar mentioned above, a palm tree cannot grow back once its branches have been cut off.

Isaiah compared Pekah's kingdom to a lake or marsh, where the head (the king) is surrounded by tails (the false prophets) who nod in meaningless agreement. This is a classic image of false prophets, who seek only to please their leader.[3] This sin, and its punishment, was mentioned in Isaiah 3:1–4, during the glorious days of Uzziah. Those days might have passed, never to return, but deceitful, corrupt leaders still dreamt of returning to the lost years of greatness and glory.

The spiritual and political leaders – the "head" – often exercised their bearing on public opinion through false prophets. King Ahab of Israel had four hundred false prophets who encouraged him to go out to war in Ramoth-Gilead, where he met his death (I Kings 22). However, one lone voice pierced the false tranquility, that of Micaiah son of Imla, who stated his opinion at the urging of King Jehoshaphat of Judah. Pekah's fierce agenda, however, did not leave room for even a single voice of warning, responsibility, or restraint.

Speaking in the name of God, Isaiah warned that both the highest authorities and their mindlessly nodding "tails" would be wiped from the land, leaving Israel without leadership.

---

2. For a description of the biblical bulrush, see Y. Felix, *The Botanical World of the Bible* (Ramat Gan, 1968), 292 [Hebrew]. For a discussion of the description and humor in this verse, see id., *Nature and Land in the Bible* (Jerusalem, 1992), 164–66 [Hebrew], which includes a picture of bulrushes growing around a palm tree by the Sea of Galilee. This image is repeated in Isaiah 19:15, in a description of the drying of the Nile and the Egyptian leadership: "Nothing shall be achieved in Egypt, by either head or tail, palm branch or reed."

3. This unflattering comparison of people to reeds also appears in Isaiah 58:5, this time referring to those who nod their heads in meaningless prayer and fasting, but do not truly repent in their hearts or through their deeds. The prophet attacks this false piety: "To bend your heads like reeds…is this what you call fasting, a day the Lord desires?"

STANZA 3: CIVIL WAR IN ISRAEL, AND WAR AGAINST JUDAH

> Already wickedness has blazed forth like a fire, devouring thorn and thistle, it has kindled the thickets of the wood, which have turned into billowing smoke; through the wrath of God, the land is scorched, and the people shall be kindling for its fire, and no one shall spare his brother; on the right, they will devour, and still hunger, on the left they will consume, and not be satisfied, people will consume the flesh of their own arm; Manasseh will feed on Ephraim, and Ephraim on Manasseh, together, they will be against Judah. Yet for all this, His anger is not yet abated, and His hand is still stretched out. (Is. 9:17–20)

Evil was spreading like wildfire, consuming thorn and thistle. The warring brothers mentioned are Manasseh and Ephraim – Shechem and Gilead – who struggled against each other to rule over Samaria, and banded together against Judah in Pekah's time.

The prophet Hosea, who witnessed the fall of Samaria, expressed similar thoughts to Isaiah's. He felt the pain of the wounded Kingdom of Israel, and described Judah and Benjamin's bitter attacks against Ephraim, which were omitted from the Book of Kings. These attacks came when Israel was particularly vulnerable, following the tribute that Menahem son of Gadi was forced to pay to Assyria (II Kings 15:19–20). Judah wanted to reclaim the Beit El area on the border between Benjamin and Ephraim, an area which had significant historical significance for both kingdoms.

> Sound a horn at Gibeah, a trumpet at Ramah, raise the cry in Beit Aven; after you, Benjamin – Ephraim shall be laid waste on the day of reckoning, among the tribes of Israel I have faithfully told what is to come – Judah's leaders are like those who move the boundary markers, upon them I will pour My wrath like water. (Hos. 5:8–10)

According to these verses, Pekah's attack on Judah was spurred by vengeance against "Judah's leaders" who had attacked Ephraim several years earlier. Hosea said that the earlier attack comprised the grave sin of altering another's borders. Thus both prophets exposed the harsh, hidden history of civil war between Judah and Israel on the eve of Samaria's destruction.

STANZA 4: EXPLOITATION OF SOCIETY'S WEAK

> Woe to those who write out evil writs and compose iniquitous documents, to subvert the cause of the poor, to rob of their rights the needy of My people; that widows may be their spoil, and orphans their booty; what will you do on the day of punishment, when destruction comes from afar? To whom will you flee for help, and where will you leave your riches? From collapsing under prisoners, from falling beneath the slain – Yet for all this, His anger is not yet abated, and His hand is still stretched out. (Is. 10:1–4)

The fourth and final sin described was the corruption of justice against society's poor, its orphans and widows. Judah had been guilty of this sin since the golden days of the previous generation.

The stanza's opening with a cry of "woe" harks back to the series of prophecies in chapter 5 which contained six such cries, describing the corruption of the decadent society.

Ahaz's Final Days: Israel and Judah under Assyrian Rule

After Judah and Israel's submission to Assyria, the two kingdoms kept a low profile, at least during Tiglath-Pileser's reign. Assyria completed its conquest of the region and continued towards the north and the east, to Babylon. Similarly, the prophet Isaiah kept a low profile, becoming deeply involved with his students and studies. This may have been the first time that God's faithful ones secluded themselves away from society; for those who walked the streets of God's "faithful city" were no longer faithful. Through his visions, Isaiah guided his students to a brighter future, with deep faith in God's salvation, "And I will wait for the Lord, who is concealing His face from the House of Jacob, and I will hope for Him" (8:17).

The years from Ahaz's surrender until his death are lost to us, but they were presumably years when pagan worship was rampant, and those who feared the Lord quietly withdrew from society to worship Him in the secrecy of their own homes. While Judah no longer exercised economic power over its surrounding regions (neither over the south in Eilat and Edom; nor in the west, over the Philistines; nor in the east, in the Gilead), its inhabitants still enjoyed a certain degree of relief and security. The surrounding kingdoms which had rebelled against Assyria collapsed one by one; the stronghold, Aram-Damascus, was conquered; the Galilee and the Gilead were destroyed and their inhabitants exiled; the Philistines were attacked, and Gaza was overcome. Jerusalem survived by pledging allegiance to the right power at the right time. Jerusalem's inhabitants held their king in high esteem, for he had successfully quieted the fierce nationalist party and ensured the kingdom's continued existence. His surrender had opened the door to the new, exciting Assyrian culture and religion, and it appears that many of Jerusalem's residents abandoned their faith as King Ahaz had done. Those who kept to the old ways, like Isaiah and his students, kept a low profile.

THE END OF CHAPTER 14: PHILISTIA'S JOY "IN THE YEAR OF KING AHAZ'S DEATH" (727 BCE)

> In the year of King Ahaz's death, this pronouncement was made: Rejoice not, all Philistia, because the staff that beat you is broken. For from the stock of a snake an asp comes forth, a flying seraph branches out from it. The firstborn of the poor shall graze, and the destitute lie down secure. I will kill your stock by famine, and it shall slay the very last of you. Howl, O gate; cry out, O city; quake, all Philistia, for a stout one is coming from the north and there is no straggler in his ranks. And what will he answer the messengers of any nation? That Zion has been established by the Lord: In it, the needy of His people shall find shelter. (14:28–32)

The date given in this prophecy is the year of King Ahaz's death, and it is directed against the joy that erupted in Philistia. The prophet reminded Philistia that while they rejoice "because the staff that beat you" is broken, soon "from the stock of a snake an asp comes forth."

Despite the explicit chronological information, this prophecy is considered one of the most difficult to date. Uzziah had ruled over Philistia (II Chr. 26:6), but Judah had lost control of the region by Ahaz's time (28:18–19). Following Ahaz's death, his son Hezekiah seized control of Philistia once more: "Until Gaza and its borders, from watchtower to fortified city" (II Kings 18:8), and Judah retained control over it until Sennacherib's campaign in 701 BCE.

It is therefore problematic to attribute the Philistine's rejoicing to Ahaz's death, as he had never been their oppressor.[1] The year of Ahaz's death may have coincided with the death of Tiglath-Pileser, in which case the Philistines were rejoicing at the lifting of Assyrian oppression.[2] There is evidence of similar excitement among other nations, such as in the Kingdom of Israel during Hosea son of Elah's time. According to this reading, the "snake" which bred the "asp" was Tiglath-Pileser, the great conqueror who produced Shalmaneser (and Sargon).[3]

CHAPTER 9: CONCLUSION OF THE PROPHECY: AN OFFSHOOT FROM THE HOUSE OF JESSE

While Isaiah was immersed in his studies, cut off from the king who had filled the land with pagan ritual, his visions transported him to a brighter future:

> The people that walked in darkness have seen a brilliant light; on those who dwelt in a land of gloom, light has dawned; You have magnified that nation, have given it great joy; they have rejoiced before You as they rejoice at reaping time, as they exult when dividing spoil. For the yoke that they bore and the stick on their back – the rod of their taskmaster – You have broken as on the day of Midian. Truly, all the boots put on to stamp with, and all bloodstained garments, have been fed to the flames, devoured by fire. (Is. 9:1–4)

1. Rashi and Radak claim that there is no direct connection between Ahaz's death and the Philistine's rejoicing, which began with Uzziah's death, and mounted as Judah's humiliation mounted. There is a theory that there were continual skirmishes between Judah and Philistia that are not mentioned in the biblical text (see *Daat Mikra* ad loc.). However, it is difficult to accept this theory, given the Assyrian control over the entire region during Ahaz's time.
2. This is the explanation given in Y. Hoffman, ed., *Isaiah* (*World of the Bible*) (Tel Aviv, 1999) [Hebrew].
3. For a different interpretation, which portrays the "snake" and "asp" as Uzziah and Hezekiah, respectively, see Y. Ofer, "From the Stock of a Snake an Asp Comes Forth," *Megadim* 1 (1986): 56–60 [Hebrew].

In the Temple courtyard, an altar was built to the Assyrian gods of victory. Graven images were sold in the streets of Jerusalem. The Valley of Hinnom echoed with the screams of children being sacrificed in Moloch's fire. But in the haven of Isaiah's study house, a heavenly light burned: "The people that walked in darkness have seen a brilliant light."

The images of light and joy reminded the prophet of Gideon's miraculous victory on "the Day of Midian" (Judges 6–8). At that time, Israel had been serving Baal for eighteen years. A man named Jehoash named his son Jerubaal,[4] and an altar to Baal was established in Ofra. That same "Jerubaal" became Gideon, who cut down (*gada*; the root of the name Gideon) the terebinth and smashed the altar, reintroducing the worship of the true God and saving Israel from the hand of Midian. Darkness and desperation were transformed into the triumph of few over many.

Isaiah emphasized the heavy burden that the people suffered and the rod that continued to strike them (Assyria in Isaiah's time, like Midian in Gideon's). His gleaming vision of a wondrous savior-king hints at an imminent miracle, and at the shattering of the alien gods and their altars.[5]

Although the identity of the child that is born is not specified, the prophecy seems to imply that Hezekiah, Ahaz's son, will bear the messianic mantle upon his shoulders. Hezekiah may already have been one of Isaiah's students, deeply involved in Torah study and prophecy. Isaiah burst out in wondrous revelatory song, concluding the series of prophecies that began with his first appeal to Ahaz (in chapter 7):

---

4. "Jerubaal, that is, Gideon" (Judges 7:1; 8:35; ch. 9). "Jeru" means a firm, solid foundation, as in "Jerusalem." Jehoash gives an alternative meaning for the name, "Let the Baal contend (*yariv*) with him" (Judges 6:31), when defending his daring son following Gideon's destruction of the altar. See Yehiel Bin-Nun's explanation of naming in the story of Gideon, in *The Land of Moriah*, 18–23.

5. Taking into account the many connections between this story and the wars of Gideon, many commentators, old and new alike, have taken the beginning of chapter 9 out of the context of Ahaz's reign, and consider it to have taken place after Sennacherib miraculously abandoned Jerusalem. The difficulty with this reading is that Isaiah speaks of a child being born, which seemingly refers to the birth of Hezekiah, rather than to Hezekiah at the end of his reign. The allusions to Gideon and the smashing of the altar are also less relevant at the end of Hezekiah's reign, for Hezekiah destroyed the pagan altars at the beginning of his reign.

For a child is born to us, a son is given to us, and authority shall settle upon his shoulders, and his name shall be called Wondrous Counselor, Mighty God, Everlasting Father, Prince of Peace – Bringing abundant[6] authority, and endless peace, upon David's throne and kingdom, that it may be firmly established in justice and in equity now and evermore. The zeal of the Lord of Hosts shall bring this to pass. (Is. 9:5–6)

This was a song about the resurrection of the House of David. Although Ahaz still sat upon the throne, the king of Assyria had control over the Kingdom of Judah (and most of the ancient world). Yet Isaiah could see what was to come. He saw the light that shone from the child Hezekiah's face. Hezekiah would grow, guided by God, to wear the royal title with true authority. He would grow and be deserving of the divine names that Isaiah had bestowed upon him: "Wondrous Counselor, Mighty God," and he would abolish the practices of his father. The names "Everlasting Father, Prince of Peace" anticipated his messianic qualities and the peace he would bring to Jerusalem in the future.[7] For those who had heard them, the language of this prophecy evoked Isaiah's earliest prophecies, the otherworldly visions of the end of days.

---

6. The Masoretic text contains an anomaly; a final *mem* appears instead of a *mem* in the middle of the word *lemarbe*, abundant. This will be discussed in Appendix 1.

7. See Y. Zakovitch, *David: From Shepherd to Messiah* (Jerusalem, 1996), 163 [Hebrew]; and see Yehiel Bin-Nun, *The Land of Moriah*, 25.

Part Three

The Days of Hezekiah

Hezekiah's Revolution: A Return to Former Glory (727–715 BCE)

AHAZ'S SHAMEFUL BURIAL

There are several conflicting accounts of the death of King Ahaz. In the Book of Kings, his death and burial are described with the usual formula for kings of Judah:

> Ahaz lay with his fathers and was buried with his fathers in the City of David; his son Hezekiah succeeded him as king. (II Kings 16:20)

However, a different picture is presented in Chronicles:

> Ahaz slept with his fathers and was buried in the city, in Jerusalem; his body was not brought to the tombs of the kings of Israel. His son Hezekiah succeeded him as king. (II Chr. 28:27)

The author of Chronicles is not willing to accept Ahaz's burial among the righteous kings of Judah, and records instead that he was buried in a commoner's grave.

Tannaitic literature presents a third, even more condemnatory tradition; that King Hezekiah of Judah "dragged his father's bones on a rope bier."[1]

We can only imagine Ahaz's funeral, conducted by his successor Hezekiah under the prophet Isaiah's watchful eye. The Judahite royalty and ministers anticipated a royal funeral; protocol dictated that the heir lead the deceased king's coffin to the royal burial grounds. But Isaiah's study house buzzed with feverish excitement. No one was happier than he. For almost twenty years, Hezekiah had been raised on the prophet's knee. His grandfather had placed him under the prophet's care, and under his father's nose, he had become one of Isaiah's greatest students. For years, the prophet and his students had been ensconced in the study house. His visions simmered within its walls as he waited for the right moment. The scene was finally set for an earthly kingdom rooted in its faith in the heavenly kingdom. Since the bitter disappointment of Uzziah's last days, the prophet had not known a moment of joy. Bitter civil war between Israel and Judah led to the king's humiliating appeal to the Assyrian Empire. The darkest hour had been Ahaz's decree to close the study houses and cease all Torah study. Ahaz's war against Israel's heritage had made Isaiah and his students into persecuted lawbreakers. With daring dedication, Isaiah's students hid themselves away with the prophet and nurtured themselves on his vision. Once a regular guest at the palace, Isaiah had not walked freely in Jerusalem's streets for years. He shut himself off from the present, and focused on the promise of the future.

Isaiah sat with the royal heir, and together they planned Ahaz's send-off. Hezekiah needed to prove to Jerusalem that the days of idolatry were over. All would know that honoring one's father was secondary to

---

1. This story is from the *Tosefta*, and appears at the end of chapter 6 of Mishna Pesaḥim (see Berakhot 10b; Pesaḥim 56a). See Y. N. Epstein, *An Introduction to the Text of the Mishna* (Jerusalem, 1948), 950–51 [Hebrew]. In his commentary on Tractate Pesahim, Rashi explains that the act was: "For atonement. And they did not bury him with honor, in a presentable bed, for the sanctification of God's name; he was condemned for his wickedness, so that the wicked would suffer." Others claim that he dragged his father's bones because it was the day of bone gathering, which was a custom in the Second Temple period. This may mean that Ahaz was buried with his forefathers, but then his bones were taken to a regular grave.

honoring God's name. Isaiah coached his student with fierce devotion as he prepared to ascend the throne.

At the appointed time, the royal court prepared the royal coffin, ornate and grand, fit for a king. Silken shrouds lined a coffin set with jewels. The customary heaps of fragrant herbs and incense surrounded the dead king's head. The court and the heads of state gathered around, waiting for the heir's first royal entrance.

Suddenly, a voice proclaimed, "In the name of Hezekiah son of Ahaz: Place the body on a bier of ropes." Confused whispers erupted in the crowd. A bier of ropes? Like the burial of a commoner? At that moment, the proud figure of Hezekiah appeared in all his glory. He stood tall in the entrance to the palace, his eyes burning with fierce authority.

No one dared to question him. Slowly, awkwardly, Ahaz's body was transferred to the rope bier, and the silent procession began to march towards the royal burial grounds. But once again, a surprise awaited them. The royal heir stopped the party in their tracks, and directed the bier to the city graveyard. There, the body was lowered into a plot in the unmarked section, where there were no gravestones to mark the names of the people who were buried, and no one came to visit. From a distance, the prophet-mentor Isaiah looked on and blessed the new king in the name of the One whose name had just been sanctified.

SMASHING THE BRONZE SERPENT

Ahaz's funeral became the talk of the town. All understood that the new king would not yield to the authority of his father's government. A new era had begun in Jerusalem. The young king assembled a new council of those close to him, his fellow students from Isaiah's study house. Together, they planned Jerusalem's return to its heritage. The years that Ahaz had spent in office had a poisonous effect on the city. Hezekiah needed to take drastic measures to redirect the people's hearts back to their God, and to this end, the king and his new advisors planned a spectacular demonstration.

For as long as anyone could remember, a bronze snake, mounted on a pole, had hung in the royal courtyard. Tradition held that this was the snake that Moses himself had cast at God's command during the plague of serpents in the wilderness:

> And the Lord said to Moses: Make yourself an asp and mount it
> on a pole, and if anyone who is bitten looks at it, he shall recover;
> and Moses made a bronze serpent and mounted it on a pole, and
> when anyone was bitten by a serpent, he would look at the bronze
> serpent and recover. (Num. 21:8–9)

For hundreds of years, this statue had been kept by the Temple priests.
Now, a century after the Temple was built, the young king decided to
crush the bronze statue into powder. One can imagine the reaction of
the priests and the people at this defiant act. The people had looked
at the ancient handiwork of Moses himself as an ancient legacy, and a
testimony to the nation's continuity.[2] Suddenly, Hezekiah ordered the
destruction of this legacy. Encouraged by Isaiah, he did not fear public
opinion. The smashing of the bronze serpent symbolized the oblitera-
tion of all cult worship, all ritual that was not in the service of the God
of Israel. Even icons that had endured for centuries would no longer
be tolerated in the wake of Ahaz's idolatry. While Hezekiah's burial of
Ahaz may have first been perceived by some as the result of a private dispute between father and son, it was now clear that the new king would
not tolerate his father's ways. Assyrian ritual worship would no longer
endure in Jerusalem.

It seems that Hezekiah, who succeeded his father in the same year
that Shalmaneser succeeded Tiglath-Pileser, maintained his father's foreign policy, running Judah as a province of Assyria without participating
in the rebellions of the surrounding nations. While he paid monetary
tribute to Assyria, however, the religious tribute of his father came to an
abrupt end, and he began to direct his nation's hearts back to their Father

---

2. The sages marveled that the statue had been preserved for that long, and that none of
Judah's righteous kings had destroyed it. Was Hezekiah indeed the most righteous?
The Talmud answers: "It must therefore be that his ancestors left something undone
whereby he [Hezekiah] might distinguish himself" (Ḥullin 7a). Radak favors a more
rational explanation: "It had been preserved since the days of Moses as a commemora-
tion of the miracle, like the jar of manna, and Asa and Jehoshaphat did not destroy it
when they destroyed the rest of the idols because when they ruled no one worshiped
or offered incense to the serpent, so they left it to commemorate the miracle." That
is, the statue only became an object of ritual worship in Ahaz's time.

in heaven. Ahaz had abandoned God on his own initiative rather than under pressure from Assyria, who did not enforce their religion upon the nations they conquered. Assyria sought Judahite taxes, not Judahite worship, so Hezekiah was able to conduct religious reform without fear of Assyrian intervention.

REMOVING THE SHRINES

After these two acts that clarified Judah's new path, Hezekiah undertook the final, most difficult stage of his religious reform. For years, the people had been sacrificing and burning incense at local shrines. In direct violation of the Torah's command, which clearly demands central ritual worship, the people continued worshiping at shrines throughout the land.[3] Like the serpent, which had been an integral part of the Judahite landscape since before the establishment of the royal dynasty, the local shrines had been there too, and none of the kings of Judah had removed them. The prohibition had never been enforced; the monarchy preferred to overlook the shrines. However, Hezekiah was determined to take action where his predecessors had not. Hezekiah overlooked nothing, and tackled everything. One can imagine the shock throughout Judah and Jerusalem when the king's officers removed altars that had been used for centuries. Alongside his religious objectives, the removal of the shrines served Hezekiah's national-political purpose; the centralization of worship also strengthened the house of David's standing within the kingdom.

"HE BANNED THE BOOK OF HEALING"

The same ancient tradition that describes Hezekiah's reform mentions a curious detail: "He banned the book of healing" (Pesaḥim 56a). This

---

3. There is clear archaeological evidence for Hezekiah's revolution. In Tel Beersheba (north of Beersheba), a magnificent horned altar of hewn ashlar (forbidden according to Ex. 20:21), that had been dismantled, was found in a storage house from Hezekiah's time; see *The New Archaeological Encyclopedia*, ed. A. Stern, vol. 1 (Jerusalem, 1992), 140 [Hebrew]. An altar of similar dimensions to the one described in Ex. 27:1 was found, stored under the floor, in Tel Arad; see Z. Herzog, *Arad* (Tel Aviv, 1997), 182–209 [Hebrew]. See also Yehuda Elitzur, *Proceedings of the Twelfth World Congress of Jewish Studies*, vol. A (1999) [Hebrew].

act raises many questions: What is this book, and why did Hezekiah ban it? In his commentary on the Mishna, Maimonides explains that the book was a collection of magical remedies related to Torah-prohibited idolatry.[4]

However, a more widely accepted opinion holds that it was a book of conventional medicine. In his work *Ein Ayah*, Rabbi Kook explains Hezekiah's purpose in banning the book of remedies:

> Hezekiah found that the people would derive more benefit from the moral improvement that would result from growing accustomed to requesting the true needs of the heart, that is, being healed from sickness, from God through prayer, than what they would lose through being healed through natural remedies…To the extent that they would be elevated and come to recognize God's hand in nature itself, which is entirely God's handiwork. (*Ein Ayah* on Pesaḥim 56a).

In the days of Ahaz, the people's relationship with God was completely shattered. Hezekiah's revolution, guided by Isaiah, took the most radical of steps in order to undermine the central role that pagan ritual occupied in the lives of the people. Hezekiah banned the "book of healing," not because natural or conventional medicine was worthless, but because of the nation's weak spiritual condition. Banning the book of remedies was a means of directing the people's hearts back to their Father in heaven through prayer. Ahaz's disregard for the prophet who urged him to "take care and be silent, and do not fear" resulted from a profound

---

4. Maimonides wrote a lengthy commentary on this phrase, which he ends by apologizing for its length, blaming his fierce desire to counter those who claimed that the book of healing was a book of conventional medicine:

> Besides the foolishness of this matter…if a person was hungry and ate bread, which no doubt healed him from his distress, can it be said the person does not trust in God? Only fools would say such a thing, for just like how I thank God when I eat for creating something that takes away my hunger and sustains me and keeps me alive, so must we thank Him for creating medicine, which takes away my sickness when I use it; and I would not have had to contradict this ridiculous argument, if it had not been published. (Maimonides, *Commentary on the Mishna*, Pesaḥim 6)

lack of faith, which bore despair. After his death came Hezekiah, who chose to walk in the path of that same prophet, and strived to restore the people's faith. The destruction of the bronze serpent and the banning of the book of healing stemmed from the same source, the young king's desire to heighten the nation's awareness of God's hand in the world.

The Days of Hosea Son of Elah: Samaria's Impending Destruction (727–722 BCE)

Tiglath-Pileser's death awakened hope among the defeated kingdoms in the area, igniting a spate of rebellions. The king's successor, Shalmaneser V (who reigned from 727 to 722 BCE) left no records, and it is thus difficult to reconstruct the period of his reign. The Bible, on the other hand, presents a clear account of the final years of Samaria. Hosea son of Elah made contact with King So of Egypt, and formed a rebellion against Shalmaneser, who besieged Samaria for three years in retaliation. During this time, the Assyrian ruler died, and Sargon II exiled Samaria. This change of leadership is hinted to in the grammar of the biblical account: "And Shalmaneser attacked Samaria, and besieged it, and *they* captured it at the end of three years" (II Kings 18:9–10). Although "and *he* captured it," would have been the logical continuation of the verse, *he* (Shalmaneser) died before the actual capture of Samaria, while Sargon was the ruler who oversaw its exile.

II Kings (18:9) relates that Shalmaneser's attack on Samaria occurred during the seventh year of Hosea son of Elah's reign and the fourth year of Hezekiah's reign. It was 725 BCE, the Assyrian ruler's second year on the throne. Tiglath-Pileser's death sparked hope in the region that the Assyrian yoke would be lifted, and this is what moved Hosea to rebel. Indeed, the fact that Assyria besieged Samaria for three years before they were able to conquer it testifies to their relative weakness at that time.[1]

We have no firsthand descriptions of the Samarian rebellion or of Israelite society in the final years of Samaria's existence as the Israelite capital. However, Hosea and Isaiah's prophecies draw a partial picture.

THE PROPHET HOSEA'S DESCRIPTION
OF THE KINGDOM OF ISRAEL

> When I would heal Israel, the guilt of Ephraim and the wickedness of Samaria reveals itself, for they have acted treacherously, with thieves breaking in and bands raiding outside; and they do not consider that I remembered all their wickedness, that now their misdeeds have been all around them, that they have been ever before Me. Their wickedness gladdens the king, and their treachery, the officers... Ephraim assimilates among the nations, Ephraim has become like a cake that has not been turned. Strangers have consumed his strength, but he has not realized; also, mold is scattered over him, but he has not realized. Though Israel's pride has been humbled before it, they have not returned to the Lord their God; they have not sought Him in spite of everything. Instead, Ephraim has acted like a foolish, mindless pigeon: They have appealed to Egypt – they have gone to Assyria. (Hos. 7:1–11)

The final verse of this prophecy is clear; the "foolish pigeon," Israel, sought help from Egypt, and as a result, it will be exiled to Assyria. No other period in Israelite history corresponds so plainly with this prophecy. The Malbim noted this in his commentary on Hosea, dating the

---

1. A. Malamat, "Wars of Israel and Assyria," in *The Military History of the Land of Israel in Biblical Times*, ed. J. Liver (Tel Aviv, 1973), 255 [Hebrew].

entire chapter to the time of Israel's final defeat. In his view, the chapter describes Israel's internal collapse, which preceded its destruction by external forces:

> And afterwards, Hosea son of Elah smote Pekah and ruled in his place, "and King Shalmaneser of Assyria marched against him and Hosea became his servant... and the king of Assyria found that Hosea had conspired against him by sending messengers to King So of Egypt... and the king of Assyria arrested him and imprisoned him in prison... and he ascended to Samaria and captured it... and he exiled Israel to Assyria" (II Kings 17:3–6). And it emerges that the king of Assyria's discovery of conspiracy was the result of a conspiracy against Hosea, because some Israelites wanted Hosea's downfall, and therefore betrayed him, exaggerating his rebellion against Assyria in order to cause his destruction, and the seer condemns these acts in his prophecy, from here until the end of the book. (Malbim on Hos. 7:1)

This verse ties Hosea's prophecies to the days of Hosea son of Elah, the final king of Israel. The chapter's opening ("when I would heal Israel") fits in with the historical context; Pekah's assassination was Samaria's last chance to survive, if it could resolve its problems of internal corruption (which is hinted at in Hosea 6:1, and mentioned explicitly in chapter 14). Such a reform could have been conducted simultaneously to Hezekiah's efforts in Judah. What was needed was an upright, strong leader who would abandon all thoughts of rebellion against Assyria, and focus upon healing Israel from within. The prophet was aware, however, that God saw the depths of Samaria's corruption. Deception and depravity wracked the kingdom. Society's sins had not been wiped away by the wrath of Tiglath-Pileser, nor had Israel been moved to repentance: "They do not consider that I remembered all their wickedness." Israel's sinful past, shameful and exposed, was laid bare before the eyes of God.

In verse 3, Hosea's words become harsher. Hosea criticized those who gladdened the king and his officers in their wickedness. This paints a familiar picture of social, moral, and political corruption, which had led to the earlier foolish Israelite rebellion. Instead of healing society from within, those in power attempted to stanch their wounds by seeking Egypt's assistance, but their internal injuries were bleeding and festering all the while. "Ephraim has become like a cake that has not been turned," burnt on one side, raw on the other, appealing to no one, and slowly rotting.

In verse 4, the prophet likens the kingdom to a burning oven:

> They are all treacherous – like an oven fired by a baker, who fails to stoke the fire, to knead the dough until it rises. On the day of our king, the officials became inflamed from wine, he gave his hand to traitors. For they approach their ambush with their hearts like an oven: Through the night their baker has slept; by the morning, it flares up like a blazing fire. (Hos. 7:4–6)

This unusual metaphor conjures up the image of an oven that is fired up and ready to bake dough, but instead of kneading and shaping the loaves, its workers drank themselves into a stupor, leaving the oven to burn throughout the night. They awakened from their drunken states to discover that their oven is entirely aflame, blazing out of control.

The parable's meaning is clear, and the prophet used only a few words to explain it:

> They have all heated like an oven and consumed their own judges. All their kings have fallen, and none among them call to me. (7:7)

Samaria was a blazing oven in its final days. The metaphor expresses precisely how its leaders had drunk themselves into a wretched state of debauchery and corruption, and had forgotten to keep watch over the loaves baking in the fire, and over the fire itself. Watching over a flame is a basic, crucial safety measure; neglecting it can easily lead to disaster and irreparable destruction. Yet the leaders of Samaria failed to do so, and they awakened from their "drunken" state to watch helplessly as their homes burned. The tragic blaze resulted from their blindness and neglect. With simple precautions, disaster could have been prevented.

As noted, the verse: "They have appealed to Egypt – they have gone to Assyria" dates this prophecy to the time of Tiglath-Pileser's death. Hosea son of Elah attempted – or was tricked into attempting – the formation of another alliance with Egypt against Assyria. While his actions were those of an important king, he was surrounded by corrupt sycophants who toasted their own death as the flames rose up around them. Meanwhile, Shalmaneser prepared for Samaria's destruction.

EPHRAIM'S DRUNKENNESS IN ISAIAH'S PROPHECIES (CHAPTER 28)

The Kingdom of Samaria, lost in drunken self-destruction, was described with cutting detail by Isaiah in what is one of his only prophecies about the Kingdom of Israel. This prophecy was a warning to the Judahite "scoffers who rule this people in Jerusalem" (28:14), who had acted as Ephraim (the Kingdom of Israel) did, especially in the days of Ahaz. This description of Ephraim corresponds to, and completes, Hosea's prophecy:

> Woe to the proud crowns of the drunkards of Ephraim, whose glorious beauty is but wilted flowers who, atop the rich valley, are overcome by wine, behold, my Lord has something strong and mighty, like a storm of hail, a devastating vapor; something like a mighty flow of torrential rain shall be hurled with force to the ground. Trampled underfoot shall be the proud crowns of the drunkards of Ephraim, the wilted flowers – atop the rich valley – that are his glorious beauty, shall be like an early fig before the first fruit harvest; whoever sees it devours it while it is still in his hand. On that day, the Lord of Hosts shall become a crown of beauty and a diadem of glory for the remnant of His people, and a spirit of judgment for he who sits in judgment; and of valor for those who repel attacks at the gate. But these are also muddled by wine and dazed by liquor: Priest and prophet are muddled by liquor; they are confused by wine, they are dazed by liquor; they are muddled in their visions, they stumble in judgment; for all tables are covered with vomit and filth, no space is left; to whom would he give instruction, and to whom expound

a message? To those newly weaned from milk, just taken away from the breast? For sign by sign, line by line, here a little, there a little, with stammering lips and foreign tongue he will speak to this people; this is the resting place, let the weary rest; this is the place of repose; they refuse to listen. To them the word of the Lord is sign by sign, line by line, here a little, there a little. And so they will march, but they shall fall backward, and be injured and snared and captured. (Is. 28:1–13)

A major question on this prophecy addresses the identity of the "remnant of His people"? This may refer to the remainder of the Samarians, before their destruction and exile, or the prophet may be speaking about Jerusalem, who has yet to learn from Samaria's mistakes.

Isaiah's prophecy opens with the drunken arrogance of Ephraim before its destruction. The kingdom sat atop a "rich valley," from both a geographical perspective (Samaria overlooks valleys planted with olives that are rich in oil), and a figurative perspective; their heads and minds were engrossed in earthly pleasures, such as rich food and wine. Samaria's destruction is described as "a devastating vapor…a mighty flow of torrential rain," unstoppable supernatural forces that would push Samaria down and trample it underfoot.

The nation (or its leaders) mocked the prophet for this vision, "To whom would he give instruction, and to whom expound a message? To those newly weaned from milk, just taken away from the breast?" They sneered that the prophet's words were only fit for children, and not for a proud, established society. His words were presented "sign by sign, line by line," as small children are taught to read, using simple formulations that have no real meaning. This is how Isaiah describes the mockery at the hands of the arrogant leaders. Ironically, it is they who were like children, irresponsible and foolish, mistaking God's word for senseless formulations that predicted only gloom and doom. Ultimately, Isaiah declared, they would "be injured and snared and captured." Isaiah presented the grim reality of the proud feast of drunkards, and the blind profligacy of the leaders of Ephraim, as a rowdy schoolroom of children mocking their teacher. Hosea's Samaria was a blazing oven, burning out of control.

THE DESTRUCTION AND EXILE OF SAMARIA

One of Sargon's records describes the rebellion, siege, conquest, and exile of Samaria as though they all happened during Sargon's reign:

> The Samarians came to an agreement with another king who threatened me, in order not to keep bearing the yoke of my rule, and in order to stop paying taxes to me, and began hostilities. I fought against them – 27,280 men they were, together with their chariots, and together with the gods in whose name I put my trust, they were for my spoil; 200 [or 50, according to a different version] chariots I took for the royal guard; and the rest I returned to the land of Assyria. I colonized the city of Samaria with new inhabitants, and made it bigger than before. I brought people from the lands that I had conquered, and appointed my officials over them. I counted them among the people of Assyria.[2]

The destruction of Samaria was followed by a significant change in the ethnic composition of parts of what had recently been the Kingdom of Israel, particularly in the capital and other strategic areas. This is evident from archaeological findings in areas such as Megiddo and Samaria. For the first time since the People of Israel had entered the land, in Joshua's time, some of them were exiled beyond its borders, to other parts of the Assyrian Empire. The exiles were deported in staggering numbers, and many fled of their own volition. The numbers in Sargon's records show that over 27,000 people were exiled, a number significantly larger than Jeconiah's exile from Jerusalem 124 years later (which was around 10,000 people, according to II Kings 24:14). Nevertheless, this exile was only partial. Despite the extent of the destruction, a small segment of the Israelite population remained within its borders. However, the king of Assyria introduced a new, foreign population to colonize Israel, who came from other lands that Assyria had conquered: Mesopotamia, Syria, and Arabia.

According to II Kings (18:11), the Samarian exiles were led to "Halah, in Gozan on the Habor River and the towns of the Medes." The

---

2. Cogan, *Historical Texts*, 64.

Habor River is in Upper Mesopotamia (East Turkey), Halah is just north of Nineveh (northern Iraq), and Medea is Rama, northwest of Iran. These are places that Sargon conquered in the years that followed (716–713 BCE). The exile of Samaria continued gradually, throughout the reigns of Esarhaddon and Ashurbanipal.[3] The colonists who were brought to the cities of Samaria "from Babylon and Kut" (17:24) are referred to as "Samaritans" in the Bible, and "*Kutim*" in rabbinic literature. They perceived local worship as "the law of the gods of the land" (17:26), that is, as necessary worship for the appeasement of the local gods. They learned about Israelite worship from the priest of the Temple of Beit El, and combined the Israelite religion with their own pagan rituals:

> They feared the Lord, while serving their own gods, according to the practices of the nations from which they had been deported. To this day, they follow their former practices; they do not fear the Lord, they do not follow the laws and practices, the Torah and commandment that the Lord commanded the descendants of Jacob, who was given the name Israel. (II Kings 17:33–34)

This colonization posed a religious threat to the remnant of Israel who still lived in Samaria, and even endangered the religion of Israel itself.

---

3. Concerning the origins of the peoples who colonized Samaria, see Na'aman, "Population Changes in the Land of Israel following the Assyrian Exiles," 43–69.

Sargon Continues his Military Campaign (717 BCE)

THE BUILDING OF THE NEW CAPITAL, DUR-SHARRUKIN, "THE FORTRESS OF SARGON"

Sargon II reigned over Assyria for seventeen years, from 722–705 BCE. It is not clear where he came from or how he rose to power, and there is basis to the claim that he was not Shalmaneser's son. This is even expressed in his name; in Akkadian, Sargon is *Sharru-kinu*, meaning "true king," a description which may have been a compensatory title.

Sargon's first military achievement was to strike the final blow against Samaria, destroying the city and exiling its inhabitants. His reign was characterized by relentless war and military campaigns across his vast empire. Whenever a whiff of rebellion was detected in some Assyrian province, Sargon's army would swiftly arrive and quash it. Sargon met his death on one such military campaign, and his body was never found, so he was not buried with dignity.[1]

---

1. This description is taken from H. Tadmor, "The Sin of Sargon," *Eretz Yisrael* 5 (1959): 153–63 [Hebrew].

Rising from nowhere and vanishing without a trace, Sargon nonetheless made his mark on history, and is considered one of Assyria's cruelest kings. In the fifth year of his rule, 717 BCE, he conquered Carchemish, on the Euphrates River just north of Syria, and had its last king, Pisiri, put to death. Carchemish became an Assyrian province. The city held command of the region's main ford across the Euphrates, controlling major trade routes, and many battles had been fought over this strategic stronghold. By conquering Carchemish, Sargon was able to seize control of the area that connected the nations of the north and the east to Anatolia and the west (today's Turkey). He then began building a new capital city, bearing his own name: Dur-Sharrukin. The new city boasted a magnificent palace, temples and a ziggurat (a holy tower that represented the meeting place of heaven and earth) forty-three meters high, with eight separate floors. The city was surrounded by a wall seven kilometers long and twenty meters high. Sargon's records specify that the wall was seven chariot-lanes wide. Square towers, twenty-four meters tall, were built upon the wall at intervals of twenty-seven meters. In the year 707 BCE, in the month of Tishrei, a dedication ceremony was held for the new city. Statues were placed in the temples, including images of the major Babylonian gods, who Sargon worshiped. He was considered the most pro-Babylonian of all the Assyrian kings.

"WOE TO ASSYRIA, ROD OF MY WRATH" (IS. 10:5): THE PROPHET'S REACTION TO THE ARROGANCE OF SARGON

For years, Isaiah had predicted Assyrian's invasion, describing its formidable chariots and storming cavalry (see end of chapter 5). After his prophecies about the destruction of Samaria and the exile of the brawling tribes (9:7–10:4), and the arrogant proclamation of Sargon, who declared himself king of the universe[2], Isaiah delivered a harsh vision of Assyria's historical role and its future downfall on its own Day of Judgment.

---

2. *Brick with inscription of Sargon II,* from Khorsabad, Royal Palace of Sargon II, 706 BC. Vatican Museums, Gregorian Eqyptian Museum. http://mv.vatican.va/3_EN/pages/x-Schede/MEZs/MEZs_Sala09_05_038.html.

Isaiah began his prophecy with a formal prophetic declaration, a general monotheistic statement about the rise and fall of empires that attribute their success to their own gods. Such empires are only executing God's will in the world and carrying out His mission, and they are but the rod that delivers God's punishment:

> Woe to Assyria, rod of My wrath – in whose hand, as a staff, is My fury – I send him against an ungodly nation, I charge him against a people that provokes Me, to take its spoil and to seize its booty, And to make it a thing trampled like the mire of the streets. (10:5–6)

Assyria's task was to bring destruction upon nations deserving of punishment, and they were successful. However, it may be asked how God could leave His people's fate in the hands of an evil, violent nation like Assyria. Isaiah's answer is that the Assyrian Empire is not actually in control, but rather God is ruling the world *through* the Assyrian rulers. Assyria is an emissary for the punishment of wayward nations, and the Kingdom of Israel in particular.[3]

Sargon, however, is unaware that he is but a messenger, the rod of God's wrath. His arrogance surpasses all his predecessors:

> But this is not what he intends, this is not what he has in mind; his purpose is to destroy, to put an end to many nations. Are not my commanders all kings? He says. Has not Calno fared like Carchemish, is not Hamath like Arpad, and Samaria like Damascus? As my hand seized the kingdoms of the idols, kingdoms whose images exceeded those of Jerusalem and Samaria – Shall I not deal with Jerusalem and her images as I dealt with Samaria and her idols? (10:7–11)

This imaginary monologue is a summary of the Assyrian conquest up until Sargon's time. Carchemish and Samaria, like Arpad, Hamath and Damascus before them, had become Assyrian provinces, and this was

---

3. Oppenheimer, "The Unique Historical Approach of Isaiah," 8–9.

attributed to the Assyrian gods who looked on and controlled it all. Sargon perceived himself as the supreme ruler of all kingdoms, and he viewed his ever increasing subjects as dirt beneath his feet. He mocked the "kingdoms of the idols," and promised that Jerusalem would meet the same end as Samaria. At this point, the prophet begins a description of Assyria's "Day of Judgment":

> Does an ax raise itself over the one who hews with it, or a saw boast against the one who wields it? As though the rod raised him who lifts it, as though the staff lifted the man! Therefore, the Sovereign Lord of Hosts will send a wasting disease against his sturdy ones, and under its body shall burn a burning like that of fire; the Light of Israel will become a fire and its Holy One a flame. It will burn and consume its thorns and its thistles in a single day, and the mass of its forest and its farm land shall be destroyed, flesh and spirit, as when a sick person wastes away. What trees remain of its forest shall be so few that a boy may record them. And in that day, the remnant of Israel and the escaped of the House of Jacob shall lean no more upon him that beats it, but shall lean sincerely on the Lord, the Holy One of Israel. Only a remnant shall return, only a remnant of Jacob, to God Almighty. Even if your people, O Israel, should be as the sands of the sea, only a remnant of it shall return. Destruction is decreed; retribution comes like a flood! For my Lord God of Hosts is carrying out a decree of destruction upon all the land. (10:15–21)

Here, Isaiah contributed to the development of the theory of reward and punishment. If the Assyrian conqueror was indeed but a tool in God's hand, then it would seem that he had no will of his own, and there is no point in judging, condemning, or punishing him. According to the prophecy, however, every person is created in God's likeness, and has freedom of choice, the most important aspect of which is their consciousness and intent. The king of Assyria was unaware that he was fulfilling God's will, and he would be punished for his own intentions, which violated the mission that he was given.

Although the prophet presented the view that Assyria was sent to destroy Israel and threaten Jerusalem because of their desertion of God and covenant with Assyria, he concluded with the promise that Judah would be saved and a remnant would be preserved, following his usual pattern. Although crisis ravaged Israel and Jerusalem, a faithful remnant would always be preserved, a holy seed that would blossom anew. This was Isaiah's reinterpretation of the verses of the Torah: "I will not reject them or abhor them so as to destroy them completely...for I am the Lord their God" (Lev. 26:44). Although the inhabitants of Jerusalem trembled at the Assyrian wrath raging around them, Isaiah encouraged them to have faith in God, together with their new king Hezekiah:

> Therefore, so says the Lord of Hosts: Do not fear, My nation dwelling in Zion, from Assyria, who beat you with a rod and lift up a club against you, as Egypt did. Very soon My anger against you will end and My wrath will be directed to their destruction. The Lord Almighty will lash them with a whip, as when He struck down Midian at the rock of Oreb, and He will raise his staff over the waters, as He did in Egypt. And on that day, their burden will be lifted from your shoulders, their yoke from your neck; the yoke will be broken because of the oil. (Is. 10:24–27)

Once again, Isaiah conjured up the sweet, ancient memory of Gideon's victory over the Midianites at the rock of Oreb, which had become a legendary, miraculous tale of victory, passed down from generation to generation. The notion of the few overcoming the many in a seemingly hopeless situation brings another of God's principles of governance to light. Isaiah concluded his prophecy with the words: "The yoke will be broken because of the oil." Judah will grow rich with oil, becoming fresh and vital once more. Judah will slip out of Assyria's heavy yoke, and succeed in crushing it.

In a Talmudic discussion, R. Yitzḥak Napaḥa, a third century scholar from the Land of Israel, connects this passage to Hezekiah's reform:

The yoke of Sennacherib [a generic name for Assyrian kings] was broken because of the oil of Hezekiah, which burned alight in synagogues and study houses. What did he do? He stuck a sword in the entrance of the study house, and said: Whoever is not involved with the Torah, will be stabbed with this sword. They searched from Dan to Beersheba and could not find any simple folk…any young girl or boy, man or woman, who were not familiar with the laws of purity and impurity [a euphemism for complete disassociation from idolatry]. (Sanhedrin 97b)

JERUSALEM'S EXPANSION FOLLOWING SAMARIA'S DESTRUCTION

The deportation of myriads from Samaria to distant Assyria and the escape of countless others resulted in the collapse of the Israelite kingdom. The nearest neighboring kingdom was Judah, who was of no interest to Assyria at that time. Some believe that many refugees from Samaria fled to Jerusalem following the destruction of their kingdom in 721 BCE, contributing to the city's bustling growth at that time. Jerusalem expanded, mainly to the northwest of the city of David, and new neighborhoods were erected. The discovery of the Broad Wall in the 1970s in the old city of Jerusalem, and another wall next to the Kidron Valley in the east, contribute to our understanding of how the city expanded in Hezekiah's time. Some, however, claim that the Broad Wall was built over an earlier wall, which would imply that this expansion occurred before Samaria's destruction.[4]

---

4. See Y. Meitlis, *Digging the Bible* (Jerusalem, 2008), 255 [Hebrew].

Hezekiah's New Vision: A United Kingdom (716–715 BCE)

Following the destruction of Samaria and its survivors' renewed connection to Jerusalem, King Hezekiah envisioned a new era – the formation of a united kingdom that had not been known since the days of David and Solomon. In the first decade of his reign, Hezekiah focused on purifying Jerusalem and his people's spiritual state. He had no wish to incur Assyria's wrath and cleansed Judah of its gods quietly and discreetly within the borders of his own kingdom. During these years, there was no mention of an expansion. With the destruction of Samaria and the exile of the ten tribes, however, Hezekiah understood that Jerusalem, the House of David, and the remnant of Israel had been thrown into a new reality. The historical rift between Ephraim and Judah was no longer relevant, and the physical barriers between the kingdoms had been removed during the reign of the final king of Israel, Hosea. The old tension over which dynasty was the chosen one had dissipated with Pekah's assassination.

As there was no king ruling in Ephraim, Hezekiah wanted to reign over whoever remained in the northern kingdom. He determined that the best way to achieve this without causing political or military outrage in Assyria was to host a Passover celebration in Jerusalem for the entire People of Israel. This was the first step that Hezekiah took towards realizing his vision of reunification. Some commentators count the number of years that Hezekiah reigned over all of Israel separately from his reign in Judah. Similarly, David had two coronations, one in Hebron to mark his rule over Judah, and another in Jerusalem to celebrate his rule over all of Israel (I Chr. 11–12).[1] This theory explains a difficulty regarding timing in a passage that describes Hezekiah's religious reforms:

> He, in the first month of the first year of his reign, opened the doors of the House of the Lord and repaired them … They began the sanctification on the first day of the first month; on the eighth day of the month they reached the porch of the Lord. They sanctified the House of the Lord for eight days, and on the sixteenth day of the first month they finished … Hezekiah and all the people rejoiced over what God had enabled the people to accomplish, because it had happened so suddenly. (II Chr. 29:3, 17, 36)

At first glance, the timing seems unlikely. In the first year of his reign, Hezekiah opened the doors of the House of God. After eight days, the priests entered the Temple to purify it. Only eight days later, the Sanctuary was already entirely pure. Only then did they decide to postpone the Passover offering by one month in order to purify the priests and allow the northern tribes time to arrive. After years of corruption during Ahaz's reign, such reform could not possibly have transpired in such a short time, cleansing Jerusalem from its pagan lifestyle within a few days. If, however, this purification took place during the second stage of Hezekiah's reign, which began about eleven years after Ahaz's death, then the time would have been ripe for such rapid progress. Chapter 30

---

1. This was suggested by R. Raviv, "The Holy One Blessed be He Wished to Make Hezekiah the Messiah," *Shmaatin* 73/74 (1983): 38–47 [Hebrew]. This theory also explains the date given in the Bible of Sennacherib's campaign to Jerusalem: "In the fourteenth year of King Hezekiah" (Is. 36:1; II Kings 18:13). This refers to the years he had reigned over the unified kingdom.

of II Chronicles describes the preparations for the Passover celebration itself, and the great efforts to draw the remnant of the Israelite tribes in from the north:

> Hezekiah sent word to all Israel and Judah; he also wrote letters to Ephraim and Manasseh to come to the House of the Lord in Jerusalem, to keep the Passover for the Lord God of Israel. The king and his officers and the congregation in Jerusalem had agreed to keep the Passover in the second month, for at the time, they were unable to keep it, for not enough priests had sanctified themselves, nor had the people assembled in Jerusalem. And the matter was right in the eyes of the king and the entire congregation to issue a decree and proclaim throughout all Israel from Beersheba to Dan that they come and keep the Passover for the Lord God of Israel in Jerusalem for not often did they act in accord with what was written. The couriers went out with the letters from the king and his officers through all Israel and Judah, By order of the king, proclaiming, O you Israelites! Return to the Lord God of your fathers, Abraham, Isaac, and Israel, and He will return to the remnant of you who escaped from the hand of the kings of Assyria… As the couriers passed from town to town in the land of Ephraim and Manasseh till they reached Zebulun, they were laughed at and mocked. Some of the people of Asher and Manasseh and Zebulun, however, were contrite, and came to Jerusalem. (II Chr. 30:1–11)

In this chapter, we get a sense of the aftermath of the Assyrian exile of the Kingdom of Israel. The text describes Hezekiah's careful efforts to seek out the remnant of Ephraim and Manasseh, the sons of Rachel, as well as the tribes of the Galilee, in order to welcome them back into the fold. From this perspective, Hezekiah's move was not merely another religious reform, but a progression to the next stage of the redemption. He sought to create a national and political revolution through the celebration of Passover, a major festival of redemption that marked the nation's birth through its exodus from Egypt. In order to celebrate in purity, with the majority of the nation, Hezekiah took unconventional measures, and postponed the Passover festival by a month.

The verse relates that: "The matter was right in the eyes of the king and the entire congregation," but according to rabbinic tradition, postponing the Passover celebration was one of three acts by Hezekiah that were criticized by the sages (Pesaḥim 56a). The concept of moving a festival was introduced by Jeroboam son of Nebat, who changed the date of the Sukkot festival to the eight month ("in the month of his own choosing," I Kings 12:33). This act earned Jeroboam his notoriety as an uprooter of the Torah. Jeroboam may in fact have chosen to insert a second Elul (the sixth month) into the calendar that year, so that the "eighth month" (Marheshvan) in Judah coincided with the seventh month (Tishrei, the month of Sukkot) in the north.[2] We may assume that this calendric disparity still existed in Hezekiah's time, which may have led to the Israelites' initial scorn for Hezekiah's messengers, as it was not yet time to celebrate Passover in the north. When Hezekiah learned of this, he decided to add another month to the Judahite calendar year in order to realign the calendars and attract the Israelite tribes to Jerusalem, and indeed, they came in their masses, all in need of purification. This took place during the month of Nisan (the first month), so Passover was postponed until the "second month."

Hezekiah knew that he had been granted a rare opportunity, which would slip away if he failed to seize it. He rapidly launched into a campaign to secure Israel's loyalty and revolutionize its religious lifestyle, although the nation was not yet ready. Hezekiah's prayer can be read in this light:

As many in the congregation had not sanctified themselves, the Levites were in charge of slaughtering the paschal sacrifice for everyone who was not clean, so as to consecrate them to the Lord. For most of the people – many from Ephraim and Manasseh, Issachar and Zebulun – had not purified themselves, yet they ate the paschal sacrifice in violation of what was written. Hezekiah prayed for them, saying, the good Lord will provide atonement for everyone who set his mind on worshiping God, the Lord God of his fathers, even if he is not purified for the sanctuary. (II Chr. 30:17–19)

---

2. This was proposed by Rabbi R. Margaliot, *The Bible and Tradition* (Jerusalem, 1964), 54–56 [Hebrew].

This was the prayer of a great leader who knew that violation of the Torah law was a problematic but necessary step in this critical situation. He was surrounded by righteous people who did not recognize the potential of the moment, and clung to the law. Hezekiah's prayer that "the good Lord will provide atonement" requested mercy and understanding for those who had left His path because of fear and doubt.[3]

The dream of reuniting all of Israel's tribes into a single kingdom once more had burned in the heart of every king of Judah since David's palace had moved from Hebron to Jerusalem. This explains the great joy and thanksgiving at the Passover celebration:

> King Hezekiah and the officers ordered the Levites to praise the Lord in the words of David and Asaph the seer; so they praised rapturously, and they bowed and prostrated themselves. (29:30)

"AN OFFSHOOT SHALL ISSUE FORTH FROM THE STUMP OF JESSE": THE PROPHECY OF THE MESSIAH KING (CHAPTER 11)

Hezekiah's revival of the united kingdom brought Isaiah, who had been awaiting the renewal of the Davidic dynasty for years, to a prophetic climax. A new prophecy of hope and growth blossomed after the dissipation of Samaria and the exile of most of its people. This vision spoke of God's Messiah arising from the seed of Jesse:

> An offshoot shall issue forth from the stump of Jesse, a twig shall sprout from his roots. The spirit of the Lord shall rest upon him: a spirit of wisdom and insight, a spirit of counsel and valor, a spirit of devotion and reverence for the Lord. He shall scent the truth by his reverence for the Lord: He shall not judge by what his eyes behold, nor decide by what his ears perceive. Thus he shall judge the poor with equity and decide with justice for the lowly of the land. He shall strike down a land with the rod of his mouth and slay the wicked with the breath of his lips. Justice shall be the girdle

---

3. S. Lieberman, "Hezekiah's Passover according to the Yerushalmi," *Sinai*, Jubilee Edition (1958): 80–88 [Hebrew].

of his loins, and faithfulness the girdle of his waist. The wolf shall
dwell with the lamb, the leopard lie down with the kid; the calf,
the beast of prey, and the fatling together, and a little boy shall herd
them. The cow and the bear shall graze, their young shall lie down
together; and the lion, like the ox, shall eat straw. A babe shall play
over a viper's hole, and an infant pass his hand over an adder's den.
In all of My sacred mount nothing evil or vile shall be done; for
the land shall be filled with devotion to the Lord as water covers
the sea. On that day, the root of Jesse that has remained standing
shall become a banner for the peoples – Nations shall seek his
counsel and his abode shall be honored. (Is. 11:1–10)

By the end of Uzziah's reign, Isaiah had despaired of earthly kingship. Now,
he envisioned a wondrous leader who combined the greatness of Moses
and Solomon, a leader who was graced with the divine spirit of God. This
ideal king, a seed of the House of David, would not be a conqueror or hero
of war. Instead of weapons, he would gird his loins with justice and faith.[4]

During this messianic reign, all the beasts of the earth would live
in harmony, and "The land shall be filled with devotion to the Lord as
water covers the sea." After this wondrous description, the second half
of the chapter depicts the ingathering of the exiles:

On that day, the Lord will apply His hand again to redeeming the
other part of His people, from Assyria – as also from Egypt, Pathros,
Nubia, Elam, Shinar, Hamath, and the coastlands. He will hold up
a banner to the nations and assemble the banished of Israel, and
gather the dispersed of Judah from the four corners of the earth.
Then Ephraim's envy shall cease and Judah's harassment shall end;
Ephraim shall not envy Judah, and Judah shall not harass Ephraim.
They shall pounce on the back of Philistia to the west, and together
plunder the peoples of the east; Edom and Moab shall be subject
to them and the children of Ammon shall obey them. The Lord
will dry up the tongue of the Egyptian sea. He will raise His hand
over the Euphrates with the might of His wind, and break it into

---

4. Kaufmann, *The Religion of Israel*, vol. 3, 277.

seven wadis, so that it can be trodden dry-shod. Thus there shall be a highway for the other part of His people out of Assyria, such as there was for Israel when it left the land of Egypt. (11:11–16)

Samaria's refugees fled in every direction, escaping southwards towards Egypt and Kush (Ethiopia), eastwards towards Elam (Persia) and Shinar (Babylon), and even west, towards the coastlands. Hezekiah's Passover, which attracted many of these exiles, paved the way for the return of those scattered towards the four corners of the earth.

ASHDOD'S REBELLION AND THE PROPHECY OF THE "NAKED AND BAREFOOT" (CHAPTER 20; 713–711 BCE)

Hezekiah awakened hope in the heart of the prophet, who began likening him to the Messiah in earnest. Hezekiah's efforts to strengthen ties with the Ephraimite refugees who had fled to Jerusalem, and the remaining Samarians in the north, as well as his Passover celebration, were indicative of the reestablishment of Davidic rule over the entire, reunited nation. There was only one thing Isaiah feared – rebellion against Assyria.

God had promised that Assyria would fall, but His message to the king of Judah was to focus his efforts on strengthening his kingdom from within, governing his land with charity and justice, and concentrating on the needs of his people.

As time passed, however, and Hezekiah's power grew, he began to take an interest in what transpired outside the borders of Israel. The kingdoms around him – now Assyrian provinces – buzzed with political activity, and Hezekiah was compelled to decide whether to join the regional efforts to expel the Assyrian forces, or to remain loyal to Assyria and risk tension with his neighbors. This is documented in a short, obscure chapter, the only passage in Isaiah that explicitly mentions Sargon's name.

POLITICAL BACKGROUND: "THE YEAR THE TARTAN CAME TO ASHDOD"

In the year the Tartan came to Ashdod, as sent by Sargon, the king of Assyria, he fought against Ashdod and captured it. (20:1)

By the third year of Sargon's reign, following the exile of Samaria, he conquered Gaza, capturing King Hanun of Gaza "with his own hands" and exiling him to Assyria. Over the next few years, he enslaved Arabian tribes near the border of Egypt, and even established an Assyrian trade colony in the area (near Arish of today). The kings of Assyria considered Philistia a strategic stronghold due to its proximity to Egypt.[5]

Ashdod's rebellion against Sargon and its suppression (which led to the conquest of the city) is documented at length in Sargon's records.[6] From the existing information, we can reconstruct the main sequence of events.

In Sargon's eighth year (715 BCE) the king of Ashdod, Azuri, rebelled against the Assyrian government. He sent out delegations in an attempt to form alliances with other kings in the area. Two years later, a Tartan (a general title for high-ranking Assyrian officers) was sent to conquer the rebellious city. Azuri was ousted and replaced by his brother Ahimati, who was loyal to the Assyrian Empire.

In Sargon's twelfth year (711 BCE), the Assyrians returned to Ashdod, because the city had rejected Ahimati and appointed Yamani, a warrior who fortified Ashdod, formed local alliances against Assyria, and even managed to form a pact with Egypt. Sargon himself led this campaign to ensure that the rebellion was smothered. He flattened Ashdod to ruins, exiled its inhabitants, and stationed Assyrian soldiers in the area.

The rebel Yamani fled to Egypt and formed an alliance with the king. However, at that time, a Kushite dynasty conquered Upper (southern) Egypt and Lower Egypt, and for about seventy-five years, a line of "Black Pharaohs" held the throne. The Egyptian ruler, who had agreed to be Ashdodite Yamani's patron, was assassinated, and King Piye, founder

---

5. Tadmor, "The Sin of Sargon"; G. Galil, "Relations between Judah and Assyria in Sargon II's Time," *Zion* 57 (1992): 113–33 [Hebrew]; N. Na'aman, "Ahaz and Hezekiah's Policy towards Assyria in Sargon's Time," *Zion* 59 (1994): 5–30 [Hebrew].

6. These records were discovered on the walls of Sargon's palace in his capital of Dur-Sharrukin (dated 706 BCE). Sargon's "Concluding Address" in Nineveh also describes Ashdod's rebellion against Sargon; see Na'aman, "The Assyrian Missions to Judea in Light of New Assyrian Evidence".

of the "Black Pharaohs," sent the head of Yamani to the Assyrians as a token of goodwill.[7]

This political background informed Isaiah's prophecy:

> At that time, the Lord had spoken to Isaiah son of Amoz, saying, go, untie the sackcloth from your loins and take your sandals off your feet, which he had done, going naked and barefoot. And now the Lord said, it is a sign and a portent for Egypt and Kush. Just as My servant Isaiah has gone naked and barefoot for three years, so shall the king of Assyria drive off the captives of Egypt and the exiles of Kush, young and old, naked and barefoot and with bared buttocks – to the shame of Egypt! And they shall be dismayed and chagrined because of Kush their hope and Egypt their boast. On that day, the dwellers of this coastland shall say, if this could happen to those we looked to, to whom we fled for help and rescue from the king of Assyria, how can we ourselves escape? (20:2–6)

JERUSALEM TREMBLES AT THE TARTAN'S ARRIVAL

During Assyria's first campaign against Ashdod (713 BCE), God commanded the prophet to remove the sackcloth that he was wearing. This raises several questions; why was Isaiah wearing sackcloth, and why was he commanded to remove it? He was then commanded to remove his shoes and walk "naked and barefoot" through the streets of Jerusalem for three years. What prophetic message was this meant to convey to the king and people of Jerusalem?

Maimonides claims that this was a prophetic vision (*Guide of the Perplexed*, II:46). In his opinion, whoever thinks that the prophet really wandered the streets of Jerusalem naked for three long years is of "weak mind." It is tempting to adopt Maimonides' explanation, for it is difficult, even painful, to contemplate the prophet, a man of royal bearing, being an object of ridicule for so long, at God's command.

---

7. For a feature article about this dynasty, see R. Draper, "The Black Pharaohs," *National Geographic* (February 2008).

However, in light of historical events it is possible to understand that it actually occurred, and is not merely a metaphor or prophetic parable.[8]

The sackcloth that Isaiah had been wearing when the Tartan arrived is not necessarily a symbol of mourning, which Radak suggests. Although sackcloth often symbolizes mourning in the Bible,[9] it also represents supplication, pleading for salvation, and prayer (see Ben Haddad's words in I Kings 20:31–32, and Ahab's deeds in I Kings 21:20, among others), and this seems to be the case in this chapter of Isaiah.

One of Sargon's records documents that the initiator of the Ashdod rebellion turned to some of his neighbors: "King Azuri of Ashdod secretly plotted that he would no longer pay tribute to Assyria, and he sent out delegates to his neighboring kings."[10]

We have no documentation to confirm whether or not the king of Ashdod approached the king of Judah. Until this point, we have heard nothing of Hezekiah's external political affairs, but this may have been the first case of such delegates being sent to him. They would be followed later on by Merodach-Baladan's delegates (ch. 39) and an eventual treaty with Egypt.

Isaiah saw the seeds of this process begin to sprout, and became deeply disturbed. Twenty years earlier, he had stood before Ahaz, desperately trying to convince him to stay out of the Aram-Israel-Assyria conflict, but to no avail; Ahaz appealed to the king of Assyria, who turned Judah into an Assyrian province. During the years that Ahaz considered himself to be Tiglath-Pileser's servant and son, Jerusalem became defaced, a city of idolatry.

---

8. This interpretation is taken from Yehuda Elitzur, "In the Year that the Tartan Came to Ashdod," in *Israel and the Bible*, ed. Yoel Elitzur and A. Frisch (Ramat Gan, 2000), 192–200 [Hebrew]. See also S. Vargon, "Isaiah's Prophecy in Light of the Ashdod Rebellion against Sargon II and its Suppression," *Beit Mikra* 152 (1998): 1–20 [Hebrew].

9. E.g. "And Jacob tore his clothing and donned sackcloth on his loins and mourned his son for many days" (Gen. 37:34); "And I will change your festivals into mourning and all your songs into lamentation and I shall place sackcloth on every loin and a bald spot on every head" (Amos 8:10); "You opened my sackcloth and girded me with joy," (Ps. 30:12), that is, you put an end to mourning.

10. Cogan, *Historical Texts*, 58.

After these difficult years, Ahaz's son Hezekiah redeemed and purified Jerusalem. These were years of returning to God and the traditions, of Jerusalem's expansion, and of reunion with the remaining tribes of Israel. All this restored the city to its former glory, and renewed the prophet's faith in the institution of earthly rule. Perhaps this king was worthy to sit upon David's throne, for he clung to his God in faith and devotion.

But now, Isaiah's old fears crept back; would this king, too, be sucked into local politics and hopeless, useless treaties? Would Isaiah once again be forced to explain that a rebel coalition was nothing but a fantasy that would lead the people away from God's will? A local rebellion would rely upon Egypt, who promised aid, but was locked in fierce internal struggles.

The Tartan's campaign to Ashdod was no secret. As the Assyrian forces marched towards their destination, the people knew that doom and destruction were on their way. Terror and panic seized the people of Jerusalem. The Assyrians were on their way to punish Ashdod, but there was no guarantee of safety for those who had joined their alliance, or even those who received their delegates.

The Assyrian army descended upon Ashdod, and Jerusalem held its breath. Isaiah donned sackcloth and prayed for salvation from the sword of Sargon. Presumably, he began his supplications as soon as he heard that the Tartan's campaign had commenced. For the moment, Isaiah's firm opposition to Hezekiah's interference in international affairs was replaced by prayer and supplication.

BETWEEN CAMPAIGNS: THE MEANING OF REMOVING SACKCLOTH AND SHOES

Once the campaign was over, Jerusalem breathed a sigh of relief, and the prophet removed his sackcloth. At that moment, however, he received the divine command not only to remove his sackcloth, but to take off his shoes, and walk "naked and barefoot" through the streets of Jerusalem. This was a strange, jarring scene; while the people of Jerusalem celebrated, the prophet circled the palace, naked and barefoot.

After the Tartan's departure, Yamani, who was appointed king of Ashdod by the people after they rejected the king appointed by the

Assyrians, quickly renewed the coalition against the empire. He turned to Philistia, Judah, Edom and Moab, and finally to Egypt, who extended its patronage.[11]

When Sargon saw that Ashdod would not surrender, he set out to punish and destroy it. During these years, 713–711 BCE, Isaiah walked naked and barefoot when delegations from Ashdod were sent to Hezekiah, in order to warn the king not to join their coalition. The prophet saw the bloody civil war that was tearing Egypt apart from within, and cried out, "And they shall be dismayed and chagrined because of Kush their hope and Egypt their boast." The prophet intentionally combined Kush and Egypt to reflect the complex political situation. Yamani formed a treaty with one, but by the time he called for help, another ruler was in power, and this king handed him over to the Assyrians. Isaiah's prophecy warned that not only would Ashdod be destroyed, but Egypt would also be harmed: "So shall the king of Assyria drive off the captives of Egypt and the exiles of Kush, young and old, naked and barefoot and with bared buttocks – to the shame of Egypt."

The naked, barefooted figure of the prophet reminded all who saw him of the fate of those who incurred Sargon's wrath. This bold, theatrical protest went on for three years. Whenever Jerusalem buzzed over Ashdod's rebellion, Isaiah stood there to act out God's word, to hold Hezekiah back from joining the new incarnation of an old alliance. Hezekiah's dream of regional power was what Isaiah feared most.

---

11. See Tadmor, "The Sin of Sargon."

Isaiah 38

Hezekiah Falls Ill

Hezekiah was struck by severe illness, described in both Kings and Isaiah. Although the descriptions of the illness follow the story of Sennacherib's campaign in the text (Is. 38; II Kings 20), it appears that Hezekiah became ill before that miraculous victory in Jerusalem.[1] Considering external factors (such as his age), it may be assumed that this episode took place during the regional rebellions against Assyria, while Isaiah was trying to dissuade the king from joining the rebel alliances.

There are differences between the story of Hezekiah's illness as depicted in Kings and in Isaiah:

> At that time, Hezekiah became deathly ill, and the prophet Isaiah son of Amoz came to him, and said to him: So says the Lord, Give command to your household, for you are dying, and you shall not live! And he turned his face to the wall and he prayed to the Lord, saying: Please, O Lord, please remember how I have

---

1. Commentators almost unanimously regard this episode as being out of its correct chronological place in the biblical narrative. Some date it a short period before Sennacherib's campaign against Jerusalem (e.g. Rashi argues that it took place only three days before), while others date it to a few years before.

walked before You, truly, and with a full heart, and that I have
done what is good in your eyes, and Hezekiah wept, with great
weeping, and it came to pass that before Isaiah had left the inner
courtyard, the Lord's word was upon him, saying: Go back and
say to Hezekiah, the prince of My people, thus says the Lord, the
God of David your father: I have heard your prayer, I have seen
your tears, behold, I am healing you, and on the third day you
shall go up to the House of the Lord; and I shall extend your life
by fifteen years, and from the hand of the king of Assyria I shall
save you, and this city, and I shall protect this city for My sake
and for the sake of David My servant; and Isaiah said: Take a
cake of figs, and they took it and put it on the boils, and he lived.
(II Kings 20:1–7)

The tension between the prophet and the king is immediately obvious
from this passage. Isaiah went to visit the suffering patient bearing a
death sentence: "Give command to your household, for you are dying,
and you shall not live." Isaiah's words were piercing, offering no comfort.
The sages sense the harshness of the prophet's words and sketch out the
story behind Isaiah's visit to the king:

R. Hamnuna said, What [is the meaning] of that which is written: "Who is like the wise man, and who knows the meaning of
the matter?" (Eccl. 8:1). Who is like the Holy One, Blessed be
He, Who knows how to effect compromise between two righteous ones, between Hezekiah and Isaiah. Hezekiah said: Let
Isaiah come to me, as that what is found in regard to Elijah, who
went to Ahab, as it is stated: "And Elijah went to appear to Ahab"
(I Kings 18:2). And Isaiah said, Let Hezekiah come to me, as that
is what is found in regard to Jehoram son of Ahab, who went to
Elisha. What did the Holy One, Blessed be He, do? He brought
suffering upon Hezekiah, and told Isaiah, Go and visit the sick,
as it is stated: "In those days Hezekiah became deathly ill, and
Isaiah son of Amoz came to him." What is the meaning of "You
are dying and you will not live"? You are dying – in this world,
and you will not live [you have no share] – in the World to Come.

He said to him: What is all this? He said to him: Because you did not marry and engage in procreation. He said to him: [I had no children] because I foresaw that the children who will emerge from me will not be virtuous. He said to him: Why do you deal with the secrets of the Holy One, Blessed be He? Do what you have been commanded to do, and let the Holy One, Blessed be He, do his work. He said to him: So give me your daughter, perhaps my merit and your merit will cause virtuous children to emerge from me. He said to him: The decree has already been decreed against you. Hezekiah said to him: Son of Amoz, cease your prophecy and leave. I have received a tradition from the house of my father's father. Even if a sharp sword rests upon a person's neck, he should not prevent himself from [praying for] mercy. (Berakhot 10a–b).

R. Hamnuna senses the tension between the prophet and the king, but does not explain its source. He claims that God had brought illness upon Hezekiah in order to bring Isaiah to him. However, the visit did not end well; the king told him to "cease your prophecy and leave." The commentator alludes to the wickedness of Manasseh son of Hezekiah, who would eventually return to the ways of his grandfather Ahaz and wipe out all that Hezekiah had toiled to achieve.

The tension between Isaiah and Hezekiah is evident in this passage. When Isaiah entered with his tidings of death, Hezekiah did not reply, but rather turned his face to the wall and prayed. The prophet left, but immediately returned to announce that the king's prayers had been answered. Like Isaiah, the king had communicated directly with God.

This episode, like the "naked and barefoot" prophecy of chapter 20, can be explained by the ideological-political struggle between Isaiah and Hezekiah. As long as Hezekiah had been engaged in restoring the Sanctuary, purifying and expanding Jerusalem, and absorbing refugees from Ephraim, the prophet had revered him as if he were the Messiah. However, once the king began to show signs of interest in the rebellion against Assyria, the prophet turned against him. The king pursued power, and the prophet protested against his actions. This is what tore the "two righteous ones" apart, in the words of R. Hamnuna.

Hezekiah's direct, urgent prayer was accepted. Not only was he healed and his life extended, but he received a divine promise that Jerusalem would be saved: "And I shall protect this city, to save it" (Is. 37:35). Hezekiah now knew that God would not let Jerusalem fall, "for My sake and the sake of My servant David" (37:35).

However, according to the Book of Kings, Hezekiah was not certain that his prayer would indeed succeed, and he asked for a sign from God:

> And Hezekiah said to Isaiah: What is the sign that God will heal me, and I will go up to the House of the Lord on the third day? And Isaiah said: This shall be your sign from the Lord that the Lord will do as He has spoken – Shall the shadow advance ten steps or recede ten steps? And Hezekiah said: Shadows can easily lengthen by ten steps, but not recede backwards ten steps! And the prophet Isaiah called to the Lord, and He made the shadow which had descended on the dial of Ahaz recede by ten steps. (II Kings 20:8–11)

Yigal Yadin found a sundial in the Museum of Cairo which was a flat-topped pyramid with steps leading down its eastern and western sides, with a wall on each side.[2] In the morning, the eastern wall cast its shadow over the adjacent steps. As the sun rose, the shadow receded down the steps, and disappeared completely by noon. Over the course of the afternoon, the steps on the western side fell into shadow.

The sundial in the Judahite palace had at least ten steps on each side. The prophet's visit to the king took place around noon, when the sundial was entirely bathed in sunlight, and the shadow was expected to gradually climb the ten steps on the western side. Instead, incredibly: "He made the shadow which had descended on the dial of Ahaz recede by ten steps."

In the parallel narrative in Isaiah, it was the prophet, and not Hezekiah, who introduced the idea of a sign of the king's recovery:

> And this is the sign for you from the Lord, that the Lord will do the thing that He has promised: I am going to make the shadow

---

2. Y. Yadin, "The Dial of Ahaz," *Eretz Yisrael* 5 (1958): 91–96 [Hebrew].

on the steps, which has descended on the dial of Ahaz because
of the sun, recede ten steps. And the sun['s shadow] receded ten
steps, the same steps as it had descended. (Is. 38:7–8)

The Book of Isaiah also includes Hezekiah's song of thanksgiving:

> A song of King Hezekiah of Judah when he recovered from the
> illness he had suffered: I had thought: I must depart in the mid-
> dle of my days; I have been consigned to the gates of She'ol for
> the rest of my years. I thought, I shall never see Yah, Yah in the
> land of the living, or ever behold men again among those who
> inhabit the earth. My dwelling is pulled up and removed from
> me like a tent of shepherds; my life is rolled up like a web and
> cut from the thrum. Only from daybreak to nightfall was I kept
> whole, then it was as though a lion were breaking all my bones;
> I cried out until morning. Only from daybreak to nightfall was I
> kept whole. I piped like a swift or a swallow, I moaned like a dove,
> as my eyes, all worn, looked to heaven, "My Lord, I am in straits;
> be my surety!" What can I say? He promised me, and He it is who
> has wrought it. All my sleep had fled because of the bitterness
> of my soul. My Lord, for all that and despite it my life-breath is
> revived; you have restored me to health and revived me. Truly, it
> was for my own good that I had such great bitterness: You saved
> my life from the pit of destruction, for You have cast behind Your
> back all my offenses. For it is not She'ol that praises You, not [the
> Land of] Death that extols You; nor do they who descend into
> the Pit hope for Your grace. The living, only the living can give
> thanks to You as I do this day; fathers relate to children your acts
> of grace: The Lord has saved me, that is why we offer up music all
> the days of our lives at the House of the Lord. (38:9–20)

This song concludes the episode of Hezekiah's illness. In the Book of
Isaiah, the king is portrayed in a more favorable light than he is in the
Book of Kings. He was deeply and directly connected to God, and sang
His praises. He is represented as being even stronger in his faith than
Isaiah himself.

Isaiah 39

The Delegation from Babylon

Following Hezekiah's recovery, a delegation arrived from Babylon:

> At that time, Merodach-Baladan son of Baladan, the king of Babylon, sent a letter and a gift to Hezekiah, for he had heard about his illness and recovery. Hezekiah was pleased with them, and he showed them his treasure house – The silver, the gold, the spices, and the fragrant oil, and all his armory, and everything that was to be found in his storehouses. There was nothing in his palace or in all his realm that Hezekiah did not show them. (39:1–2)

According to the text, Hezekiah received anti-Assyrian delegates, and the prophet Isaiah reacted violently. The story substantiates Isaiah's "naked and barefoot" prophecy, which protests against Judah's participation in the rebellion of Ashdod. The Babylonian delegation was not merely sent to wish Hezekiah well. In order to understand the significance of this visit, it is important to appreciate Babylonia's position in relation to the Assyrian Empire.[1]

During the reign of Merodach-Baladan (in the second half of the eighth century BCE), the Chaldeans held influential positions in Babylonia, and Merodach ruled over them. According to Assyrian sources, he was a prince of the royal house of Yakin and the head of a Chaldean tribe not far from the Persian Gulf. Merodach is considered a founder of Babylonian-Chaldean leadership, which would grow to immense power a century later, in Nebuchadnezzar's time. Initially loyal to Assyria, Merodach later united the Chaldean tribes in an effort to fight against it. This began in Tiglath-Pileser III's time, but Merodach was forced to surrender. After the death of Shalmaneser V in 722 BCE, Merodach-Baladan believed that his time had come. He made contact with the regional powers – Elam and the Arabian tribes – reaching as far as Syria and Israel. Gathering the Chaldeans and Arameans together, he appointed himself ruler over the Chaldean nation. He then conquered Babylon, and Sargon, unable to gather sufficient resistance, was forced to recognize his supremacy there. Merodach's power endured for about a decade. In his heyday, he formed connections with many local rulers in an attempt to overthrow the Assyrian Empire. There are several opinions regarding the timing of the delegation to Jerusalem, but the explicit biblical reference to Hezekiah's illness, and the documentation of many delegations sent at that time, indicate that the delegation was part of this bid, in 712 BCE. Sargon attacked the Chaldean alliance preemptively in 710 BCE. Merodach fled to the border of Elam, and according to Sargon's records, was taken captive. Upon Sargon's death, Merodach made yet another attempt to seize power. He could not have foreseen that Sargon's son and successor, Sennacherib, was to become one of the cruelest and most skilled rulers of Assyria. Merodach gathered his forces and reconquered Babylon. Two years later, in 703 BCE, Sennacherib attacked Babylon and banished Merodach to the Yakin region. Three years after that, Sennacherib's forces banished

---

1. Yehuda Elitzur, "Isaiah against Hezekiah and Merodach-Baladan," in *Israel and the Bible,* ed. Yoel Elitzur and A. Frisch (Ramat Gan, 2000), 201–9 [Hebrew].

him from this bastion as well, whereupon he fled to the Persian Gulf and died shortly afterwards.

Hezekiah received the delegation from Babylonia around the time that its ruler was forming ties with the rebels of Ashdod and Egypt. Through his reception of them, Hezekiah included Judah in the circle of nations who sought Assyria's demise. Isaiah set out to protest this step. Every time a delegation approached, Isaiah would appear "naked and barefoot," crying out that this was an illustration of the fate that awaited those who rebelled against Assyria. Hezekiah ignored the prophet's cries and showed the Babylonians his entire treasury, as kings of equal standing commonly did in those days in order to strengthen the ties between them.

With the delegation's departure, Isaiah launched into a furious rant against the king:

> Then the prophet Isaiah came to King Hezekiah. And he said, what did those men say to you? Where have they come to you from? And Hezekiah said, they have come to me from a far country, from Babylon. And he asked, what have they seen in your house? And Hezekiah said, they have seen everything there is in my house. There was nothing in my treasuries that I did not show them." Then Isaiah said to Hezekiah, Hear the word of the Lord: A time is coming when everything in your house, which your ancestors have stored up to this day, will be carried off to Babylon; nothing will be left behind, said the Lord. And some of your sons, your own issue, whom you will have fathered, will be taken to serve as eunuchs in the palace of the king of Babylon. Hezekiah declared to Isaiah, The word of the Lord that you have spoken is good. For he thought, it means that safety is assured for my time. (Is. 39:3–8; II Kings 20:14–19)

It seems that Hezekiah initially failed to understand the prophet's questions. "What did they say...where have they come from," were not innocent questions. In all likelihood, the entire city had heard of the royal visit. Despite the diplomatic cover story (congratulating the king on his recovery), everyone knew that the delegation had come for a political purpose. Hezekiah did little to hide his pride at the fact that they had come all the way "from a far country, Babylon." He was pleased that word of his power and capabilities had reached as far as Babylonia. His answer also hinted that he considered this delegation to be of a different caliber than the nearby Ashdod rebellion. Hezekiah proudly continued, telling of how he had shown his entire treasury to the Babylonians, at which point Isaiah launched into his attack: "A time is coming when everything in your house, which your ancestors have stored up to this day, will be carried off to Babylon; nothing will be left behind, said the Lord. And some of your sons, your own issue, whom you will have fathered, will be taken to serve as eunuchs in the palace of the king of Babylon."

Hezekiah's reaction seems strange, perhaps because his tone of voice is unknown to us. The Malbim explains Hezekiah's intent: "For in any case, [the prophet's words say] that it will surely come to pass that there will be safety in my day, but as for the prophecy about my children (and the Children of Israel in the future), that could change if they improve their deeds." According to this, Hezekiah considered the prophecy as comprising two separate parts. He was pleased with the first part; he had been promised that there would be peace in his time, and so he responded, "the word of the Lord that you have spoken is good." As for the harsh punishment in store for his children, Hezekiah believed that their fate could change for the better if their deeds were worthy. Once again, the prophet and the king held opposing views. Hezekiah was certain that he was executing God's will. When Isaiah had predicted Hezekiah's death, the decree was amended due to Hezekiah's deep, sincere prayer. So, too, Hezekiah believed that if he and his children acted for the sake of Jerusalem and its people, God would look favorably upon them.

Isaiah, however, was firmly set in the view that he had held his entire life. He rejected earthly politics, dismissing both rebellion and submission. Isaiah demanded of Hezekiah what he had demanded of his father before him; that the only kingdom he would submit to would be the Kingdom of Heaven. Let the nations act out their earthly, bloody games, said the prophet, without Judah joining in. Isaiah viewed Hezekiah's display of his treasuries to the Babylonians as an omen of that kingdom's rise a century later. Merodach-Baladan failed to leave his mark on history, but 125 years later, Nebuchadnezzar would seize everything Hezekiah had displayed to his predecessor, destroying Jerusalem and the House of God, and fulfilling every last detail of Isaiah's terrible prophecy.[2]

---

2. Professor Yehuda Elitzur gave a lecture on this topic in David Ben-Gurion's series of Bible lectures (1965). Ben-Gurion responded: "So faith requires us to eschew any covenant [with another nation]?" Whereupon Elitzur replied: "Heaven forbid, Heaven forbid… right now, you are not worthy of being an empire." Elitzur's answer was that international treaties must be undertaken at the right time, and must stem from internal strength at home.

The Conquest of Babylonia and the Death of Sargon (710–705 BCE)

Merodach-Baladan's coalition was destroyed with only the feeblest of protest (710 BCE). Sargon conquered Babylonia, and from then on, referred to himself as "King of Assyria, Prince of Babylonia." This ancient expression was used by Assyrian kings because of Babylonia's importance.[1] Sargon considered himself to be a pro-Babylonian king, and even served its gods. His son Sennacherib, on the other hand, destroyed Babylonian temples and palaces (in 703 BCE).

This sheds light on Sennacherib's actions at the beginning of his reign. There are records that document Sennacherib's inquiries of oracles and sorcerers about the circumstances of his father's death on the battlefield somewhere in the north: "They will explain to me about the death of Sargon, and why he was not buried in his house [grave]."[2]

---

1. This was suggested in Kaufmann, *The Religion of Israel*, vol. 3, 177.
2. From Winkler's publication of the document K4730, see Tadmor, "The Sin of Sargon," 145–55.

From this record, it is clear that Sargon died an unconventional death and was not buried in the royal "house." His body may have been burnt or desecrated; in any case, it disappeared.[3]

Sennacherib investigated the circumstances of his father's death, eventually reaching the conclusion that Sargon died because he had offended the Assyrian gods. Some proposed that Sargon's sin had been the relocation of the empire's capital to another place.[4] Following his father's death, Sennacherib moved the capital city from Dur-Sharrukin back to Nineveh to rectify his father's arrogance. This would have been considered an act that abased the Babylonian gods, and glorified Assyria.

CHAPTER 14: "HOW YOU HAVE FALLEN FROM HEAVEN, O SHINING ONE, SON OF DAWN"; ISAIAH'S PROPHECY OF SARGON'S DEATH

Chapters 13–23 of Isaiah contain prophecies about the surrounding nations. They begin with the word *massa,* "pronouncement," which may come from the expression "lifted up," as they were a lifting up of the prophet's voice. Chapters 13–14 contain the pronouncement of Babylonia; the end of chapter 14 contains the pronouncement of Philistia; chapters 15–16, the pronouncement of Moab; chapter 17, the pronouncement of Damascus; chapter 19, the pronouncement of Egypt; chapter 21, the pronouncements of the Desert by the Sea, Edom, and Arabia; chapter 22, the pronouncement of the "Valley of Vision," (the only pronouncement against Jerusalem); and chapter 23, the pronouncement of Tyre.

Where is the pronouncement of Assyria? How could a series of prophecies regarding the nations omit the greatest empire of the day? The prophecies concerning Babylonia in chapters 13–14 are addressed to a mighty empire, the nation that Babylonia was to become a century later. At that time, it was still a small collection of tribes near the Persian

---

3. Sargon was the only king in Isaiah's lifetime who died on the battlefield, apparently during a failed campaign. See B. Oppenheimer, "The Prophecy of the Shining One, Son of Dawn," *Beit Mikra* 41 (1996): 12–13 [Hebrew].

4. H. Tadmor, "Hezekiah and Sennacherib," in *Conversation in the Bible*, ed. B. Tzvieli (Jerusalem, 1974) [Hebrew].

Gulf, threatening to no one. Why, then, did Isaiah relate to a powerful kingdom and its fall at the hands of Persia eighty years after its rise; how was this relevant to Isaiah's day?

Yehezkel Kaufmann contends that the portrayal of the king in the pronouncement of Babylonia is inconsistent with contemporary descriptions of the kings of Babylonia. Babylonian kings were considered figures of culture, and were deeply involved in religion, temples and architecture. In contrast, the king in chapter 13 is depicted as a bloody warmonger, a more typical characterization of the Assyrian kings. Kaufmann concludes that the pronouncement of Babylonia was in fact referring to Assyria:

> They were all crueler than wild beasts. Each would "strike people in their wrath with strokes unceasing." Hangings, dismemberment, gruesome and unusual execution, destruction of entire cities, trampling of fields and vineyards, torture of prisoners, etc. – they never tired of such acts of cruelty. In Isaiah's generation (beginning in Tiglath-Pileser's day), the uprooting of nations and their transferal from place to place was a routine procedure of the Assyrian government. The forced migration of masses of men, women and children at the hands of bloodthirsty warriors undoubtedly involved mass destruction. This is all reflected in chapter 14…The content of the pronouncement of "Babylonia" and the description of its king clearly attest that this pronouncement was not made about Babylonia, but rather about Assyria… Here, [the prophet] calls Assyria "Babylonia", but this should come as no surprise. Babylonia was the most ancient and revered of empires, "the most glorious of kingdoms," and the kings of Assyria, as well as the first Persian kings, reveled in the title of "King of Babylonia."[5]

Support can be found for Kaufmann's claim that "Babylonia" refers to Assyria in the prophecy's conclusion, where the prophet presents God's famous warning: "To break Assyria in My land, to crush him on My

---

5. Kaufmann, *The Religion of Israel*, vol. 3, 176.

mountain, and his yoke shall drop off them, and his burden shall drop from their backs" (14:25). It may be inferred that if the passage culminates with Assyria, then the entire prophecy was about Assyria.

The pronouncement of Babylonia can be read as describing the death and defeat of Sargon. At the end of the pronouncement, Isaiah mocked the Assyrian king who came crashing down from his lofty position, to the great joy of the trees of the Lebanon, who would never again be cut down to build his palaces. He described the king's fall into the underworld, where he was greeted by all the spirits he himself had sent there:

> All the earth is calm, untroubled; loudly it cheers. Even pines rejoice at your fate, and cedars of Lebanon, "Now that you have lain down, none shall come up to fell us." She'ol below was astir to greet your coming – Rousing for you the shades of all earth's chieftains, raising from their thrones all the kings of nations. All speak up and say to you, "So you have been stricken as we were, you have become like us! Your pomp is brought down to She'ol, and the strains of your lutes! Worms are to be your bed, maggots your blanket!" How are you fallen from heaven, O Shining One, son of Dawn! How are you felled to earth, O vanquisher of nations! Once you thought in your heart, "I will climb to the sky; higher than the stars of God I will set my throne. I will sit in the mount of assembly, on the summit of Zaphon: I will mount the back of a cloud – I will match the Most High." Instead, you are brought down to She'ol, to the bottom of the Pit. They who behold you stare; they peer at you closely, "Is this the man who shook the earth, who made realms tremble, who made the world like a waste and wrecked its towns, who never released his prisoners to their homes?" All the kings of nations were laid, every one, in honor each in his tomb; while you were left lying unburied, like loathsome carrion, like a trampled corpse wearing the clothing of slain gashed by the sword who sink to the very stones of the Pit. You shall not have a burial like them; because you destroyed your country, murdered your people. Let the breed of evildoers nevermore be named! (Is. 14:7–20)

Knowing Sargon's story, it is plain to see that Isaiah's pronouncement of Babylonia referred to the only Assyrian king of the prophet's time who worshiped the gods of Babylonia, the king who was not buried in a grave, "You were left lying unburied like loathsome carrion, like a trampled corpse...you shall not have a burial like them."

Maimonides uses the example of the pronouncement of Babylonia to show that while prophetic narrative often uses metaphorical language, descriptions of supernatural upheaval are (allegorical) references to actual historical events, with no real disruptions to the world order. Maimonides famously discusses this at the end of the Laws of Kings (*Mishneh Torah*) in relation to the Messianic Age. He explains our chapter thus:

> When Isaiah received the divine mission to prophesy the destruction of the Babylonian Empire, *the death of Sennacherib and that of Nebuchadnezzar,* who rose after the overthrow of Sennacherib, he commences in the following manner to describe their fall and the end of their dominion, their defeat, and such evils as are endured by all who are vanquished and compelled to flee before the victorious sword [of the enemy], "For the stars of heaven, and the constellations thereof, shall not give their light: the sun is darkened in his going forth, and the moon shall not cause her light to shine" (13:10) ... He speaks in a similar manner when he describes the poverty and humiliation of the People of Israel, their captivity and their defeat, the continuous misfortunes caused by the wicked Sennacherib when he ruled over all the fortified places of Judah, or the loss of the entire Land of Israel when it came into the possession of Sennacherib. He says, "Fear, and the pit, and the snare, are upon thee, O inhabitant of the earth" (24:17) ... At the end of the same prophecy, when Isaiah describes how God will punish Sennacherib, destroy his mighty empire, and reduce him to disgrace, he uses the following figure: "Then the moon shall be confounded, and the sun ashamed, when the Lord of Hosts shall reign" (24:23) ... The prophet then pictures the peace of the Children of Israel after the death of Sennacherib, the

> fertility and the cultivation of their land, and the increasing power of their kingdom through Hezekiah. He employs here the figure of the increase of the light of the sun and moon. (*Guide of the Perplexed,* II:29)

Maimonides understands that the pronouncement of Babylonia refers to Assyria, however he believes that it also includes the Chaldean-Babylonian Empire, ruled by Nebuchadnezzar, who rose up after Assyria and destroyed Jerusalem. Maimonides claims that Isaiah's prophecy referred to Assyria in his own day, however, it repeats itself over the course of history: "But you must know that a day of great salvation or of great distress is called 'the great and terrible day of the Lord'" (*Guide of the Perplexed,* II:29).

On this meta-historical plane, Isaiah's prophecy transcends specific dates, people, and events, and rather represents a model that recurs throughout history, "The great and terrible day of the Lord." This is a day when world order changes based on humanity's moral decisions, and it may manifest itself through political upheaval. These key moments in time open up the door for Israel's salvation.

The Rise of Sennacherib: Preparations for Rebellion in Jerusalem (705 BCE)

Sargon's death rekindled the sparks of rebellion that had lain dormant during his reign of terror. In Egypt, Shabaka rose to power. Shabaka was the uncle of the heir, Taharqa, who was too young to rule at the time. Unlike his older brother Piye, whose cautious relationship with Sargon had bordered on friendship, Shabaka decided that the regime change in Assyria was an auspicious moment for the strengthening of his own kingdom. He began to gather forces against Assyria. He saw King Hezekiah of Judah as his main ally. From an international political perspective, this was Hezekiah's finest hour. His diplomatic ties, carefully nurtured over the past decade, allowed him to boldly declare his official participation in the rebellion.

It appears that the first stage of his rebellion took place in the Philistine city of Ekron. This is evident from the Book of Kings as well as Sennacherib's records. According to II Kings (18:7–8), Hezekiah rebelled against the king of Assyria, did not serve him, and "smote the Philistines until Gaza and its borders, from watchtower to fortified town." According to Sennacherib's records, Hezekiah managed to stir up rebellion in Ekron, whereupon its citizens chained up their governor, Padi, who was loyal to the Assyrians, and delivered him to Hezekiah: "And the people of Ekron, who had rejected their king, bound him with an oath and a curse against Assyria, and delivered him to the hands of Hezekiah the Judean. And he put him in captivity like an enemy."[1]

Other military activity is briefly mentioned in the Book of Chronicles, but it took place far from Jerusalem, on the border between Gaza and the central Negev. The text relates an event that occurred in the Negev and in Mount Seir to the south (today's Negev highlands and eastern Sinai), concerning groups of nomad shepherds from the tribe of Simeon, who found ample pasture in the desert:

> They went to the approaches to Gedor, to the eastern side of the valley, in search of pasture for their flocks. They found rich, good pasture, and the land was ample, quiet, and peaceful. The former inhabitants were of Ham; those mentioned by name came in the days of King Hezekiah of Judah, and attacked their encampments and the Me'unim who were found there, and wiped them out forever, and settled in their place, because there was pasture there for their flocks. And some of them, five hundred of the Simeonites, went to Mount Seir…And they destroyed the last surviving Amalekites, and they live there to this day. (I Chr. 4:38–41)

The tranquility of the Hamite nomads and the "last surviving Amalekites" near them was shattered by a group of people "mentioned by name" in Hezekiah's time. According to some modern commentators, those "mentioned by name" are people in Hezekiah's army, who set up posts in the south and in the highlands and desert south of Gaza, as far as Mount Seir.[2]

---

1. From the records of Sennacherib, column II, lines 73–78, in Cogan, *Historical Texts*, 78–79.
2. In *World of the Bible* it is explained that those "mentioned by name" refers to Hezekiah's population census. Most commentators overlook the entire event entirely and fail to discuss it. Mazer suggests that these verses are an enlistment record and population census from Hezekiah's time; B. Mazer, "Sennacherib's Campaign to the Land of Judah," in *The Military History of the Land of Israel in Biblical Times*, ed. J. Liver (Tel Aviv, 1964), 286–95 [Hebrew].

Sargon launched considerable military and economic efforts against the nomadic tribes on the Egyptian border in 716 BCE, even before the Ashdodite rebellion. This may have been due to Hezekiah's encouragement of the southern tribes of Israel, particularly the Simeonite nomads, to take over the area, replacing Assyrian control with an Egyptian-backed Judahite presence.

These are indications of Hezekiah's preparations for rebellion, including his establishment of territorial proximity to Egypt and the coastal strip of Philistia. These preparations would only have been possible if Hezekiah had made an alliance with Egypt, who stoked the blazing fire in order to drive the Assyrian conquerors out of the area.

THE FORTIFICATION OF JERUSALEM

Hezekiah's main preparations for war took place in Jerusalem itself. His greatest efforts were devoted to Jerusalem's water system, as he realized that this was a weak point in the city's defenses. With technological ingenuity that far surpassed his time, he engineered a water system that would enable Jerusalem's survival under siege.

The Book of Kings only briefly mentions this massive enterprise, while Chronicles describes it in more detail:

> When Hezekiah saw that Sennacherib had come, intent on making war against Jerusalem, he consulted with his officers and warriors about stopping the flow of the springs outside the city, and they supported him. A large force was assembled to stop up all the springs and the wadi that flowed through the land, for they thought, why should the king of Assyria come and find water in abundance? (II Chr. 32:2–4)

Testimony of this remarkable feat of engineering was found in a Hebrew inscription carved in a stone near the tunnel's opening, the Shiloah (Pool of Siloam) inscription. The ancient Paleo-Hebrew letters describe the momentous meeting between the men who worked on either side of the tunnel:

> …the tunnel…and this is the story of the tunnel while…the axes were against each other and while three cubits were left

to cut(?)…the voice of a man…called to his counterpart, (for) there was *zada* in the rock, on the right…and on the day of the tunnel (being finished) the stonecutters struck each man towards his counterpart, ax against ax and flowed water from the source to the pool for 1200 cubits, and 100(?) cubits was the height over the head of the stonecutters…[3]

3. Regarding the tunnel's winding route, see Yoel Bin-Nun, "He Shall Not Shoot an Arrow at it," 29–43.

Micah vs. Isaiah: For and Against the Rebellion

The study house was in turmoil. A heated battle had been playing itself out for days, its duelers alight with prophetic fire. Fiercely devoted to each other, each one nevertheless blazed with a holy intensity that threatened to reduce the other to ashes. A new prophet had come from the foothills of Judah to challenge the prestigious, prophetic veteran, and his name was Micah the Morasthite.[1] Isaiah prophesied about the need to withdraw, to remain passive, to avoid war, and to trust in God. Micah prophesied about the need to become stronger, to be swift and aggressive, and to crush the enemy. The study house was torn in two. Each of Isaiah's prophecies was countered by a prophecy of Micah's. Isaiah urged the people to withdraw into their shelters and let the wrath of nations burn itself out around them; Micah called for the army to penetrate the enemy's borders, to strike in the heat of battle. Isaiah cautioned that only God's hand should strike; Micah insisted that the remnant of Jacob must wield a sword against the enemy. On one front, however, the prophets agreed; they both strongly disapproved of King Hezekiah's political tactics, bitterly opposing the

---

1. See S. Vargon's discussion of the Book of Micah in *Micah* (*Mikra LeYisrael*) (Ramat Gan, 1994), 11–12 [Hebrew].

alliance with Egypt. Isaiah considered it a dangerous move that threatened Israel's security in relation to Assyria, while Micah claimed that it threatened Israel's military independence as it showed dependence on other nations.[2]

ISAIAH'S PROPHECIES AGAINST THE ALLIANCE WITH EGYPT (CHAPTERS 30–31)

Isaiah watched the preparations for rebellion with growing trepidation. Since Sargon's time, he had walked "naked and barefoot" in scathing protest of joining the Ashdodite rebellion, and he had vehemently denounced Hezekiah's display of wealth to the Babylonian delegation. After Sargon's death, the prophet remained a fierce opponent of all such political moves. The chasm between Isaiah and his once-protégé, Hezekiah, widened, and the prophet began to openly protest the alliance with Egypt:

> Oh, disloyal sons! – declares the Lord – Making plans against My wishes, weaving schemes against My will, thereby piling guilt on guilt – Who set out to go down to Egypt without asking Me, to seek refuge with Pharaoh, to seek shelter under the protection of Egypt. The refuge with Pharaoh shall result in your shame; the shelter under Egypt's protection, in your chagrin. (Is. 30:1–3)

The entire kingdom was bustling with preparations for war. Convoys set out from Judah towards the south, to Philistia and the Egyptian border, and delegations streamed to Egypt to ensure Egyptian military assistance against the Assyrians. In the next verses, Isaiah bitterly described the movement southwards as the antithesis of the exodus from Egypt:

> The "Beasts of the Negev" Pronouncement: Through a land of distress and hardship, of lion and roaring king-beast, of viper

---

2. Appendix 2 of this book traces this dispute from biblical times and discusses its implications in later Jewish political thought.

and flying seraph, they convey their wealth on the backs of asses, their treasures on camels' humps, to a people of no avail. For the help of Egypt shall be utterly useless. Therefore, I call this, "The arrogant do-nothings." (30:6–7)

Was anyone listening to the prophet during their intensive preparations for war? Who was prepared to stop and hear the words of a sworn opponent of the kingdom's foreign and defense policies? The answer can be found in the prophet's next words:

> For it is a rebellious people, faithless children, children who refused to heed the instruction of the Lord; who said to the seers, "Do not see," to the prophets, "Do not prophesy truth to us; speak to us falsehoods, prophesy delusions. Leave the way! Get off the path! Let us hear no more about the Holy One of Israel!" (30:9–11)

Isaiah described a government completely engrossed in bustling preparations, leaders who averted their eyes from the prophet's black predictions. No one stopped to hear his criticism. The prophet's words of warning went unheeded.

Isaiah stood there repeating the same tired old prophecies he had pronounced to Ahaz and his rebellious enemies, the supporters of Pekah and Rezin, thirty years earlier. In both prophecies he called for the king to avoid military action; the king should not grovel, but he should also not revolt, nor show any aggression towards the empire in power, whom God had appointed. The Kingdom of Judah would only be saved through its steady faith. But the visionary's words fell upon deaf ears, and he uttered his words in total despair:

> For thus said the Lord God, the Holy One of Israel, "You shall triumph by stillness and quiet; your victory shall come about through calm and confidence." But you refused. "No," you declared. "We shall flee on steeds" – Therefore you shall flee! "We shall ride on swift mounts" – Therefore your pursuers shall prove swift! (30:15–16)

Yet as always, even in the depths of his misery and the black vision of Sennacherib's time, Isaiah saw the remnant who would endure:

> Truly, the Lord is waiting to show you grace, truly, He will arise to pardon you. For the Lord is a God of justice; happy are all who wait for Him. (30:18)

Isaiah returned to his treasured vision of utopia. Gazing into the future, he saw not only a world at peace, but a world created anew, a world without idolatry, a world brimming with blessing, new life, and light:

> And the light of the moon shall become like the light of the sun, and the light of the sun shall become sevenfold, like the light of the seven days, when the Lord binds up His people's wounds and heals the injuries it has suffered. (30:26)

The next chapter is also directed against the military alliance with Egypt. Isaiah once again contrasted the reliance upon earthly rule with reliance upon heavenly rule, and the exodus from Egypt with the return to Egypt and all it represents:

> Woe to those who go down to Egypt for help and rely upon horses they have put their trust in abundance of chariots and in vast numbers of riders, and they have not turned to the Holy One of Israel, they have not sought the Lord … And the Egyptians are man, not God, and their horses are flesh, not spirit; and when the Lord stretches out His arm, the helper shall trip and the helped one shall fall, and both shall perish together. For thus the Lord has said to me: As a lion and the young lion growls over its prey and, when the shepherds gather in force against him, is not dismayed by their cries nor cowed by their noise – So the Lord of Hosts will descend to make war against the mount and the hill of Zion. Like hovering birds, even so will the Lord of Hosts shield Jerusalem, shielding and saving, protecting and rescuing. Return, O Children of Israel, to Him to whom they have been so deeply false; for on that day everyone will reject his idols of silver and

idols of gold, which your hands have made for you in sin. Then Assyria shall fall, not by the sword of man; a sword, not mortal, shall devour him. He shall flee before the sword, and his young men shall be put to forced labor. His rock shall melt with terror, and his officers shall collapse from weakness – declares the Lord, who has a fire in Zion, who has an oven in Jerusalem. (31:1–9)

Isaiah held fast to his beliefs, focusing on charity and justice, and on obeying the voice of God and following in His path, for these are a person's sole purpose in this world. Isaiah did not favor any particular international policy; rather, he rejected all participation in international politics. His vision for Judah and its king was a vision of divine peace between all nations. Jerusalem was to be the ultimate model of this peace, exemplifying morality. While the nations around him battled, Isaiah maintained that Hezekiah must take care of his city and people, governing Jerusalem as an island of peace and reason in a sea of violent madness.

ISAIAH'S REACTION TO JERUSALEM'S FORTIFICATION (CHAPTER 22)

Isaiah wandered the streets of Jerusalem and saw a bustling city, buzzing with activity. The east resonated with the racket of the tunnel's construction, and the north was filled with the sounds of stone upon stone as the Broad Wall grew. By night, the rooftops echoed with the sounds of drinking and feasting. Victory is at hand, said the people, and if not, then we might as well die with a full stomach. Against this electrifying atmosphere, Isaiah projected his vision:

> The Valley of Vision Pronouncement: What can have happened to you, that you have gone, all of you, up on the roofs, O you who were full of tumult, you bustling town, you city so gay? Your slain are not the slain of the sword nor the dead of battle. Your officers have all departed, they fled far away; your survivors were all taken captive, taken captive without their bows. That is why I say, "Let me be, I will weep bitterly. Press not to comfort me for the ruin of my poor people." (22:1–4)

This passage appears towards the end of the series of "pronouncements" against the nations (ch. 13–23), and is the only pronouncement about Judah. Instead of referring to Jerusalem by name, the prophet calls it, "Valley of Ḥizzayon (Vision)." The prophet watched the rowdy rooftop celebrations and wept bitterly. Unlike the buzzing, excited people, he could foresee the enemy approaching the city walls:

> For a day of tumult and trampling and terror has the Lord of Hosts for the Valley of Vision, a day of battering down walls and of crying out to the mountains. Elam takes up the quiver, with her charioteers and horses; and Kir uncovers the shield. Your choicest valleys are full of chariots, and horsemen are posted at the city gates. They stormed at Judah's gateway and pressed beyond its screen. You gave thought on that day to the arms in the forest house. (22:5–8)

Isaiah also called Hezekiah to account for his massive efforts to fortify Jerusalem:

> And you took note of the many breaches in the City of David. And you collected the water of the Lower Pool; and you counted the houses of Jerusalem and pulled houses down to fortify the wall; and you constructed a basin between the two walls for the water of the old pool – But you did not look unto its Maker, you took no note of Him who designed it long before. (22:9–11)

The houses of Jerusalem became mere building materials for the new wall. Their inhabitants were cast aside like the farmers of the Kidron Valley, whose land had dried up because the Gihon Spring was blocked. Instead of the careful consideration of the physical and spiritual needs of the people, blind, fervent activity ruled the city.

> My Lord God of Hosts summoned on that day to weeping and lamenting, to tonsuring and girding with sackcloth. Instead, there was rejoicing and merriment, killing of cattle and slaughtering of sheep, eating of meat and drinking of wine, "Eat and drink, for

tomorrow we die!" Then the Lord of Hosts revealed Himself to my ears, "This iniquity shall never be forgiven you until you die," said the Lord God of Hosts. (22:12–14)

PROPHETIC ARROWS ARE DIRECTED TOWARDS SHEBNA, IN CHARGE OF THE HOUSE (22:15–25)

After crying out against Jerusalem, fortifying itself for war, Isaiah prophesied against Shebna, who was in charge of the house. He was the personification of evil in the prophet's eyes:

> Thus said my Lord God of Hosts: Go in to see that steward, Shebna, in charge of the house: What have you here, and whom have you here that you have hewn out a tomb for yourself here? O you who have hewn your tomb on high; O you who have carved out for yourself an abode in the cliff! (22:15–16)

We have not encountered "Shebna, in charge of the house" before now, so we extract what little information we can from this passage, about the man, his position, and his crime. At the end of the prophecy, Isaiah promises that God will strip Shebna of his special clothing and confiscate his keys to the House of David, entrusting its care to another. From this description it is clear that Shebna held an esteemed position in the palace.[3] This is also indicated in the description of the delegation sent to meet the Rabshakeh, Sennacherib's senior envoy, who demanded Jerusalem's surrender: "And Eliakim son of Hilkiah who was in charge of the house and Shebna the scribe went out to him" (36:3). It is not clear whether this Shebna is the same person,

---

3. Similarly, in Ahab's court, Obadiah was "in charge of the house" (I Kings 18:3–6), although the sages of the Land of Israel interpreted this in a slightly different way: "If it is the anointed priest [who has incurred guilt, so that blame falls upon the people]: This is Shebna, as it is written (Is. 22:15): 'Go in to see that steward, Shebna, in charge of the house' – R. Elazar said: He was the High Priest; R. Yehuda [Rebbe] said: He was the treasurer." (Leviticus Rabba 5:5) The midrash goes on to explain Shebna's sin according to each opinion; in R. Elazar's view, Shebna (the High Priest) benefited from the sacrifices, while according to R. Yehuda, he (the treasurer) benefited from what had been consecrated.

relegated to a secondary position, but Hezekiah had obviously heeded the prophet's words and replaced the official "in charge of the house." What informed this harsh prophecy?

It appears that this senior governor, bearer of the keys of Jerusalem, took advantage of the crazed excitement that had seized the city and commissioned a magnificent tomb for himself in the most important section of the city's graveyard, upon the Mount of Olives. This was the perfect opportunity to exploit public labor for personal gain; the city's engineers and construction workers were all at the government's full disposal, and Shebna seized his chance. At a time of national emergency, Shebna was busy digging his own grave (literally and figuratively), and Isaiah would not let this selfish act go unnoticed. Isaiah wailed and wept at the people's preparations for war and simultaneous indulgent celebrations, but he attacked Shebna's deed with vehement opposition:

> The Lord is about to shake you severely, fellow, and then wrap you around Himself. Indeed, He will wind you about Him as a headdress, a turban, off to a broad land! There shall you die, and there shall be the chariots bearing your body, O shame of your master's house; for I will hurl you from your station, and you shall be torn down from your stand; and on that day, I will summon My servant Eliakim son of Hilkiah, and I will dress him in your tunic, gird him with your sash, and deliver your authority into his hand; and he shall be a father to the inhabitants of Jerusalem and the men of Judah. I will place the keys of David's palace on his shoulders; and what he unlocks none may shut, and what he locks none may open. He shall be a seat of honor to his father's household. I will fix him as a peg in a firm place, on which all the substance of his father's household shall be hung. (22:17–22)

The sages of the Land of Israel proposed that Shebna was the head of the party that opposed the rebellion and supported submission to Assyria:

> R. Birkhiya, in the name of R. Abba b. Kahana said: What did Shebna and Yoah [who opposed Sennacherib with Eliakim son of Hilkiah, but were not worthy like him, Isaiah 36:3] do? They

wrote a letter and affixed it to an arrow and shot the arrow through the window, and it was given to Sennacherib. What did it say? We, and all of Israel, wish to submit to you, but Isaiah and Hezekiah do not wish to submit to you. This is what David perceived with the Divine Spirit and said, "For the wicked bend the bow" – this is Shebna and Yoah, "they set their arrow on the string to shoot from the shadows at the upright" (Ps. 11:2) – at two upright people, these are Isaiah and Hezekiah. (Leviticus Rabba 5:5)

This party acted as a pro-Assyrian "fifth column," continuing Ahaz's policy, and undermining Hezekiah's authority. This sparked Isaiah's rage. In the Talmud, the midrash is developed more dramatically:

Shebna was supported by thirteen thousand, Hezekiah was supported by eleven thousand. When Sennacherib came and besieged Jerusalem, Shebna wrote a note and sent it by arrow to the king of Assyria: Shebna and his supporters surrender, Hezekiah and his supporters do not surrender. Hezekiah was concerned that the Holy One, Blessed be He, would go according to the majority opposing the rebellion, and because the majority of the people have surrendered to Assyria, I too must give myself up … into their hands. The prophet came and said to him that the Holy One, Blessed be He, does not consider a majority of wicked people, for a conspiracy of the wicked does not count. (Sanhedrin 26a)

This Talmudic legend combines different biblical sources, especially from Isaiah, and fits them into the historical-political background. The verse Isaiah quotes to encourage Hezekiah is adapted from his words to Ahaz: "You must not call conspiracy, all that this people calls conspiracy" (Is. 8:12), which referred to the party that favored joining the Aram-Israel coalition against Assyria. The sages of the Talmud, however, reformulate this verse and place it in the prophet's mouth as condemnation of Shebna, the head of the party in favor of surrendering to Assyria. Isaiah favored neither party, and he had become weary of this same old conflict. Nevertheless, once Hezekiah had joined the rebellion, and Sennacherib had besieged Jerusalem, Isaiah prayed for the city's welfare (ch. 37). He did not oppose Hezekiah, even though he had foreseen the city's punishment. Shebna's party and conduct was disgraceful in Isaiah's eyes, no less than forming a conspiracy against Assyria, especially on "a day of crisis, reproach, and disgrace" (37:3), while the city was under siege. The prophet encouraged Hezekiah to stand firm, not to surrender, for in the end, God would save Jerusalem. And indeed, after Hezekiah's prayer in the Temple, God put harsh words in Isaiah's mouth against Sennacherib and those who offended the God of Israel (37:21–32).

The two sections of chapter 22 highlight Isaiah's opposition both to the preparations for the rebellion, and to the notion of surrender. This is consistent with Isaiah's approach from the days of Ahaz (who surrendered) until the days of Hezekiah (who rebelled).

MICAH THE MORASTHITE JOINS ISAIAH'S PROTEST

Jerusalem was fortifying its walls in preparation for the rebellion, but within, society was crumbling under the strain. At this point, the prophet Micah joined Isaiah in his protest. The two proponents of the burning study house argument combined, and together they blazed their way to the palace. Despite their initial differences, Isaiah and Micah had both always maintained that Jerusalem's strength lay not in its broad walls, but in its moral and social strength:

> Hear this, you rulers of the House of Jacob, you chiefs of the House of Israel, who detest justice and make crooked all that is straight, who build Zion with crime and Jerusalem with iniquity; her rulers judge for bribes, and her priests give rulings for a fee, and her prophets divine for pay; yet they rely upon the Lord, saying, "The Lord is in our midst; no calamity shall overtake us." Assuredly, because of you Zion shall be plowed as a field, and Jerusalem shall become heaps of ruins, and the Temple Mount, a shrine in the woods. (Mic. 3:9–12)

The text of this chapter does not reveal when the prophecy was uttered, or its precise political and social circumstances. This criticism is similar to Isaiah's criticism during Uzziah's reign, rather than Hezekiah's. After all, Hezekiah instituted moral and spiritual reform. How could a prophecy about bribery, government corruption, and false prophecy be about Hezekiah's time? There is, however, textual evidence that Micah's words were spoken in Hezekiah's time, for his prophecy was quoted a century later, when the prophet Jeremiah's life was in danger because he dared to utter that Jerusalem would not withstand destruction.[4] In chapter 26 of Jeremiah, the elders of Jerusalem recall the distant past:

> And some of the elders of the land arose and said to the entire assemblage of the people, Micah the Morasthite, who prophesied in the days of King Hezekiah of Judah, said to all the people of Judah: Thus said the Lord of Hosts: Zion shall be plowed as a field, Jerusalem shall become heaps of ruins and the Temple Mount a shrine in the woods. Did King Hezekiah of Judah, and all Judah, put him to death? Did he not rather fear the Lord and implore the Lord, so that the Lord renounced the punishment He had decreed against them? We are about to do great injury to ourselves! (Jer. 26:17–19)

Based on this, Micah's prophecy was indeed said in Hezekiah's day, and it is apparent that bribery and corruption survived and thrived, even during the reign of a leader as righteous as Hezekiah. Hezekiah's ambitious fortifications and excavations required untold planning, expenditures and manpower. The king was occupied with preparations, and during that time there was ample opportunity for people to exploit the system. Isaiah's condemnation of Shebna strengthens this theory. As always, the weakest sector of society became the victims of this corruption. Micah did not spare Hezekiah and his government in his rebuke. This is the first time in the Bible that a prophet openly announced Jerusalem's impending destruction.[5]

---

4. For a detailed discussion of this shocking episode, see B. Lau, *Jeremiah: The Fate of a Prophet* (Jerusalem: Maggid, 2013), 87–92.

5. See M. Broshi's description in "The Population of Ancient Jerusalem," in *From Hermon to Sinai: Memorial to Amnon*, ed. M. Broshi (Jerusalem, 1977), 65–74 [Hebrew].

Not only did the elders of Jerusalem in Jeremiah's day recall Micah's words; they also recalled Hezekiah's reply. The king prayed and begged for mercy for the city. In their distant recollection, the elders fused the prophecy of destruction with Sennacherib's actual attack and siege, and attributed the city's salvation to Hezekiah.

From the description of Shebna's replacement by Eliakim son of Hilkiah, as per Isaiah's request, we learn that not only did Hezekiah pray, but he also attempted to repair the corruption that he encountered during his fortification of the city. Hezekiah was one of the only kings of Judah (or Israel) who was open to prophetic criticism. He was a righteous leader who continually strived to elevate the moral state of his kingdom.

THE KING'S REACTION TO THE PROPHETIC PROTEST

Isaiah and Micah's prophecies were harsh. They could not be ignored, and they could not be silenced. King Hezekiah did neither, and invited the prophets to a special assembly of the people with his ministers of war. This gathering is described in Chronicles, immediately following the description of construction of the water tunnel and the fortification of Jerusalem:

> He appointed battle officers over the people; and he gathered them to him in the square of the city gate, and he heartened them, saying, be strong and of good courage; do not be frightened or dismayed by the king of Assyria, or by the horde that is with him, for we have more with us than he has with him. With him is an arm of flesh, but with us is the Lord our God, to help us and to fight our battles. The people were encouraged by the speech of King Hezekiah of Judah. (II Chr. 32:6–8)

These verses were a dialogue with the prophet's words. The prophet's claim: "But you did not look unto its Maker," (Is. 22:11) pained Hezekiah, and he therefore declared to the people that Sennacherib comes with "an arm of flesh," while, "with us is the Lord." This is a continuation of Hezekiah's prayer during his illness. The king did not cease his preparations for the rebellion following his illness, but when the prophet pointed out a serious flaw in the nation's faith, and described the reckless feasting on the rooftops, Hezekiah rallied the nation to instill in them a renewed confidence in God. This was a difficult, decisive moment in Hezekiah's life. He accepted the prophet's criticism and showed him true respect. At the same time, however, he maintained that it was God's will that the people were to fight with weapons, and not just with prayer. The king showed honor to the prophet, yet undercut his words in the same breath.

"WOE, ARIEL, ARIEL": THE PEOPLE OF JERUSALEM SERVE GOD SUPERFICIALLY (CHAPTER 29)

Isaiah's words in chapter 29 can be read as a continuation of the pronouncement of the Valley of Vision (ch. 22), and a reaction to Hezekiah's gathering and his declaration that faith in God was the guiding principle in his preparations for war. At the beginning of the chapter, Judah is in deep disgrace. Isaiah questioned its people and king, describing another side of the people of Jerusalem in Hezekiah's time:

> Act stupid and be stupefied! Act blind and be blinded! They are drunk, but not from wine, they stagger, but not from liquor; for the Lord has spread over you a spirit of deep sleep, and has shut your eyes, the prophets, and covered your heads, the seers; so that all prophecy has been to you like the words of a sealed document. If it is handed to one who can read and he is asked to read it, he will say, "I can't, because it is sealed"; and if the document is handed to one who cannot read and he is asked to read it, he will say, "I can't read." (Is. 29:9–12)

Isaiah saw the frenzied preparations of the city as a fit of drunkenness, followed by a drunken stupor; no ear, nor eye, was open to the prophets' words or visions. The prophet returned to his introverted state of Ahaz's time, when he had cried: "Bind up the message, seal the instruction with my students, and I will wait for the Lord, who is concealing His face from the House of Jacob, and I will hope for Him" (8:15–17). Those were the days of the "sealed book," when no one read God's words. Hezekiah had been one of the children who studied with the secluded prophet. Isaiah had hung all of his hopes for a better future for Israel upon the future king. Now, once again, the book seemed sealed shut: "And the wisdom of its wise ones shall be lost, and the insight of its insightful ones shall be hidden" (29:14). Here, the prophet adds another interesting perspective:

> My Lord said: Because that people has approached with its mouth and honored Me with its lips, but has kept its heart far from Me, and its worship of Me has been a human rule, learned by rote – Truly, I shall further baffle that people with bafflement upon bafflement; and the wisdom of its wise ones shall be lost, and the insight of its insightful ones shall be hidden. Woe to those who would hide their plans deep from the Lord, who do their work in dark places and say, "Who sees us, who takes note of us?" How perverse of you! Should the potter be accounted as the clay? Should what is made say of its Maker, "He did not make me," and what is formed say of Him who formed it, "He did not understand?" Surely, in a little while, Lebanon will be transformed into farm land, and farm land accounted as mere brush. On that day, the deaf shall hear even written words, and the eyes of the blind shall see even in darkness and obscurity. Then the humble shall have increasing joy through the Lord, and the neediest of men shall exult in the Holy One of Israel. (29:13–19)

Hezekiah's assembly, and his declaration of faith in God, moved the people to talk about their own trust in God: "And the people were encouraged by the words of King Hezekiah of Judah" (II Chr. 32:8). There is no doubt that Hezekiah's words were sincere; the righteous king spoke directly to God during his illness and during Sennacherib's siege. But can the same be said of the people, who began repeating the words of the king? Did their faith in God come from their hearts, or were they merely paying lip service to the prophet's demands?

Here, Isaiah made a critical statement. Fear of God is not measured by public declarations, nor by reverberating speeches of fleeting effect; this kind of faith is merely "a human rule, learned by rote," and it is not sincere. Years had passed since Hezekiah's reform, and the Temple service and religious culture had been instituted thoroughly and officially, but the people were not wholehearted. Deep down, they asked themselves, "Who sees us, who takes note of us?" The prophet lashed out against this shallow faith, "How perverse of you! Should the potter be accounted as the clay? Should what is made say of its Maker, 'He did not make me?' And what is formed say of Him who formed it, 'He did not understand?'"

Isaiah's answer lay in his vision of the future, when the darkness will be lit up: "On that day, the deaf shall hear even written words, and the eyes of the blind shall see even in darkness and obscurity." Then, "the humble shall have increasing joy through the Lord, and the neediest of men shall exult in the Holy One of Israel." Only those with humility will be able to meet their Maker, and only those who look towards God for their needs will be able to rejoice in Him.

The king's work was done. His monumental tasks had been accomplished. A colossal new wall surrounded Jerusalem, and the city's water supply was safe. Now, all was eerily silent as the people awaited the Assyrian attack. No one knew where the mighty army would come from. Sennacherib had recently conquered the Philistine coast, so he might tear in from the west to the east. On the other hand, he already ruled Samaria, so he might strike from the north. The city was on full alert, tense and expectant. As the prophets herded their students into the study house, the Assyrian army sharpened their swords and prepared for the great invasion of Jerusalem.

Sennacherib's Campaign (701 BCE)

SENNACHERIB'S JOURNEY[1]

Sennacherib began his destructive path with the conquest of the Phoenician towns that controlled the coastline. Sailing southwards, he made several stops along the way to exercise Assyrian authority. He laid anchor at Akko and conquered Jaffa, Beit Dagon, Benei Berak and Azur, which were all under the protection of Tzidka king of Ashkelon, one of the leading members of the anti-Assyrian alliance. From there, he made his way to Ashdod, where, for the first time, he faced military resistance from Egypt. The first battle took place in the Yavneh region (the fields of Althaka, according to Sennacherib's records):

> And the members of the alliance called to the kings of Egypt and to the archers of the king of Kush and his chariots and horses, and innumerable forces, and they came to their aid. In the fields of Althaka they waged battle against me…I fought them and defeated them. During the battle, I caught the royal Egyptian chariot and the son of their king alive, and the royal chariot of the king of Kush.[2]

---

1. Mazer, "Sennacherib's Campaign to the Land of Judah"; Na'aman, "The Assyrian Missions to Judea in Light of New Assyrian Evidence."
2. Cogan, *Historical Texts*, 79.

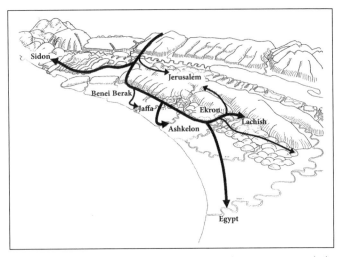

Map of Sennacherib's campaign (relief map by Meir Kahana; conquests marked
by Megalim Institute, City of David)

Following this victory, Sennacherib continued to the Philistine towns
under Judah's rule. He conquered Ekron, the town that had delivered their
ruler, Padi, to Hezekiah as a token of its loyalty. Sennacherib hung the officials who had rebelled against him on high pillars around the town. From
there, he continued to the western region of Judah and the Shephelah.

The first stronghold he encountered in the Shephelah was the
town of Azeka, situated atop the hilly range guarding the entrance to
the Elah Valley, on the way to Bethlehem and Judah. In another Assyrian record, Sennacherib described Azeka as a town whose walls "reach
the skies" like "an eagle's nest," and how his army managed to climb the
hills, attack the wall, and besiege and capture the town.[3] At the same
time, he captured and destroyed Gath, the Philistine capital, and burnt
it down to the ground, after looting it and taking captives.

The destruction of the Shephelah is not described at length in
the Book of Kings, however the prophet Micah, a local, compared it to
Samaria's destruction, and likened Lachish, the large city captured by
Sennacherib, to Jerusalem:

---

3. These records were discovered in two different museums by Nadav Na'aman; see
"The Assyrian Missions to Judea in Light of New Assyrian Evidence," 164–80.

The word of the Lord that came to Micah the Morasthite, who prophesied concerning Samaria and Jerusalem during the reigns of Kings Jotham, Ahaz, and Hezekiah of Judah; listen, all you peoples, give heed, O earth, and all it holds; and let my Lord God be your accuser – My Lord from His holy abode. For behold, the Lord is coming forth from His dwelling place, He will come down and stride upon the heights of the earth. The mountains shall melt under Him and the valleys burst open – Like wax before fire, like water cascading down a slope. All this is for the transgression of Jacob, and for the sins of the House of Israel. What is the transgression of Jacob, but Samaria, and what the shrines of Judah, but Jerusalem? So I will turn Samaria into a ruin in open country, into ground for planting vineyards; for I will tumble her stones into the valley and lay her foundations bare. All her sculptured images shall be smashed, and all her harlot's wealth be burned, and I will make a waste heap of all her idols, for they were amassed from fees for harlotry, and they shall become harlots' fees again. Because of this I will lament and wail; I will go stripped and naked! I will lament as sadly as the jackals, as mournfully as the ostriches. For her wound is incurable, it has reached Judah, it has spread to the gate of my people, to Jerusalem. In Gath, do not tell it, do not weep; in Beit Ophrah [lit. *house of dust*], scatter dust. Pass on, inhabitants of Shaphir! Did not the inhabitants of Zaanan have to go forth naked in shame? There is lamentation in Beit Ezel – It will withdraw its support from you. The inhabitants of Maroth hoped for good, yet disaster from the Lord descended upon the gate of Jerusalem. Hitch the steeds to the chariot, inhabitant of Lachish! It is the beginning of Fair Zion's guilt; Israel's transgressions can be traced to you! Truly, you must give a farewell gift to Moresheth-Gath. The houses of Achzib are to the kings of Israel like a spring that fails. A dispossessor will I bring to you who dwell in Mareshah; at Adullam the glory of Israel shall set. Shear off your hair and make yourself bald for the children you once delighted in; make yourself as bald as a vulture, for they have been exiled from you. (Mic. 1:1–16)

Sennacherib's next stop was Lachish, considered the second most important city in Judah. Sennacherib besieged and conquered the fortified stronghold, and stationed his forces there to retain control over the road to Hebron, at the heart of Judah's rebellion. The Assyrian army then continued southwards towards Beersheba. They did not advance on Jerusalem at that time. Much information about Lachish's harsh siege, war and conquest was discovered in Sennacherib's reliefs in Nineveh. The conquest of Lachish was chronicled to a surprising extent, as if it had been the capital of Judah.[4] These reliefs depict the painful fulfillment of Isaiah's prophecies; the humiliated Judeans are shown as prisoners, being led naked and barefoot into captivity. There are also depictions of battle scenes in which the Judeans use the weaponry and fortifications that Uzziah had prepared in the previous generation.

Sennacherib's records describe his military success:

> And as for Hezekiah the Judahite, who did not submit to my yoke: forty-six of his strong, walled cities, as well as the small towns in their area, which were without number, by levelling with battering-rams and by bringing up siege-engines, and by attacking and storming on foot, by mines, tunnels and breaches, I besieged and took them. 200,150 people, great and small, male and female, horses, mules, asses, camels, cattle and sheep without number, I brought away from them and counted as spoil. (Hezekiah) himself, *like a caged bird* I shut up in Jerusalem his royal city.[5]

It is not known how many of the 200,150 were people, horses, donkeys or camels, but it is clear that many thousands of Judeans from the Shephelah and its surroundings were exiled, just like their Samarian brothers. This

---

4. Some scholars claim that Sennacherib's records emphasize his victory over Lachish in order to compensate for his failure to conquer Jerusalem. Tadmor, "Hezekiah and Sennacherib," for example, asserts that Jerusalem was the only rebellious capital city that Sennacherib failed to conquer, and the Assyrians therefore exaggerated the importance of Lachish to claim that it was a substitute for Jerusalem.
5. D.D. Luckenbill, *The Annals of Sennacherib*, Oriental Institute Publications 2 (Chicago: University of Chicago, 1924), 31–36.

destruction was mourned and lamented by the prophet Micah, who witnessed it with his own eyes: "Shear off your hair and make yourself bald for the children you once delighted in; make yourself as bald as a vulture, for they have been exiled from you."

In desperation, Hezekiah was forced to surrender to the king of Assyria. From Sennacherib's records, we learn that Hezekiah paid him a heavy fine, including thirty talents of gold and eight hundred talents of silver (according to the Bible, three hundred talents of silver), precious stones, furnishings inlaid with ivory and costly wood, as well as women and concubines, princes and princesses. Hezekiah was also required to release Padi of Ekron and restore him to power.

Judah's humiliation at this point is briefly described in the Book of Kings:

> In the fourteenth year of King Hezekiah, King Sennacherib of Assyria marched against all the fortified towns of Judah and seized them. King Hezekiah sent this message to the king of Assyria at Lachish, "I have done wrong; withdraw from me; and I shall bear whatever you impose on me." So the king of Assyria imposed upon King Hezekiah of Judah a payment, of three hundred talents of silver and thirty talents of gold. Hezekiah gave him all the silver to be found in the House of the Lord and in the treasuries of the palace. At that time Hezekiah cut down the doors and the doorposts of the Temple of the Lord, which King Hezekiah had overlaid [with gold], and gave them to the king of Assyria. (II Kings 18:13–16)

The text hints that when Hezekiah overlaid the Temple doors with gold, he was considered "King Hezekiah of Judah"; however, when he removed them, he lost this prestigious title, and is referred to merely as "Hezekiah." Like Micah, Isaiah described the destruction of Judah (Rashi attributes these verses to Hezekiah's time, during Sennacherib's campaign):

> Why do you seek further beatings, that you continue to offend? Every head is ailing, and every heart is sick. From head to foot, nothing is untouched: All bruises, and welts, and festering

sores – Not pressed out, not bound up, not softened with oil. Your land is a waste, your cities burnt down; before your eyes, the yield of your soil is consumed by strangers – A wasteland as overthrown by strangers! The daughter of Zion is left like a booth in a vineyard, like a hut in a cucumber field, like a city besieged. (Is. 1:5–8)

Assyrian records end with Hezekiah's submission. Sennacherib certainly would have had no interest in documenting his failure to conquer Jerusalem, instead preferring to emphasize his victory over Lachish. He commemorated his triumph with a relief of a procession of defeated Judeans passing before his throne.

SENNACHERIB'S CAMPAIGN IN ISAIAH'S EARLY PROPHECIES (10:24–33)

Sennacherib received Hezekiah's heavy tribute, but it failed to satisfy him. He decided to increase the pressure on Jerusalem in order to penetrate its defenses and punish the rebellious city. To this end, he sent the Tartan and Rabshakeh, among his highest officials, to instigate a psychological war. The Assyrian army had little time to spare on fortified Jerusalem, for its real enemy, Egypt, was waiting on the coast.

While Jerusalem was busy with preparations for rebellion, Isaiah withdrew into his study house and wept at the people's imperviousness. The Assyrian army marched before his eyes, and he knew that Hezekiah was leading the people into a hopeless campaign of death and destruction. Once the war began, however, all his harsh reproach ceased; when news of the defeat of Judah's outlying cities reached Jerusalem, Isaiah became a source of consolation and encouragement, lifting the spirits of the people and their king. This is apparent from the narrative in Isaiah 37.

This prophecy describes the moments before the siege in graphic, realistic language. The people were seized with panic, but Isaiah stood before the king, a pillar of strength and faith, speaking of the salvation that would swiftly come. This prophecy, about Assyria's arrogance since the days of Tiglath-Pileser, was one of Isaiah's first prophecies of consolation:

ot fear, my nation dwell-
ing in Zion, from Assyria, who beat you with a rod and lift up a
club against you, as Egypt did. Very soon my anger against you
will end and My wrath will be directed to their destruction. The
Lord Almighty will lash them with a whip, as when He struck
down Midian at the rock of Oreb, and He will raise his staff over
the waters, as He did in Egypt. And on that day, their burden will
be lifted from your shoulders, their yoke from your neck; the
yoke will be broken because of the oil. He advanced upon Aiath,
he proceeded to Migron, at Michmash he deposited his bag-
gage. They made the crossing: "Geba is to be our night quarters!"
Ramah was alarmed; Gibeah of Saul took to flight. "Give a shrill
cry, O Bath-gallim! Hearken, Laishah! Take up the cry, Anathoth!"
Madmenah ran away; The dwellers of Gebim sought refuge. This
same day at Nob, He shall stand and wave his hand. O mount
of Fair Zion! O hill of Jerusalem! Behold, the Sovereign Lord of
Hosts will hew off the tree-crowns with an ax: The tall ones shall
be felled, the lofty ones cut down: The thickets of the forest shall
be hacked away with iron, and the Lebanon trees shall fall in their
majesty. (10:24–34)

The prophecy's opening: "Do not fear, my nation," might apply to any
of Assyria's campaigns, but a closer reading reveals that it was referring
to a specific campaign whose purpose was to reach Egypt. It is tempting to identify the prophecy with Sennacherib's campaign, which is
well documented in Assyrian records, but the main problem with this
lies in the route that is described. According to Sennacherib's records,
he came from the coast, entering Judah from the southwest through
Azeka and Lachish, from where he sent messengers to Jerusalem
(Is. 36:2; II Kings 18:17). The march to Jerusalem described in chapter 10
came from the northeast, thus it is not the same campaign. Nonetheless,
it is apparent that chapter 10 describes an actual campaign, rather than
just a vision. The locations mentioned form an eastern route, from the
Jordan Valley towards the East of the land of Benjamin, connecting to
the main mountain route near "Ramah," and not to the main road to

gn (701 BCE)*

Jerusalem that came from the north.[6] Scholars have attempted to identify this route among Assyria's known campaigns to Judah.[7]

It seems that Assyria sent troops from other areas to deal with
rebellious Jerusalem, while most of its forces remained in the Philistine region in order to face Egypt, the real enemy, whose troops had
begun advancing towards Gaza. Jerusalem was thus approached on its
northern frontier, as described in chapter 10, while its western front
was not threatened.[8] Isaiah, living in Jerusalem, received accounts of
the progression of the Assyrian forces, which had already reached Nob
and could be seen observing the capital from its vantage point, ready
to strike at any moment.

JERUSALEM AT WAR (ISAIAH 36; II KINGS 18)

> And the king of Assyria sent the {Tartan and the Rabseris and}
> Rabshakeh from Lachish, with a large force, to King Hezekiah in
> Jerusalem. And they went up and came to Jerusalem, And they
> took up a position near the aqueduct of the Upper Pool, which
> is by the path to the Washer's Field; and Eliakim son of Hilkiah
> who was in charge of the palace, and Shebna the scribe, and Joah
> son of Asaph the recorder went out to him. (Is. 36:2–3; {} mark
> additions found in II Kings 18:17–18)

The confrontation by the aqueduct took place between high ranking officers, one step below royalty. Hezekiah retained Judah's dignity by refusing

---

6. Yoel Elitzur, "The Diagonal Path from Jerusalem to the Plains of Edom in Biblical Times,"
   Judea and Samaria Research Studies 2 (1992): 111–24 [Hebrew]. A team of researchers
   made the journey on foot and discovered a small stronghold and pottery near the
   Michmash crossing, dating back to the monarchic era; see also Yoel Bin-Nun, "He
   Advanced Upon Aiath," *Judea and Samaria Research Studies* 2 (1992): 43–64 [Hebrew].
7. S.Z. Aster, "Historical Background of the Campaign," *Shnaton: An Annual for Biblical
   and Ancient Near Eastern Studies* 19 (2009): 105–24 [Hebrew].
8. Mazer, "Sennacherib's Campaign to the Land of Judah," 292. Mazer suggests that the
   Assyrian troops mentioned in chapter 10 came from Samaria and took a roundabout
   route; however, they may have come from Damascus or the Transjordan, and passed
   through Michmash. Recent findings attest that an Assyrian camp was stationed above
   Jerusalem at the end of the eighth century BCE.

to meet the delegation himself, and instead sent officers of equivalent rank to the delegates. These verses also show that Shebna, detested by Isaiah, was no longer "in charge of the house," and had been demoted to "scribe." He was still a senior official, but, as Isaiah had envisioned, he was outranked by Eliakim son of Hilkiah. Once both parties were present, Rabshakeh revealed the purpose of the delegation. The Book of Kings mentions two officers before Rabshakeh: "The Tartan and the Rabseris," who presumably outranked Rabshakeh. Apparently, Rabshakeh was elected as spokesperson because of his ability to speak "Judean."

An analysis of his words shows that the Assyrians used psychological tactics to crush their enemies' spirits, mocking the weakness of the besieged nation. Rabshakeh's words were carefully calculated to undermine Jerusalem's confidence in every respect: politically, religiously, and militarily.

(1) POLITICAL SCORN: "THE SPLINTERED REED OF A STAFF"

> The Rabshakeh said to them, "You tell Hezekiah: Thus said the Great King, the king of Assyria: What makes you so confident? Does mere talk make counsel and valor for war – Look, on whom are you relying, that you have rebelled against me? You are relying on Egypt, that splintered reed of a staff, which enters and punctures the palm of anyone who leans on it. That is what Pharaoh king of Egypt is like to all who rely on him. (Is. 36:4–6; II Kings 18:19–21)

Everyone in Jerusalem knew that Hezekiah's rebellion depended upon a military alliance with Egypt. Isaiah had condemned this treaty, and now the Rabshakeh repeated the prophet's warnings almost word for word. By undermining their greatest political ally, the Assyrian official deflated the hopes of Jerusalem's soldiers.

(2) RELIGIOUS SCORN FOR HEZEKIAH'S REFORM

> And if you tell me that you are relying on the Lord your God – He is the very one whose shrines and altars Hezekiah did away

with, telling Judah and Jerusalem, 'You must worship only at this altar!' (Is. 36:7; II Kings 18:22)

The effective Assyrian intelligence network had discovered Judah's resentment at Hezekiah's removal of the shrines and altars. The people had worshiped God at these altars for so long, and Hezekiah had insisted upon their destruction. The Rabshakeh taunted the weary guards of Jerusalem's walls, bringing their long-buried resentments to the surface. Playing upon this source of religious tension, the Assyrian openly questioned Hezekiah's religious achievements by claiming that his destruction of the altars resulted in divine anger and punishment.

(3) MILITARY SCORN: MOCKING JUDAH'S WEAKNESS

Come now, make this wager with my master, the king of Assyria: I'll give you two thousand horses, if you can produce riders to mount them. How then can you repulse one officer of the least of my master's officials, when you are depending on Egypt for chariots and horsemen? (Is. 36:8–9; II Kings 18:23–24)

Although the precise size of Judah's army is not known, Sennacherib's great pride at its destruction, as seen in the records of his third campaign, gives some indication of the power of Hezekiah's forces and fortifications. Rabshakeh's mockery of Judah for its "weakness" may instead stem from Judah's conception of the Assyrian army. Playing on Assyria's infamous reputation, Rabshakeh sought to intimidate Judah's soldiers before he struck, emphasizing one of Judah's perceived weaknesses in order to destroy Judahite confidence.

(4) ASSYRIA HAS RISEN THROUGH THE WILL OF GOD

Now, do you think I have ascended to destroy this place without the Lord? The Lord said to me, Ascend against this land, and destroy it!" (Is. 36:10; II Kings 18:25)

Half a century earlier, Isaiah had warned that Assyria was the "rod of God's wrath." Now, Rabshakeh repeated this concept, so familiar to Jerusalemites, in order to crush the people's spirits.

The Judahite delegates who met with the Assyrian representatives were well aware of the dangers of this psychological war, and sought to minimize the damage:

> Eliakim, Shebna, and Joah said to the Rabshakeh, "Please, speak to your servants in Aramaic, since we understand it; do not speak to us in Judean in the hearing of the people on the wall." But the Rabshakeh said to them, "Was it to your master and to you that my master sent me to speak those words? It was precisely to the men who are sitting on the wall – who will have to eat their dung and drink their urine with you." (Is. 36:11–12; II Kings 18:26–27)

Deliberately, in his loudest voice, the Rabshakeh turned to the men on the walls:

(5) THE KING OF ASSYRIA PROPOSES IMMIGRATION TO ASSYRIA

> And the Rabshakeh stood and called out in a loud voice in Judean, "Hear the words of the Great King, the king of Assyria! Thus said the king: Do not let Hezekiah deceive you, for he will not be able to save you. Don't let Hezekiah make you rely on the Lord, saying, 'The Lord will surely save us; this city will not fall into the hands of Assyria!' Do not listen to Hezekiah. For thus said the king of Assyria: Make your peace with me and come out to me, so that you may all eat from your vines and your fig trees and drink water from your cisterns, until I come and take you away to a land like your own, a land of bread and wine, of grain and vineyards, {A land of olive oil and honey, and you shall live and you shall not die}. (Is. 36:13–17; {} are additions found in II Kings 18:28–32)

Assyria's exile policy differed according to the compliance of the conquered nation. It is infinitely easier to transfer a population from one place to another if the population in question is willing to move, rather than having to be dragged to their destination in chains, under the watchful eyes of soldiers. Rabshakeh offered the people of Jerusalem a new home in a bountiful land, where they would be able to start anew. He presented the Assyrian king as a merciful, benevolent ruler who was concerned about the welfare of his new subjects.

(6) SCORN FOR THOSE WHO RELY UPON GOD'S HAND AGAINST ASSYRIA

> Beware of letting Hezekiah mislead you by saying, 'The Lord will save us.' Did any of the gods of the other nations save his land from the king of Assyria? Where were the gods of Hamath and Arpad? Where were the gods of Sepharvaim? And did they save Samaria from me? Which among all the gods of those countries saved their countries from me, that the Lord should save Jerusalem from me?" (Is. 36:18–20; II Kings 18:32–35)

Here, Rabshakeh contradicted himself. He had initially spoken of the God of Judah with respect, as the One who had appointed Assyria to destroy the land; now he equated him with the gods of the other conquered nations.

The Rabshakeh's speech ended and was met with silence, as King Hezekiah had commanded:

> And the people were silent and did not answer him with a single word; for the king's order was, "Do not answer him." (Is. 36:21; II Kings 18:36)

The delegation reported to Hezekiah in despair:

> And so Eliakim son of Hilkiah who was in charge of the palace, and Shebna the scribe, and Joah son of Asaph the recorder came to Hezekiah with their clothes rent, and they recounted the words of the Rabshakeh to him. (Is. 36:22; II Kings 18:37)

Isaiah's Prophetic Revolution: From Reproach to Reassurance

King Hezekiah's reaction to the Assyrian's haughty words recalls his sickbed prayer. He rent his clothes, donned sackcloth, and broke out into a direct appeal to God. He then sent a delegation to the now elderly Isaiah and implored him to join the struggle for Jerusalem's existence:

> They said to him, "Thus said Hezekiah: This day is a day of distress, of chastisement, and of disgrace. The babes have reached the birthstool, but the strength to give birth is lacking. Perhaps the Lord your God will listen to the words of the Rabshakeh, whom his master the king of Assyria has sent to blaspheme the living God, and will mete out judgment for the words that the Lord your God has heard – If you will offer up prayer for the surviving remnant." (Is. 37:3–4; II Kings 19:3–4)

Hezekiah's words reflect great tension. They also reflect the longstanding relationship between the king and the prophet. The king did not ask the prophet whether or not God would listen, but rather placed responsibility upon Isaiah's venerable shoulders: "Perhaps the Lord *your God* will listen." Hezekiah did not wish to hear the prophet's opinion; his words were a plea that they pray together on this day "of distress, of chastisement, and of disgrace."

The prophet's reply was short and simple, in sharp contrast to Hezekiah's lengthy expressions of fear:

> Isaiah said to them, "Tell your master as follows: Thus said the Lord: Do not be frightened by the words of blasphemy against Me that you have heard from the minions of the king of Assyria. I will delude him; he will hear a rumor and return to his land, and I will make him fall by the sword in his land." (Is. 37:6–7; II Kings 19:6–7)

At this point, the Rabshakeh returned to Sennacherib, who had already advanced from Lachish to Libnah. There, a rumor reached Sennacherib that the Egyptian-Kushite pharaoh, Taharqa, was again rebelling against him. Sennacherib dispatched explicit, frank threats to Hezekiah.

HEZEKIAH'S PRAYER AND THE PROPHECY OF SALVATION

Upon reading Sennacherib's threat, Hezekiah broke out into a prayer of supplication, standing alone before God:

> And Hezekiah prayed to the Lord and said, "O Lord of Hosts, Enthroned on the Cherubim! You alone are God of all the kingdoms of the earth. You made the heavens and the earth. O Lord, incline Your ear and hear; open Your eyes and see. Hear the words that Sennacherib has sent to blaspheme the living God! True, O Lord, the kings of Assyria have annihilated the nations and their lands, and have committed their gods to the flames and have destroyed them; for they are not gods, but man's handiwork of wood and stone. But now, O Lord our God, deliver us from his hands, and let all the kingdoms of the earth know that You alone, O Lord, are God." (Is. 37:15–20; II Kings 19:15–19)

This bold prayer reveals Hezekiah's true loyalty, as a God-fearing person and king who turned to God in his time of need. In response, God sent Isaiah a poetic vision that promised Jerusalem's protection from every evil:

> "Thus said the Lord, the God of Israel: I have heard the prayer you have offered to Me concerning King Sennacherib of Assyria. This is the word that the Lord has spoken concerning him: Fair Maiden Zion despises you, she mocks at you; fair Jerusalem shakes her head at you. Whom have you blasphemed and reviled? Against whom made loud your voice and haughtily raised your eyes? Against the Holy One of Israel!? (Is. 37:21–23; II Kings 19:20–22)

Prophet and king were united once more, joining forces in supplication, prayer and vision. This was reflected in Isaiah's prophecy of the remnant that would spring forth.

> For a remnant shall come forth from Jerusalem, survivors from Mount Zion. The zeal of the Lord of Hosts shall bring this to pass. (Is. 37:31–32; II Kings 19:30–31)

At the end of his condemnation of Sennacherib's arrogance, and the assurance that he would be punished, the prophet explicitly promised that God would protect Jerusalem:

> Therefore, thus said the Lord concerning the king of Assyria: He shall not enter this city: He shall not shoot an arrow at it, or advance upon it with a shield, or pile up a siege mound against it. He shall go back by the way he came; he shall not enter this city – declares the Lord. I will protect and save this city for My sake, and for the sake of My servant David." (Is. 37:33–35; II Kings 19:32–34)

THE MIRACULOUS LIBERATION

The miracle of the reconciliation between the prophet and the king, through Hezekiah's prayer and Isaiah's vision of God's answer, was the climax of Hezekiah's reign and of Isaiah's prophecy.

The miracle of Jerusalem's salvation is described in a brief prophetic narrative:

> And it came to pass on that night, an angel of the Lord went out and smote the Assyrian camp, one hundred and eighty-five thousand, and the following morning they were all dead corpses. So King Sennacherib of Assyria broke camp and retreated, and stayed in Nineveh. (Is. 37:36–37; II Kings 19:35)

Early historians such as Josephus explained this as the plague, which occasionally struck military camps or besieged cities during wartime (*Antiquities* X, 1:5). Herodotus (2.141) bases his version of this episode on an Egyptian tradition that the Assyrian army encroached on its border was struck by a plague of rats (who were often carriers of disease). Nonetheless, the Egyptians believed that their pharaoh, Taharqa, was responsible for Sennacherib's retreat.

Modern historians have shown skepticism towards the biblical account, which is reminiscent of the ten plagues of Egypt. The lack of an explanation for Sennacherib's desertion of Jerusalem in the Assyrian records, however, reinforces the narrative of the miraculous salvation. Sennacherib's records only mention the conquest of Lachish and its exiles marching in front of the Assyrian king, which, as mentioned earlier, seems exaggerated, as if to compensate for his failure to conquer the capital. Jerusalem, rebelling under Hezekiah's leadership, merits an unusually brief mention:

> And as for Hezekiah the Judahite... *like a caged bird* I shut up in Jerusalem his royal city. Earthworks I threw up against him [to besiege him] – the one coming out of the city-gate, I turned back to his misery.[1]

Shalmaneser besieged Samaria for three years before he managed to conquer the city, displaying typical Assyrian obstinacy. Sennacherib, however, withdrew from Jerusalem without offering any explanation.

1. Luckenbill, *The Annals of Sennacherib*, 36.

Isaiah's prophecy echoes the arrogance of the Assyrian records, just like his prophetic response to Sennacherib's brash words to Hezekiah. In contrast to the image of the "caged bird," Isaiah portrayed God as a mother bird, flying free and hovering protectively over Jerusalem:

> Like hovering birds, even so will the Lord of Hosts shield Jerusalem, shielding and saving, protecting and rescuing. (Is. 31:5)

Hezekiah Failed to Sing

The prophecies of Isaiah were peppered with sacred songs of thanksgiving for the miraculous salvation from Assyria's hands. One such example can be found in chapter 26:

> On that day, this song shall be sung in the land of Judah: Ours is a mighty city; he makes victory our inner and outer wall. Open the gates, and let in a righteous nation, who keeps faith (Is. 26:1–2).

And in chapter 30:

> For you, there shall be singing as on a night when a festival is hallowed; there shall be rejoicing as when they march with flute, with timbrels, and with lyres to the Rock of Israel on the Mount of the Lord. (30:29)

Yet songs of thanksgiving did not burst forth from Judah with all their might. Perhaps Hezekiah had used up his strength in his prayer for salvation. Moreover, Judah and its king were mourning the destruction of the Shephelah and Lachish, and the exile of countless Judeans. Hezekiah may have been too distraught to lead the city in grateful thanksgiving. The simultaneous conflicting emotions of grief and joy illuminate certain chapters of Isaiah's prophecy, which are a disjointed, baffling collection of verses of rejoicing and despair, of war and salvation.[1]

This is reflected in the words of the sages, who discuss why Hezekiah was not worthy of being the Messiah:[2]

> R. Tanḥum said, and Bar-Kapra in Zippori said: The Holy One, Blessed be He, wanted to make Hezekiah the Messiah, and Sennacherib Gog and Magog – The attribute of justice said before the Holy One, Blessed be He: Master of the world! You did not make King David of Israel, who said so many songs and praises before You, the Messiah. Hezekiah, for whom you performed all these miracles, and didn't say songs [of thanksgiving] before You, You wish to make the Messiah? ... Straight away the earth exclaimed, "Sovereign of the Universe! Let me utter song before You instead of this righteous man [Hezekiah], and make him the Messiah." So it broke into song before Him, as it is written, "From the uttermost part of the earth have we heard songs, even glory to the righteous" (Is. 24:16). Then the ministering angel of the world said to Him, "Sovereign of the Universe! It [the earth] has fulfilled Your desire [for songs of praise] on behalf of this righteous man." But a heavenly Voice cried out, "I waste away, I waste away!" (24:16) To which the prophet rejoined, "Woe is me (24:16), woe is me: how long [must we wait]?" The heavenly Voice [again] cried out, "The faithless have acted faithlessly; the faithless have broken faith!" (24:16). (Sanhedrin 94a)

In order to understand this remarkable story, we must refer to the relevant prophecies in Isaiah (ch. 24–27), which are interspersed with verses of praise and cries of woe. During this period, the messianic dream "wasted away" because of the faithless who "acted faithlessly". Many people blamed the grave results of the war on Hezekiah for pursuing the alliance with Egypt. Some went so far as to follow in the footsteps of

---

1. Some of Isaiah's most perplexing chapters (24–27) are strewn with verses that are unrelated to the adjacent passages.
2. See Raviv, "The Holy One Blessed be He Wished to Make Hezekiah the Messiah."

Ahaz, pandering to Assyria. The heavy fine that Hezekiah was forced to pay to Sennacherib undermined his leadership in the eyes of the people. Now, once the threat had passed, all that Hezekiah had achieved – his spiritual revolution – was in jeopardy.

Those who supported Isaiah and his idea of the remnant blossoming to full glory were overpowered by the harsh atmosphere of a city grieving for its brothers. Their lone voices were drowned out by confusion and mourning, and their "song" sank into the blood-soaked earth that was struggling to renew itself, as the prophet expressed, "This year you shall eat what grows of itself, and the next year what springs from that, and in the third year sow and reap and plant vineyards and eat their fruit" (37:30).

This difficult rehabilitation moved Hezekiah's opponents to support his son, Manasseh. This period sheds light on the sharp contrast between the two kings; the father, who was one of the most righteous and God-fearing kings of Judah, and his idol-worshiping son.

Isaiah 1

An Overview[1]

T he prophet Isaiah, venerable and ancient, stood at the entrance to his study house in Jerusalem and watched the town square. Decades earlier, in his mind's eye, he had seen ragged old women begging for food and shelter, and people wandering the streets in desperation. Now, his vision had become the bitter reality. Yesterday's aristocracy was indistinguishable from the masses of refugees. Jerusalem had yet to recover from the siege and the horrors of war. Sennacherib's army had bolted from the land, but they had left their cruel mark on Judah, and the land was still covered with Assyrian hoof-prints. Isaiah lowered his gaze. There

---

1. See Rabbi M. Breuer, *Pirkei Moadot*, vol. 2 (Jerusalem, 1986), 457–75; *Pirkei Yeshayahu* (Alon Shvut, 2010), 15–18, 235–40. Rabbi Breuer draws a long list of parallels between chapters 1 and 6, claiming that chapter 1 is a "reflection" of the initial prophetic mission that Isaiah received, in chapter 6, which was delivered to the public as an irreversible decree of destruction. This, however, does not fit with the concept of prophetic mission, especially considering the plain meaning of chapters 2–5, where Isaiah was sent to warn the people to repent. It also contradicts the notion of free choice that is presented in the continuation of chapter 1: "If, then, you agree and give heed, you will eat the good things of the earth; but if you refuse and disobey, you will be devoured by the sword" (1:19–20). We follow Rashi's interpretation of chapter 1, which sees the list of the four kings during whose reigns Isaiah prophesied (v. 1) as an indication that chapter 1 is a summary of all of his prophecies.

was no doubt that the sorry sight before him was the fulfillment of his vision of ruin, which he had seen fifty years before. King Hezekiah was utterly drained, unable to continue the revolution of his youth, and he slumped tiredly on the throne of his forefather, David.

From the depths of his wounded soul, Isaiah's final lamentation burst out:

> Hear, O heavens, and give ear, O earth, for the Lord has spoken, "I reared children and brought them up, and they have rebelled against Me. An ox knows its owner, an ass its master's crib: Israel does not know, My people takes no thought." Ah, sinful nation! People laden with iniquity! Brood of evildoers! Depraved children! They have forsaken the Lord, spurned the Holy One of Israel, turned their backs. Why do you seek further beatings, that you continue to offend? Every head is ailing, and every heart is sick. From head to foot no spot is sound: All bruises, and welts, and festering sores – Not pressed out, not bound up, not softened with oil. Your land is a waste, your cities burnt down; before your eyes, the yield of your soil is consumed by strangers – A wasteland as overthrown by strangers! Fair Zion is left like a booth in a vineyard, like a hut in a cucumber field, like a city beleaguered. Had not the Lord of Hosts left us some survivors, we should be like Sodom, like another Gomorrah. (Is. 1:2–9)

As Isaiah wept over the destruction of the city, Sennacherib's scribes chronicled his campaign in Judah. As Isaiah stood in the abandoned vineyards of Jerusalem, Sennacherib arrogantly described the city's struggle: "Like a caged bird." This harsh image reflected almost half a century of Isaiah's prophetic battle to shape Judah's politics. He had implored four different kings to direct their powers inward and not outward, to focus on the moral state of their own people, and not on Judah's prestige in the eyes of surrounding nations. His protests did not affect Uzziah's thirst for power, his words fell upon deaf ears when Ahaz pandered to Assyria, and Hezekiah did not listen to him, insisting instead on forming an alliance with Egypt. Isaiah's condemnation of the rebellion against Assyria had no effect. His desperate campaign of walking "naked and barefoot" only postponed the crisis, which ended with a trembling, wounded city gasping for air after Sennacherib's miraculous departure.

Jerusalem survived, but the surrounding cities had been consumed by fire. Judah lay in ruins; countless families had become homeless. The prophet witnessed all this and was reminded of the destruction of Sodom and Gomorrah. The golden city and its surrounding fertile hills of wine and oil were laid to waste. The Judah of his childhood, of Uzziah's day, had become a ruin. The prophet mouthed weak words of gratitude that the Creator had left the city standing: "Had not the Lord of Hosts left us some survivors, we should be like Sodom," a realization which triggered his fury against those who had brought about Judah's destruction. God was not the destroyer of Jerusalem; human choices had led to its downfall. Isaiah's lament became a prophecy of harsh reproach against the Judahite leadership. His weeping shifted into wrath, and he launched into a tirade against those "chieftains of Sodom" whose arrogance and alienation had led to the city's destruction:

> Hear the word of the Lord, chieftains of Sodom; give ear to our God's instruction, people of Gomorrah! "What need have I of all your sacrifices?" says the Lord. "I am sated with burnt offerings of rams, and suet of fatlings, and blood of bulls; and I have no delight in lambs and he-goats. Who asked you to come to appear before Me and trample My courts? Do not bring anymore futile oblations, incense is offensive to Me. New moon and sabbath, proclaiming of solemnities, assemblies with iniquity, I cannot abide. Your new moons and fixed seasons fill Me with loathing; they are become a burden to Me, I cannot endure them. And when you lift up your hands, I will turn My eyes away from you; though you pray at length, I will not listen. Your hands are bloodstained with crime! (1:10–15)

Isaiah could not abide by the automatic worship of the people. Like the prophet Samuel, he attacked those who clung to the horns of the altar, continuing their empty worship and seeking to appease God through the blood and fat of sacrifices. God has no desire for prayers, offerings, Sabbaths, and festivals, he admonished them, when there is no justice and charity. Orphans and widows were downtrodden and suffering, and,

"Your rulers are rogues and cronies of thieves, every one avid for presents and greedy for gifts" (1:23), while, "Your hands are bloodstained with crime" (1:15). Only moral reform could save the sinful society. Standing before God in prayer, and offering sacrifices to Him, can only be meaningful within a moral, compassionate context.

In anger and pain, the prophet roared at those who made pilgrimages to Jerusalem: "Who asked you to come to appear before Me and trample My courts?" This verse is perhaps the clearest reflection of the humiliation that Isaiah felt before God. The most climactic encounter between a worshiper and his Creator was the pilgrimage during the festivals. There is a commandment to make an appearance before God three times a year; it was an encounter of love and yearning. Suddenly, the "Host" no longer wished to welcome His "guests"; His own children had become like intruders to Him. The Talmud describes a Babylonian sage who would burst out into weeping when he heard this verse:

> R. Huna would weep when he heard this verse. He said, "The slave who His master longs to see should become estranged from him? (Ḥagiga 3a)

How distant the people of Judah had grown from the eager pilgrims they once were, when they sought the presence of God! True, Jerusalem and its Temple still stood, but the people's corruption had broken them and distanced them from their God and His house.

After bitter lamentation and bitter reproach, the prophet turned to the people and explained the essence of Jewish faith:

> If, then, you agree and give heed – you will eat the good things of the earth; but if you refuse and disobey – the sword will devour you for the Lord has spoken. (1:19–20)

There is no consolation in this chapter, no word about how Israel is God's chosen people. Here, Isaiah established that Israel will be granted lives of dignity and peace if they choose to live their lives with responsibility and morality. Israel's special role as God's people comes with obligations, and the privilege of living the Promised Land is not unconditional. There is no assurance of physical security unless the people have spiritual and moral fortitude.

Isaiah was the mouthpiece for all those who strived for Israel's autonomy within its land. A moral code was established when Abraham was chosen, which has governed every generation since: "Keep the way of the Lord by doing what is just and right" (Gen. 18:19). This is the subtle, essential guideline that allows a king to retain the balance between the greater good of his kingdom and the individual needs of his subjects, especially the weak and vulnerable among them.

The concluding verse of Isaiah's opening prophecy encapsulates the most essential message of every true prophet of Israel, the key to Israel's continued existence upon its own Land. Where there is injustice (*mispaḥ*) and where there are cries of distress (*tze'aka*), God will avenge the cries. Where there is justice (*mishpat*) and righteousness (*tzedaka*), God will dwell among His people:

> Zion will be redeemed through justice and delivered with righteousness. (1:27)

Part Four

The Days of Manasseh

By Yoel Bin-Nun

Isaiah 40-52

Isaiah and His Disciples

Isaiah son of Amoz was very active in Jerusalem – he described the vision of God's glory (Is. 6); he went out to meet Ahaz with his son She'ar-Yashuv (7:3); for three years, he walked through the streets "naked and barefoot" (20:3); and he maintained a close relationship with his protégé, Hezekiah (ch. 37–39).

From chapter 40 onwards, however, there is no narrative whatsoever.

This is one of the reasons for the cornerstone belief in biblical scholarship that chapters 40 and onwards of Isaiah (and possibly chapters 34–35 as well) were composed by a different prophet (referred to as "second Isaiah"), who lived in the days of the return to Zion following Cyrus' declaration, the era when there was a call to leave Babylonia and return to Zion.[1]

Nevertheless, I find this hypothesis unconvincing. During the Babylonian exile, the Hebrew language was heavily influenced by Akkadian and Aramaic, as is reflected, for example, in the prophetic language

---

1. A summary of this scholarly approach can be found in the commentary on chapters 40–46 in M. Paul, *Isaiah* (*Mikra LeYisrael*) [Hebrew], and J. D. W. Watts, introduction to *Word Biblical Commentary*, vol. 25: *Isaiah 34–66* (Waco, Texas, 1987), xxiii-xxv.

of Ezekiel. However, the Hebrew of the early Second Temple period is completely different from that of the Book of Isaiah, in its entirety.

This will be clarified below, chapter by chapter, together with an alternative suggestion – that Isaiah and his students were the upholders of the "prophetic school" that Isaiah founded in Manasseh's time, when true prophets were persecuted by Manasseh and his son Amon, and went into hiding. The details will be clarified through the analysis of chapters 40–49, and especially of chapters 50–59. The later chapters are from the end of the First Temple period, and they all contain the words of Isaiah son of Amoz.

The themes and style of these chapters are clearly a continuation of Isaiah's words;[2] the Hebrew is the biblical Hebrew of the days of Judahite royalty,[3] which is distinct from the style of Ezekiel's time in exile, the return to Zion, Zerubbabel, Ezra and Nehemiah, the Second Temple prophets Haggai and Zechariah, and the Chronicler, all of whom attempted to maintain the biblical Hebrew as best as they could.

The reality of the early Second Temple period in Judah is also entirely inconsistent with the comprehensive process of consolation that gradually unfolds in the Book of Isaiah from its beginning (ch. 11) to its end (ch. 60–62). There was no ingathering of exiles during the

---

2. See R. Margaliot, *One Was Isaiah* (Jerusalem, 1954) [Hebrew], which lists dozens of phrases that are unique to Isaiah and that appear throughout the book, in both sections; and see A. Hacham, introduction to *Isaiah*, vol. 1 (*Daat Mikra*) (Jerusalem, 1984), 12–16 [Hebrew]. I believe that Hacham was the first who recognized that Isaiah was the founder of a study house, and the first to propose that the second part of the book was a continuation of Isaiah's prophecies and those of his disciples from Manasseh's time and onwards. However, while he claims that most of these later prophecies were kept in the prophetic study house until they were needed by later generations, I believe that most of them were indeed pronounced during Manasseh's time and were the source of the prophet's persecution, eventually leading to innocent bloodshed (Is. 53:7–12; 59:7; II Kings 21:16).

3. On the continuity and differences between the biblical Hebrew of the First Temple period and the Hebrew of the Second Temple period, see A. Ben David, *Biblical Language and the Language of the Sages* (Tel Aviv, 1967), 60–72 [Hebrew]; on Ezekiel's exilic Hebrew, influenced by Akkadian and Aramaic, see R. Kasher, *Ezekiel* (*Mikra LeYisrael*) (2004), 82–83 [Hebrew]. The Hebrew of Isaiah, chapters 40–66, contains none of these phenomena.

Second Temple period, nor was there any known struggle against idol-worshiping Jews at that time.

It is crucial to understand that Isaiah son of Amoz was not just a prophet. He was a teacher and mentor with students (8:16–17; 50:4). He established a prophetic school, or *beit midrash*, where they uttered lyrical prophecies as psalms (12:24–27; 30:29; 38:9–20). The prophets who continued his legacy included Micah, Zephaniah, Nahum, and Habakkuk, who echoed his verses and ideas.

Isaiah's disciple-followers struggled against idol worship and empire worship throughout the desperate days of Manasseh and afterwards, until the end of the First Temple period. These anonymous prophets, who repeated Isaiah's words, present the natural continuation of the visions of Isaiah son of Amoz.

One of them describes his prophetic election from the womb, as a continuation of his mentor's prophecy:

> The Lord has called me from birth; From my mother's insides He made mention of my name; He has made my mouth like a sharp sword. In the shadow of His hand he has hidden me ... He said to me, "You are My servant, Israel, in whom I will be glorified." (Is. 49:1–3)

CHAPTER 40:[4] PROPHECIES OF CONSOLATION – WHEN WERE THEY UTTERED, AND WHEN WERE THEY FULFILLED?

On *Shabbat Naḥamu* 1920, Viscount Herbert Samuel, a British Zionist Jew, arrived at the Hurva Synagogue in the Old City and was honored with the recitation of the *haftara* "Take comfort, take comfort, My people, says your God; Speak to the heart of Jerusalem and call out to her" (40:1–2).[5]

The congregation burst into tears from sheer excitement. After thousands of years of exile, wandering, and suffering, a Jewish authority had finally returned to Jerusalem, following the Balfour Declaration and

---

4. Chapters 40–49 are a single unit; there is no significance to the chapter divisions.
5. I read this story in my youth.

the League of Nations' historic decision, recalling Zerubbabel (and Nehemiah) at the beginning of the Second Temple era: "The deaf have heard, and the blind looked out to see" (Is. 42:18). This prophecy was neither pronounced nor written following the Balfour Declaration, nor following Cyrus' declaration; prophecies are not written down as they are fulfilled.

Marvelous descriptions of the future have been written by leaders and philosophers who did not consider themselves prophets.

In 1840, Rabbi Yehuda Alkalai predicted that the redemption would only take place after a great destruction that would occur exactly a century later.

In 1905, Yosef Haim Brenner wrote that "six million [Jews] will be hung by a burned gate … give us a cave to hide in."

On September 3, 1897, Theodor Herzl wrote in his diary: "In Basel, I founded the state of the Jews; were I to announce this today in public, the response would be laughter on every side, but perhaps in five years, or fifty years at the most, all will recognize it." The Jewish state in the Land of Israel was recognized by the United Nations on the November 29, exactly fifty years later.

If such visions are uttered by those who are not prophets, they can certainly be fulfilled when pronounced by the prophets themselves.

CHAPTERS 40–42: BELIEFS VS. CULTIC RITUAL, AND FUNDAMENTAL BELIEFS FROM THE BOOK OF GENESIS – WHO CONTROLS HISTORY?

"The Creator of the ends of the earth" (Is. 40:28), "who measures the waters in the hollow of His hand, the heavens with a span, and the dust of the earth with a measure" (40:12), is also He who "calls the generations from the beginning" (41:4), and who chose the People of Israel, "the descendants of My beloved Abraham" (41:8).

Who must repeatedly be taught this basic lesson from the Book of Genesis?[6] Jews who have despaired of their faith and belief in God.

---

6. From here, biblical scholarship determined that the fundamentals of the Jewish faith were formed only at the beginning of the Second Temple period even though the

After the destruction of Samaria and the devastating exile of the ten tribes of Israel, Hezekiah still celebrated the Passover festival in Jerusalem with many of the remaining Israelites who still remained in the north (II Chr. 30). But after the destruction of Lachish and the exile of many from Judah, he had no heart to sing about Jerusalem's salvation, and this despair prevailed with Manasseh's ascent to the throne at the age of twelve (II Kings 21).

Jerusalem was flooded with Assyrian and Babylonian idol worship, as these empires were the big victors of the ancient world wars. It was extremely difficult to cling to the idea that the God of Israel was the sole hand that shaped history.

In the first part of the Book of Isaiah (ch. 1–39), there is no mockery of worshipers of wooden idols that are coated in silver and gold, because there was no such practice at that time; but from chapter 40 and on, the phenomenon is described in all its odiousness: "The statue is crafted by the craftsman" (40:19). The deep despair of Hezekiah's time led Jews to embrace blocks of wood taken from the royal treasuries: "He chooses wood that will not rot…to make a firm idol that will not topple" (40:20).

The burgeoning comfort throughout these chapters is the believing prophet's vision of the future. He stood almost alone among the despairing Jews who had turned to idol worship. By contrast, at the beginning of the Second Temple period, with all its hardships, there was no need to teach the fundamentals of belief in God from the very beginning.

CHAPTER 42: THE VISION OF REDEMPTION VS. HARSH REALITY (I)

A selected reading of these prophecies (such as the *haftarot* read in the weeks following Tisha B'Av) may be misleading; the people's dire situation at the time of the prophecies cannot be overlooked.

Hebrew of Genesis is clearly much more ancient. It did not occur to these scholars that the prophet was attempting to address desperate Jews who had turned to idol worship out of despair.

The target audience of these prophecies did not experience consolation, but were "a people robbed and spoiled; all of them snared in holes and hidden in prisons; given to prey with no one to deliver" (Is. 42:22).

Descriptions of consolation and of the principles of faith were the only remaining tools of the prophet who attempted to alleviate the grave despair of a "people robbed and spoiled"; they recall the song of the Jewish partisans during the Holocaust: "Never say, 'This is the final road'... Our longed-for hour will yet come."

The struggle to sustain hope produces the notion of the Messiah (which also appeared in chapter 11, a prophecy from Ahaz's time), the divinely elected king who will execute true justice for Jews and the nations alike; he appears in prophecies during the darkest hours:

> An offshoot shall issue forth from the stump of Jesse... The spirit of the Lord shall rest upon him... He shall not judge by what his eyes behold... Thus he shall judge the poor with equity and decide with justice for the lowly of the land. (11:1–4)

> Behold My servant whom I uphold, My elect, in whom My soul delights, I have settled My spirit on him, He will bring out justice for the nations; he shall not cry, nor lift up his voice; a bruised reed he will not break... He shall bring forth judgment unto truth... The isles shall await his teachings. (42:1–4)

This prophetic vision (from the prophetic school of Isaiah son of Amoz) will bring a "new song" to the world (42:10–12), making the desert bloom (41:18–19), for there will be "justice in the wilderness" (32:16), which will enable the release of "prisoners from the prison, and them that sit in darkness," and God's people will have "a covenant of the people, for a light of the nations" (42:6–7). These are ideas from chapters 2 and 11, from the beginning of Isaiah's prophetic career. But would the prisoners and sufferers believe in these visions?

The earlier prophecies, which told of the coming of Assyria and Babylonia, had come true and all witnessed their fulfillment; thus, the prophet urged, have faith that these new visions of consolation and redemption will also be fulfilled: "Behold, the former things are come to pass, and new things do I declare; before they spring forth I tell you of them" (42:9).

CHAPTER 43: THE MIRACLE OF THE INGATHERING OF EXILES WAS NOT FULFILLED IN THE SECOND TEMPLE ERA

The prophecy of the ingathering of exiles "from the four corners of the earth" is also an extension and development of previous prophecies in Isaiah (11:11–16; 27:12–13):

> And it shall come to pass on that day – The Lord will set His hand a second time to recover the remnant of His people that will be left in Assyria and Egypt, from Patros and from Kush, from Elam and Shinar and Hammath and from the islands of the sea; and He will set up a banner for the nations, and gather in the outcasts of Israel, and bring together the outcasts of Judah from the four corners of the earth. (11:11–12)

> Fear not, for I am with you – From the east I will bring your seed and from the west I will gather them in; I will tell the north, "Yield," and to the south, "Do not hold back; bring My sons from afar, and My daughters from the ends of the earth." (43:5–6)

This later prophecy is heavier with prophetic persuasion, addressed as it is to a more desperate people. During the ingathering of exiles, all the nations, too, will recognize that God is the one true God, and the only One capable of gathering His lost children from the ends of the earth. These prophecies were not written during a time of ingathering of exiles because no such ingathering took place during ancient times; rather, these prophecies were pronounced at a time of great despair, just as Jeremiah's prophecies of consolation were pronounced during the time of the destruction (especially Jer. 32).

It is important to recall that there was no ingathering of exiles during the Second Temple period, or in any other era before the return to Zion in recent generations. Likewise, there is no other nation who has survived such long, scattered exiles, so there will never again be an ingathering of exiles such as this. This prophecy has been fulfilled over the last two centuries. Around 600,000 people returned with the establishment of the State of Israel, and around four million have gradually come back since then, most of them from the west, from over the sea.

Yet there are Jews in our time who do not see God's hand in this astounding ingathering of exiles, and who do not understand its religious significance. Some of these Jews even recite three times daily, "Blessed are You, who gathers in the dispersed of Israel." Many have neither read nor internalized the prophecies of Isaiah, despite the fact that thanks to these prophecies hundreds of millions of believers all around the world recognize that God is the One and only.

CHAPTER 44: THE STRUGGLE AGAINST FOREIGN WORSHIP (I)

The prophet went out of his way to explain against whom he was fighting, and why he could not stop teaching the basic principles of faith: There were senseless Jews who "have not known nor understood, for He has shut their eyes, that they cannot see, and their hearts, that they cannot understand" (Is. 44:18), who worshiped and "pray to a god who will not save them" (45:20). They could not even understand how absurd it was to take a block of wood and use half of it for a cooking fire and the other half for a carved idol.

We know for certain that Jews worshiped idols in Manasseh's time, and we have explained that this was the result of deep despair at the harsh destruction and exile that preceded his reign.

Yet even so, how could these idol worshipers be so senseless?

In general, they thought the same about the prophets who still believed in God. Pagan nations all over the world worshiped gold-wood idols, for they represented the powers of the Assyrian and Babylonian empires, while the prophet believed in a single, invisible God whom the nations of the world knew nothing about. The people had witnessed the powers of the pagan empires with their own eyes, while the prophet believed in a future ingathering of exiles the likes of which had never been seen before.

If so, then who is the fool?

Through Assyrian, Babylonian, and Chaldean eyes, the prophet's beliefs and visions were foolish and insubstantial, while the golden statues represented reality. Through the monotheistic eyes of Isaiah, the wooden (or stone) statues represented the peak of foolishness and evil, and he believed that they would be shattered and burned in the future.

Nowadays, these statues are at most showcased in museums as testimony of ancient foolishness; Babylon is an archaeological site of ruins, while the people once exiled have risen again, returned to the land of their ancestors, and fulfilled the prophet's words:

> That says to Jerusalem, You shall be inhabited, and to the cities of Judah, you shall be rebuilt, and its ruins I will resurrect. (44:26)

CHAPTERS 45–46: CYRUS – THE MESSIAH KING?

The savior king's rise to the historical stage is described in an unusual prophecy that explicitly refers to the figure of the Persian King Cyrus II:

> Whose right hand I have held, that I may subdue nations before him, and loosen the loins of kings; that I may open doors and gates before him which shall not be shut... I, the Lord, who calls you by name, am the God of Israel – For the sake of My servant Jacob and Israel, My chosen... That they may know from the rising of the sun, and from the west, that there is none beside Me. I am the Lord, and there is none else; I form the light, and create darkness, I make peace, and create evil; I, the Lord, do all of this. (45:1–7)

The prophet was familiar with the Zoroastrian faith (the original form, of Cyrus' time, had already become the official religion of Persia), which held that the world was given over to two ruling powers – good and evil. He attempted to teach that only one God – the Lord – was responsible for all, creating light *and* darkness, good *and* evil. The prophet taught that this would be proven when all gates were opened before Cyrus.

And indeed, Babylon (with the support of its temple priests) opened its gates to King Cyrus of Persia. He was accepted as the ruler, usurping King Nabonidus, the last Babylonian king, who left for the

Arabian Peninsula and devoted many years to spiritual seclusion while his regent Belshazzar held drunken feasts (Dan. 5:23) and the empire crumbled.

Cyrus, however, did not accept the one true faith. Rather, he remained a Zoroastrian, although he found a believing Jew to formulate his declaration in appropriately Jewish language: "The Lord God of heaven has given me all the kingdoms of the earth and has charged me with building Him a house in Jerusalem, which is in Judah" (Ezra 1:2; II Chr. 36:23).

The prophecy was fulfilled precisely according to the Israelite belief: The gates of Babylon opened to Cyrus, and he received the charge of rebuilding Jerusalem and the Lord's Temple seventy years after its destruction. This proved God's total control over the world. Whoever composed Cyrus' declaration for him was clearly familiar with the prophecy and its significance for the Jews.

The historical figure of Cyrus, however, was far from the messianic ideal.

CHAPTERS 46–47: THE FALL OF EMPIRES AND THE BELIEF IN ONE GOD

The fall of Babylon and its gods (46:1–2), and the opening of its gates to "the eagle from the east," an apt description of Cyrus (46:11), should have sufficed to prove the authenticity of the one true faith.

Another twelve hundred years would pass before the spread of Islam, when the faith in "the one and only Allah" would take over the "East," but in the Book of Isaiah, as we have seen, descriptions of the distant future are merged with those of the present.

Isaiah had already presented the surprising vision of the end of days, when all the nations would ascend to the mountain of the Lord to learn "the Torah from Zion" and all wars would cease – a vision that would one day be engraved upon the entrance to the United Nations headquarters in New York after two horrific world wars that took place thousands of years after Isaiah's time.

He had already explained (10:5–19) that the leaders of empires are only "rods of wrath" in the hand of God; they execute His will without meaning to, and will one day be punished for their crimes and arrogance.

These ideas are familiar from the first part of the Book of Isaiah; only one idea has not yet been presented in Isaiah's prophecies until now: A non-Jewish king, the ruler of an empire, can be considered "the Lord's Messiah," the shepherd elected to bring redemption to Judah, "to say to Jerusalem, 'You will be rebuilt,' and to the sanctuary, 'You will be founded'" (44:28), even if his religious world is very far from Judah's.

This is the highest tier in the universal dimension of Isaiah's prophecies: In addition to the vision of the end of days (at the beginning of chapter 2), and in addition to "Blessed be My people Egypt, and My handiwork Assyria, and My inheritance Israel" (19:25), it now becomes apparent that the Messiah king can also be a foreign king who will rebuild Jerusalem and reestablish the Temple.

It is hard to believe such a bold prophecy, that the Lord's anointed is not necessarily a Jew, or even a believer in the Jewish faith. Indeed, the historical figure of Cyrus restored Temples and granted autonomy to many nations, not only to Judah and Jerusalem.

No prophecies about the greatness of the kings of Persia were uttered in the days of Cyrus' declaration, nor afterwards in the time of Darius, who permitted the building of the Temple; such language is only found in Isaiah's vision of the future.

In retrospect, we believe and know that God's hand is perpetually shaping history, but the victors only see their own part in their victory. God's hand is more easily perceived when a great empire falls.

In World War I four European and Middle Eastern powers fell: the German Empire, the Austro-Hungarian Empire, the Russian Empire, and the Ottoman Empire, and the world powers began to shift. In World War II, the short-lived but momentous Third Reich fell together with the Japanese Empire. In the Cold War, the Soviet dictatorship came crashing down together with the atheist communist zeitgeist. It is still unclear what will be the outcome of the current war against Islamic terrorism.

In truth, there were no true victors in any of these wars. As has been true throughout history, the most important outcome of such wars is the downfall of great forces of evil, while the "victors" were those who were able to continue living their lives in relative peace and stability.

The prophet celebrated the expected downfall of Babylonia and the retribution for all its cruelty, though without battle: "I will not harm a man" (47:1–3): "You showed them no mercy; you placed a heavy burden on the aged" (47:6). This cruelty was clearly the product of their extreme arrogance: "You said in your heart: I am, and no-one besides me" (47:10). Hubris is generally what causes powerful rulers to overlook the iron rule of history with regard to the rise and fall of empires. Even the Babylonian rulers "who gaze at the stars" (43:13) were blind to their impending downfall: "And you said, 'I will be mistress forever' – you did not take these to heart, and you did not recall its end" (47:7).

CHAPTERS 48–49: WHY DID GOD CHOOSE SUCH A STUBBORN PEOPLE?

God chose the People of Israel out of all the nations, knowing how "stiff-necked" (Ex. 33:5) they are: "Because I know that you are obstinate; your neck is an iron sinew, and your forehead is of bronze" (Is. 48:4). But why did He choose such a stubborn people?

Had God merely wanted crowds of His creations to sing His praises and bow in obedience, there would have been no need to create humanity. Billions of stars call out "Hallelujah" (Ps. 148:3). All of creation bows before God; only humans have freedom of choice and freedom of thought. Only humans protest and argue, sometimes erring and committing sins both great and small. Humans even argue with the Creator Himself: Abraham and Moses both contested God's way of ruling the world and His people, and they would not back down. Abraham challenged God's destruction of Sodom; this was one of his trials: "For I have known him, so that he will instruct his children and his household after him to keep the way of the Lord by doing what is right and just" (Gen. 18:19). God accepted most of Moses' prayers about Israel (but rejected his own prayer to enter the Land of Israel in Deut. 3:23–27). Only a stubborn nation is capable of producing such prophets, who have the audacity to challenge how God runs His world.

But this quality also has a dark side. This grave problem already reared its head during the exodus from Egypt, when the Israelites were unwilling to trust Moses and God, when they complained at every step and doubted at every trial, and constantly sought alternatives (returning to Egypt, the Golden Calf, Pe'or). At the end of the First Temple period, Israel embraced the culture of Assyria and Babylonia out of great despair.

The Jews, "who are called in the name of Israel ... who swear in the name of the Lord" (Is. 48:1), are liable to cling to exile and foreign powers, and may not wish to be redeemed, out of fear of the birth pangs of redemption. The prophet, therefore, must take care to declare "ahead of time" that Assyria and Babylonia will fall as suddenly as they rose, "I did them suddenly, and they came to pass" (48:3). Israel must be aware of the impending downfall of these nations so that as soon as they fall, they will not cling to exile, but "Go out of Babylon, flee from the Chaldeans ... say: 'The Lord has redeemed His servant Jacob'" (48:20).

Do not cling to exile – go back up to Israel as soon as you can, and follow God's path.

CHAPTERS 50–51: IS EXILE A BILL OF DIVORCE?

Isaiah son of Amoz founded a prophetic school with a unique language and style, "the language of the learned" (50:4), and one of its characteristics was the interpretation of the Torah through prophecy. One example of this special phenomenon concerns the law of divorce in Deuteronomy (24:1–4), which the prophet deals with in the same way that he applied the laws of the king from Deuteronomy 17 in Isaiah 2. Through the law of divorce, the prophet grapples with the troubling issue of whether exile is like God's divorce bill to Israel, who is like a wife sent away by her husband. Can the divorced wife ever return home? After all, if she sins "and is with another man," the "first husband who sent her away may not take her again as his wife" (Deut. 24:2–4).

This question is not raised in the Torah, where the Israelites are generally characterized as God's children, not as his wife: "My firstborn son Israel" (Ex. 4:22); "You are sons of the Lord your God" (Deut. 14:1). Children may always return home to their parents. However, in prophetic literature, God and Israel are often characterized as husband and wife.

The prophet's decisive answer is that God never wrote a "bill of divorce" for Israel, and the gates of redemption are always open:

> Thus says the Lord, where is the bill of your mother's divorce, with which I sent you away? To which of My creditors did I sell

you? See, you have sold yourselves through your own sins, and through your own iniquities, your mother was sent away. (Is. 50:1)

There are close similarities as well as differences between Isaiah and his disciples, and Jeremiah. Jeremiah states that God indeed gives unfaithful Israel a bill of divorce (Jer. 3:8–15), and that His anger will never truly abate. When Judah, too, will betray Him, He will summon "the wayward sons" (the ten tribes) to return to Him from "the land of the north." Similarly, Hosea claims that redemption will come despite God's "bill of divorce," as a new, pure generation will arise, to whom divorce will not apply.

God also commanded Jeremiah, with Nebuchadnezzar's ascent (Jer. 25:15–29) to take "the wine cup of wrath" to distribute among all the nations including Jerusalem, for when the city "whom My name is called for" drinks, every nation must drink as well. Now, in his prophecy of consolation, Isaiah declares that Jerusalem has already drained "His cup of wrath" to the dregs (Is. 51:17, 22) and that God has taken back "the goblet of poison" and Jerusalem will no longer drink from it.

Jeremiah also writes similar prophecies at God's command. Both of them lifted up their eyes to the heaven and earth (Is. 51:6) to contemplate the laws of the sun, moon, and stars (Jer. 31:34–36) in order to promise eternal salvation to Jerusalem.

When did Jeremiah compose such powerful prophecies of consolation? Before the destruction, during the Babylonian siege, and during the depths of despair. They contain clear, indisputable dates.

The calls for Jerusalem's awakening in the Book of Isaiah were also pronounced during times of deep despair, when there was a need for prophetic faith in order to survive. These prophecies reflect utter confidence in "God's arm" paving a safe way through a stormy sea (like in the exodus from Egypt):

A way for the redeemed to pass over; and God's freed shall return, and reach Zion in joy. (Is. 51:11)

This reassurance is what gave hope and strength during times of "sorrow and sighing." In the generation of the return to Zion, especially after

Cyrus' declaration, the need for such reassurance was not as critical as it was in the time of Manasseh and Amon.

CHAPTER 52: ISAIAH AND HIS STUDENTS – AN ENCOUNTER WITH THE PROPHECY OF NAHUM

It is clear that Nahum, the prophet from Elkosh (which was apparently in the Galilee) who predicted the destruction of Nineveh, capital of Assyria, lived at the end of the period of Josiah (612 BCE). Nahum's "Pronouncement against Nineveh" recalls the Assyrian conquest of Egypt (671 BCE), which implies that he lived in Josiah's time (640–609 BCE) or at the end of Manasseh-Amon's reign (660–640 BCE). His language and style is similar to that of Isaiah, and together with the prophecies of Micah, Zephaniah, and Habakkuk, his prophecies make it clear that Isaiah had disciple-prophets who emulated his style and path.

Here is an explicit parallel between the consolations of (the disciples of) Isaiah, and Nahum's pronouncement:

Nahum

Behold on the hills the footsteps of a herald announcing good fortune! "Celebrate your festivals, O Judah, fulfill your vows. Never again shall scoundrels invade you, they have totally vanished." (Nah. 2:1)

Isaiah

How welcome on the mountain are the footsteps of the herald announcing happiness, heralding good fortune, announcing victory, telling Zion, "Your God is King!" Hark! Your watchmen raise their voices, as one they shout for joy; for every eye shall behold the Lord's return to Zion. (Is. 52:7–8)

Nahum pronounced his vision of consolation for Judah by focusing on the destruction of Nineveh and the fall of Assyria, while (the disciples of) Isaiah made a similar speech about Zion and Jerusalem, while still mentioning Egypt and Assyria; the second exile is ascribed to Assyria:

At first My people went down to Egypt to live there, and Assyria oppressed them without cause. And now, what have I here [in exile], declares the Lord, for My people have been taken away for nothing. (Is. 52:4–6)

Both prophecies predict a great vision of the return to Zion – a vision which was only partially fulfilled.

The historical background of Nahum's prophecy is almost explicit in the verse of the "footsteps of a herald," which discusses a great festival celebrated without fear of Assyria. This can only be referring to the Passover of Josiah (II Chr. 35) in the eighteenth year of his reign (622 BCE). Those who recalled the great terror of Sennacherib's campaign and his conquest of Judah may have warned the king not to "provoke" Assyria any further.

Nahum challenged these fears:

Celebrate your festivals, O Judah, fulfill your vows. Never again shall scoundrels [the Assyrian army] invade you, they have totally vanished. (Nah. 2:1)

That is, there is no point in fearing Assyria's wrath, for the Assyrian enemy has already disappeared, and Nineveh will shortly be destroyed. However, while Nahum speaks about the celebrations in Josiah's time, (the disciples of) Isaiah refer to those exiled by Assyria, who will return and rebuild Jerusalem. This vision is applicable to all time, from before Josiah's time and until today.

These consolations were partially fulfilled with the ascent of Zerubbabel, but the ingathering of exiles from all over the world did not come to pass until just a few generations ago. The glory of God's presence did not appear in the Second Temple, nor did "the Lord reveal His holy arm" (Is. 52:10) as He did in recent times, during the Six Day War, when the whole world stood in awe at Israel's victory, and Jerusalem was freed from captivity amidst great astonishment. In contrast, the reality of the Second Temple period was "a day of smallness" (Zech. 4:10) compared to this great prophetic vision.

Isaiah 50–59[1]

Chapters of Persecution – "Innocent Blood" and Reproach

T hese chapters contain harsh descriptions that fit Manasseh's time: the persecution, and even execution, of prophets (ch. 53); coarse idol worship and child sacrifice to Moloch; a king presented with tributes who sends emissaries far away (ch. 57); in short, grave sins and the spilling of innocent blood (ch. 59). These prophecies are not relevant to the days of the return to Zion; there is no testimony of any of these things occurring during the transition from Babylonian to Persian rule with the rise of Cyrus.

On the other hand, the exile from Israel and Judah is mentioned as having been the bitter reality since the days of Ahaz (at the end of chapter 11); here, too, Jerusalem is portrayed as being in mourning and disgrace, and in need of comfort and encouragement to rise up "from

---

1. These chapters should be read as a single unit; the chapters' divisions are arbitrary.

the dust" (52:2). Though she is in ruins, *she still endures*, as opposed
to the description of utter destruction at the end of the lyrical lament
(64:9–10).

Chapters 50–59 are therefore a decisive testimony to the continuation of Isaiah's prophecies from his own mouth and from the mouths
of his students during the harsh days of Manasseh's and Amon's reigns.
The description of these long years is brief in the Book of Kings, and
the mention of the "innocent blood" spilled by Manasseh is obscure
(II Kings 11:16), generating the questions of: Whose blood? What happened? How did they reach this low state? Once the historical connection with Isaiah chapters 50–59 is recognized, the full picture of one of
the most corrupt periods in Jewish history emerges.

CHAPTERS 52–53: EXECUTION – ISAIAH
AND HIS DISCIPLES

According to the sages (Yevamot 49b), the king of Judah, Manasseh,[2]
executed the prophet Isaiah, the servant of God. Based on false accusa-
tions, he was arrested, tortured, brought out for a walk of shame before
the people while in terrible pain, and finally executed. This does not
seem to have been the only such incident of killing by Manasseh. This
is the "innocent blood" that Manasseh spilled "until Jerusalem was
brimming from end to end; this was besides the sins he had led Israel
to sin, doing what was evil in the eyes of the Lord" (II Kings 21:16); this
verse refers also to his idol worship. The prophets' struggle against idol
worship and Manasseh's official policy of it turned them into enemies
of the state.

The horror of his execution after prolonged torture and being
gagged so that he was no longer able to voice any opposition, is
described in the onlookers' perspective of the fate of "the servant of
the Lord":

---

2. The only defense of Manasseh found in the Bible is not his submission in
II Chr. 33:12–13, which is not even hinted to in Kings or Jeremiah, but in the fact
that he became king when he was only twelve (II Kings 21:1), so that his guilt mainly
rests on the shoulders of the adults who initially influenced him, who were evidently
opposed to Hezekiah's path.

> He was maltreated yet he was submissive, he did not open his mouth; like a sheep being led to slaughter... he did not open his mouth. By oppressive judgment he was taken away... For he was cut off from the land of the living... And his grave was set among the wicked... Though he had done no injustice and had spoken no falsehood. (Is. 53:7–9)

From the audience, the prophet's disciples, loved ones, and friends looked on, silent and afraid, not daring to join his prophetic protest. They witnessed it in horror, unable to look the victim in the face as he bore the sins of the whole generation:

> Yet it was our sickness that he was bearing, our suffering that he endured... He was wounded because of our sins... Crushed because of our iniquities. And by his bruises we were healed. We all went astray like sheep, each going his own way; and the Lord visited upon him the guilt of all of us. (53:4–6)

The prophecy ends with a prayer of atonement and a lament for the future triumph of God's murdered servant; his descendants will keep to his path and perpetuate his memory, and his great reward will be distributed among the masses like spoils of war:

> That, if he made himself an offering for guilt, he might see offspring and have long life, and that through him the Lord's purpose might prosper. Out of his anguish he shall see it; he shall enjoy it to the full through his devotion. "My righteous servant makes the many righteous, it is their punishment that he bears; assuredly, I will give him the many as his portion, he shall receive the multitude as his spoil. For he exposed himself to death. (53:10–12)

This horrific description explains Isaiah's disappearance during Manasseh's time and why it was that his teachings were perpetuated and disseminated by his disciples. The sages transmitted this tradition in a chilling description:

> Manasseh killed Isaiah… Rabbah said: He held a trial for him
> and executed him; he said to him: Your teacher Moses said, "For
> no man shall see Me and live," but you said, "I saw the Lord sit-
> ting on the throne, lofty and exalted"!? Isaiah said: I know that
> [Manasseh] will not accept what I tell him, and if I tell him [what
> I should], his transgression will be intentional. So he pronounced
> the Holy name and he became hidden in a cedar tree. They
> brought the cedar tree and chopped him up. When they reached
> his mouth, which had uttered, "Among a people of impure lips I
> dwell," his soul departed. (Yevamot 49b)

This chapter is a chilling account of the "innocent blood" spilled by
Manasseh; it has no connection whatsoever to the struggles against
Rome at the end of the Second Temple period.

Unfortunately, the Christian faith interpreted this chapter as a
prophecy about the man from Nazareth whose name is similar to Isaiah's.
However, the one who crucified him was a foreign ruler, a Roman, who
crucified him along with thousands of other Jews (and others) who
opposed his rule. With time, Rome converted to Christianity, and
accused the Jews of this sin. They spared no effort to transfer all guilt to
the Jews, until the entire Jewish people became the persecuted "servant
of the Lord" suffering torture and execution. In this way, the Christian
interpretation of the episode resulted in a mistaken Jewish interpretation of the episode.

In the Barcelona trial of 1263,[3] Nahmanides was forced to stand
before the king and hold a public debate with a Jewish apostate, concerning this chapter in particular. This was a rare occurrence when a
Jewish sage was allowed true freedom of speech, and following the trial,
the king withdrew his demand for conversion to Christianity, and even
awarded him a handsome sum of money. The people would not accept

---

3. Nahmanides describes this debate in detail and adds his commentary on this chapter;
see *The Writings of Nahmanides*, vol. 1 (Jerusalem: Mossad Harav Kook), 299–326
[Hebrew].

the outcome of the trial, however, and Nahmanides made his way from Spain to the Land of Israel.

The Christian church only renounced its general accusation against the Jews with the birth of the new Jewish state.

CHAPTER 54: THE VISION OF REDEMPTION VS. HARSH REALITY (II)

In these prophecies it is easy to focus on the wondrous prophetic visions, but much harder to contemplate Judah's dire situation, which includes the state of the land, the kingdom, and the Jews, at the time of their utterance:

> Barren…children of desolation…the disgrace of your maiden-hood…abandoned and dour of spirit…the cast off wife of your youth…abandoned…in the overflowing of wrath I hid My face from you. (Is. 54:1–8)

These are not the days of the return to Zion but the days of exile, a desolate time of deep despair (the exile, of course, began with the exile of the Galilee and Samaria, Lachish, and the Judean lowlands, in the time of Ahaz and Hezekiah).

The prophet struggled against this harsh reality with all his might, as he did in the time of Ahaz with his prophecy of "An off-shoot shall issue forth from the stump of Jesse" and the ingathering of exiles that will be like the exodus from Egypt (ch. 11). The greatest struggle was to maintain hope and Jewish faith, and the prophet succeeded. For thousands of years, the Jews have been repeating his songs of a joyous future:

> Sing…burst into song and rejoice…Enlarge the space of your tent, for you will burst out to the right and to the left…Do not fear, for you will no longer be ashamed…With great mercy I will gather you in…With eternal loving kindness I will have mercy on you, declares the Lord, your redeemer; My loving kindness will never cease from you, and My covenant of peace will never collapse. (54:1–10)

CHAPTERS 56–57:[4] "INNOCENT BLOOD" AND
MANASSEH'S ABOMINATIONS (I)

All you beasts of the field, come to devour all the beasts in the forest – His watchmen are all blind, ignorant; they are all dumb dogs who cannot bark; dreaming, lounging about, lovers of sleep. And the dogs are greedy, never satisfied, the shepherds do not understand, they all turn their own way, each for his own gain. Come, they say, I will fetch wine and we will gorge on strong drink, tomorrow will be the same as today, but even more so. The righteous are lost but no one notices, loyal men are taken away but no one gives thought that because of evil, the righteous were taken away. But there will be peace – the honest man will rest on his couch. But as for you, come closer, you sons of witches, [rulers of Judah] the seed of the adulterer and the whore, with whom do you act so familiarly? At whom do you open your mouth and stick out your tongue? Why, you are children of iniquity, offspring of treachery – You who inflame yourselves among the terebinths, under every green tree; who slaughter children in the wadis, among the clefts of the rocks. With such are your share and portion, they, they are your allotment; to them you have poured out libations, presented offerings. Should I relent in the face of this? On a high and lofty hill you have set your couch; there, too, you have gone up to perform sacrifices. Behind the door and doorpost you have directed your thoughts; abandoning Me, you have gone up on the couch you made so wide. You have made a covenant with them, you have loved lying with them; you have chosen lust. You have approached the king with oil, you have provided many perfumes. And you have sent your envoys afar, even down to the netherworld. Though wearied

---

4. Scholarship holds that as this is written by second Isaiah, not even one verse is comprehensible, and indeed, Kaufmann, in *The Religion of Israel*, vol. 8, 139, writes that this reproach is retroactively summarizing the sins of the past, as occurs in the Book of Ezekiel. However, it actually refers to the prophet's own time, during Manasseh's reign.

by much travel, you never said, "I give up!" You found grati-
fication for your lust, and so you never cared. Whom do you
dread and fear, that you tell lies? But you gave no thought to
Me, you paid no heed. (Is. 56:9–57:11)

After witnessing the ghastly execution of "the servant of the Lord"
(ch. 53), we read the full story of Manasseh's reign. The drama begins
with an invitation to the "beasts of the field" to attack the "beasts of the
forest." The onlookers are "blind," the guard dogs are sleepy, and the
attack dogs[5] are insatiable. The "shepherds," the leaders, have concern
for none but themselves, carelessly drinking themselves into a stupor.

In the meantime, "the righteous are lost but no one notices," while
"loyal men" die. They are the lucky ones, who will not witness the coming horrors, which include ritual prostitution, repugnant idol worship
in every home, and worst of all, those "who slaughter children in the
wadis, among the clefts of the rocks."

At the same time, the king of Judah, presumably Manasseh,
accepts costly gifts: "You have approached the king with oil", manages
local and international politics: "you have sent your envoys afar", and
ensures political and cultural survival under Assyrian rule by embracing
pagan values: "even down to the netherworld".

This chapter, it emerges, holds the key to these terrible events.
The group that surrounded Manasseh considered Hezekiah's creed as the
main reason for Sennacherib's campaign against Judah and the destruction of Lachish, and therefore turned to Assyrian culture and religion to
ensure their own political survival. Whoever followed Hezekiah's path
was considered an enemy of the state.

Isaiah and his disciples, who struggled against the abhorrent
pagan culture that spread in Jerusalem, were hunted down, tortured,
and executed, as hinted to in the Book of Kings: "And what is more,
Manasseh shed so much innocent blood, until Jerusalem was brimming
from end to end; this was besides the sins he had led Israel to sin, doing
what was evil in the eyes of the Lord" (II Kings 21:16).

---

5. Oppressive governments typically make use of vicious attack dogs.

CHAPTER 59: "INNOCENT BLOOD" AND MANASSEH'S ABOMINATIONS (II)

The most detailed description of the corruption of Manasseh's generation introduces the final chapter of the most gruesome prophetic sequence in the Bible (before the Book of Ezekiel).[6] It includes "innocent blood" (Is. 59:3, 7), robbery, violence, and false words: "They hatch vipers' eggs … whoever eats of their eggs dies" (59:5).

All of these constitute "the hiding of God's face" that created a barrier between God and Judah:

> But your iniquities have been a barrier between you and your God, your sins have made Him turn His face away and refuse to hear you. (59:2)

The groups of prophets and their disciples had to feel their way around in the darkness: "Like those without eyes we grope; we stumble at noon, as if in darkness; among the sturdy, we are like the dead" (59:10). They blindly hoped for salvation, but it "is far from us" (59:11). The bitter struggle of the prophet's disciples against the stable, cruel government of Manasseh, which lasted for fifty-five years (II Kings 21:1), bore terrible prophecies of vengeance. God, seeing that "there is no one," will appear as a God of vengeance (Is. 59:15–18), for only then will fear of the Lord spread "from west … and from the east … and a Redeemer will come to Zion" (59:19–20).

The prophet concludes by renewing the eternal covenant of redemption:

> As for Me, this is My covenant with them, says the Lord, My spirit that is upon you, and My words that I have put in your mouth will never cease from your mouth or from the mouths of your descendants and the mouths of your descendants' descendants says the Lord, from now and forever. (59:20–21)

---

6. With all the focus on the prophecies of "Cyrus," theological debates do not consider that the "servant of the Lord" might be referring to chapters 50–59, which describe Manasseh's time with gruesome clarity.

Isaiah 54–58

The Redemption – in Righteousness and Justice

The prophet only makes one demand of the "wife of youth" (Is. 54:6), in order for her to be worthy of salvation and the glorious palaces that God will build for her "of sapphires" (54:11):

> In righteousness be established, keep away from oppression so you will not fear and from ruin so it will not come near you. (54:14)

This, of course, is a striking continuation of Isaiah's early prophecy:

> Zion will be redeemed through justice, and those that return to her, through righteousness. (1:27)

If this demand is fulfilled, then the children of Zion will be worthy of following in God's path: "And all your children will be the Lord's students, and there will be great peace for your children" (54:13).

Most of the prophecies of these chapters do not impart any new information about how to serve God. As was taught in chapter

1, God comes to those who call for Him and remains close to those who are close to Him. He is not swayed by empty offerings presented in the Temple, nor by prayers or fasts, but only by repentance from evil and sin:

> Thus says the Lord: Keep justice and do righteousness, for My redemption is about to come and My righteousness to be revealed. (56:1)

The prophet does not harbor reservations towards sacrifices only; in chapter 1 (1:13–15) he also refers to prayers and festivals, sacrifices and offerings, reading the Torah on Rosh Hodesh and on Shabbat, incense, and meal offerings. God does not desire any of these unless they are offered up by those who are worthy, whose hands are clean. The same is true in chapter 58, where it is stated that fasts, confessions, and Shabbat observance are worthless without genuine justice and righteousness.

Like Isaiah (1:13–17; 58:13–14), Amos (8:4–5) also criticizes Shabbat observers who wait for the day to end in order to return to their corrupt activity in the marketplace. Over the course of the book, Isaiah's perspective on how to stay close to God does not change. This closeness does not require money (55:1–2), and the "bread and water" it yields are integrity and justice, which lead to "an eternal covenant" (55:3).

The ideas about ideal worship expressed by the prophets of the period of the return to Zion (from Haggai to Malachi) are not mentioned in Isaiah chapters 40–66. Ezra's religious revolution (Neh. 8–10), as well as the prophecies of Malachi, emphasized the reading of the Torah, fasting and confession, taking tithes, and offering sincere offerings, as well as stringent observance of proper marriage (Ezra 9–10). None of these ideas are expressed in Isaiah, whose main emphasis is on righteousness and justice:

> To be sure, they seek Me daily, eager to learn My ways. Like a nation that does what is right, that has not abandoned the laws of its God, they ask Me for the right way, they are eager for the nearness of God. (Is. 58:2)

CHAPTER 56: ASSIMILATED JEWS AND FOREIGN CONVERTS TO JUDAISM

There are no differences in Isaiah's attitude towards true worship throughout the Book of Isaiah, but chapter 56 presents a surprising new prophetic idea about a completely new Jewish reality. The exiles that began with Samaria and the Judean lowlands brought masses of Jews into close daily contact with foreigners, in Israel and in exile. This generated Jewish assimilation as well as the phenomenon of foreigners who were drawn to Judaism. There was a deep fear of allowing these people to approach, and "the foreigner who has become attached to the Lord" (56:3) felt rejected by Jewish families who were afraid of contaminating their family line.

Additionally, Jewish eunuchs were no longer capable of bringing children into the world, as they were castrated in captivity in order to prevent them from having relations with the foreign queens and princess whom they were forced to serve (as alluded to in the Book of Esther).

These individuals cried out in frustration: What is the use of keeping Shabbat from a place of righteousness and justice, as the prophet demanded, if there is no continuity of the Jewish family line?

Human continuity is preserved through descendants who bear the family name: "Thus your descendants and name will stand" (66:22). Animals also have offspring, but biological continuity alone has no meaning in the human world without names and without memory. In truth, sometimes friends and students remember a person who has died, and the legacy of his name, in a more significant way than his biological descendants do.

Therefore, the prophet promises both Jewish eunuchs and foreigners drawn to Judaism that they will have continuity through "a monument and a memorial [*yad vashem*] better than sons and daughters ... an eternal name that will not be cut off" (56:5).

Recently, following the mass destruction of the Jews of Europe, a similar problem arose with regard to the thousands of Jewish families who were wiped out without a trace. At the same time, thousands of assimilated families came to Israel. The State of Israel, which is the state of the ingathering of exiles and a state of survivors, founded Yad

Vashem as a memorial for all those who were lost, and established the Law of Return to allow for the immigration of anyone with a Jewish grandparent, as a response to the Nazi laws of who was considered a Jew.

Yad Vashem on the one hand, and the Law of Return on the other, are the striking fulfillments of the prophets' visions of the Land of Israel.

CHAPTER 58: THE SONG OF REDEMPTION AND THE ANSWER TO "WHY DID WE FAST BUT YOU DID NOT SEE?" – WAYS OF REDRESS AND REDEMPTION

One fundamental idea of fasting is basic equality between people, who were all created "in the image of God" (Gen. 1:27). When fasting, all are hungry; the disparities between individuals are blurred and pushed aside. In contrast, when some are feasting like kings while others subsist on a piece of bread, economic competition abounds, gaps widen, and the lowest sectors of society grow weaker as the privileged become yet more privileged.

A day of fasting and supplication can become the catalyst for change if undertaken correctly. But if a fast day is merely another empty ritual observed with false reverence, then such a day is worthless.

One critical question is how the underprivileged will break their fast; will their hunger simply continue? If the wealthy undertake such a fast as an empty ritual, while it is merely another dreary day for the destitute, then God will not accept such a fast, nor the prayers and confessions that accompany it.

Fasting is not a late religious idea that was only born in Babylonia. Evidence of misuse of fasting can be found as early as the false trial of Naboth in Ahab's time: "Proclaim a fast, and seat Naboth in front of the people!" (I Kings 21:9).

The common denominator between fasting and keeping Shabbat is that both restore a sense of equality. Shabbat can used to bridge the gap between rich and poor, and if it is not, then it, too, is worthless. Both Amos (8:4–7) and Isaiah and his followers (1:13–14; 58:13–14) express this idea about Shabbat and fast days. True worship of God is measured according to the justice and righteousness that it engenders.

Isaiah 60–64

Complete Redemption and Devastating Destruction – Vision vs. Reality (III)

C hapters 40–49 declare "Take comfort, take comfort, My people" in the midst of a profound, harsh dispute with idol-worshiping Jews living in the time of Manasseh. The prophet repeated basic concepts of the Book of Genesis, and above all, cried out, "Believe me! I speak God's words! The Lord is the true God, and there is no other! Why do you treasure worthless, useless idols that you carve yourselves out of wood, using the leftovers for heating your stove?"

Chapters 50–59 contain prophecies of redemption and repentance, interspersed with horrific descriptions of the execution of the "servant of the Lord," innocent bloodshed, idol worship, and even child sacrifice to Moloch.

So what was happening in reality?

In the chapters of vengeance and destruction (Is. 61; 63–64), the tragic answer is revealed: There is complete destruction and desolation in Jerusalem. It is when the destruction reaches a climax that the consolation climaxes as well, for only a vision of a better future can provide the strength to carry on: "To comfort all who mourn … to give to them glory instead of ashes …" (61:2–3).

In exactly the same way, Jeremiah's prophecies of consolation (Jer. 30–33), were uttered on the very brink of the destruction (Jer. 32 even contains the dates of the Babylonian siege of Jerusalem).

Prophecies are never fulfilled at the time of their composition.

CHAPTER 63: EDOM AND JUDAH

One of the climaxes of the redemption prophecies is the domination over the territory of Edom, which was situated south of Judah. This region included the Negev, the craters, the area east of Sinai towards Eilat, and the tall mountains of Edom east of the Arabah.[1] Isaac lived in Beersheba; Esau inherited the area from Beersheba-Arad southward, while Jacob inherited the northern territory. After David defeated Amalek, removed all trace of their threat, and conquered the Edomite territory, Solomon was able to send fleets of ships from Etzion Geber, with his Phoenician friends, (I Kings 9:26–28), and even the Queen of Sheba arrived for a royal visit, from Ethiopia, (I Kings 10), apparently in response to Solomon's involvement with Phoenicia. After the kingdom split, Judah's power weakened, and the Edomites threatened the Judean border. A clay fragment was found near the Arad stronghold with a First Temple period inscription on it, an urgent military order to dispatch forces to Ramat HaNegev, "in case Edom comes there."[2] Amos (9:12) concluded his prophecy of future redemption with Judah's reconquest of Edom, and the same is described in Obadiah (ch. 19–21), and twice in Isaiah.[3]

---

1. Nowadays Edom is incorrectly thought to be the territory of the hills to the east of the Arabah, which was never the case.
2. Y. Aharoni, *Arad Inscriptions* (Jerusalem, 1976), 48 [Hebrew].
3. These prophecies were only fulfilled in our own time, when the region from the Negev until Eilat was included within Israel's borders.

Isaiah's harsh prophecy of the destruction of Edom (ch. 34)[4] hints to the bloody history between Judah and Edom.[5] Edomite slave traders would buy Judahite (and other) slaves in Gaza's and Tyre's slave markets and sell them to people from distant lands (Amos 1:6–11). The enmity only increased following Jerusalem's destruction. The Edomites assisted Babylonia in their conquest by reporting Jewish refugees who attempted to flee, and by selling prisoners as slaves. The entire Book of Obadiah is directed against Edom:

> How could you stand at the passes to cut down its fugitives! How could you betray those who fled on that day of anguish … As you did, so shall it be done to you; your conduct shall be requited. (Ob. 1:14–15)

Isaiah's description of the destruction later on (Is. 63:7–64:11) shows that this harsh prophecy against Edom will be fulfilled after the destruction of Jerusalem.

The same fierce anger against Edom is reflected in Psalm 137:

> Remember, O Lord, against the Edomites the day of Jerusalem's fall; how they cried, "Strip her, strip her to her very foundations!" (Ps. 137:7)

And similarly, in Lamentations:

> Rejoice and exult, fair Edom, who dwell in the land of Uz! To you, too, the cup shall pass, you shall get drunk and expose your nakedness. (Lam. 4:21–22)

---

4. Because of this, some scholars connected chapters 34–35 to chapters 40–66.
5. See I Kings 11:14–17; II Kings 3:8–9; 8:20–22; 14:7; 16:6; Amos 1:11–12; II Chr. 25:11–12, and see the inscription from Arad about the war against Edom at the end of the First Temple period in Aharoni, *Arad Inscriptions*, 48–51.

An unusual find, recently discovered at "Edom Rock" in Jordan,[6] illuminated and clarified these prophecies against Edom. A giant inscription was discovered on the rocks of the Edomite fortress, describing the last Babylonian king, Nabonidus, as a king "of glorious garb." Nabonidus was "the one coming from Edom with crimsoned garments from Bozrah…glorious in his apparel" (Is. 63:1). He arrived with blood-soaked garments, having destroyed Bozrah and "Edom Rock," and the prophets perceived him as a special messenger whom God had sent to punish the Edomites for their arrogance and active destruction of Jerusalem. This was the last Babylonian conquest before Cyrus' declaration: "For I had planned a day of vengeance, and My year of redemption arrived" (Is. 63:4).

CHAPTERS 63–64: PSALMS OF DESTRUCTION IN ISAIAH AND THE BOOK OF PSALMS

In general, there are profound connections between the Books of Isaiah and Psalms. In chapter 12 of Isaiah there is a full psalm of thanksgiving as an integral part of the vision of redemption and ingathering of exiles, and the sages point out a psalm scattered throughout the chapters of Jerusalem's salvation (Is. 24–27). Likewise, Hezekiah's psalm of thanksgiving for his recovery from illness (38:9–20) appears only in Isaiah, and not in the parallel chapters in the Book of Kings.

Isaiah's disciples continued on his prophetic path, with lofty ideas and a lyrical style, from Manasseh's time until Jerusalem's destruction, which is described in the final historical psalm:

> The Lord's kindnesses I will mention; the Lord's praises, for all the Lord has bestowed upon us. (63:7)

The opening mention of God's kindness, together with the mention of Moses' song at the sea after the exodus from Egypt (63:7–14), recall Psalm 106:

---

6. C. Ben-David, "'You Who Live in the Clefts of the Rocks' (Jer. 49:16): Edomite Mountain Strongholds in Southern Jordan," ARAM 27 (2015): 227–38.

Who can express the Lord's might or proclaim all his praises. (106:2)

He blasted the Sea of Reeds and it dried up, and He led them through the deep as if through the wilderness. (106:9)

They forgot God their savior. (106:21)

What follows in Isaiah is:

But they rebelled, and vexed His holy spirit … Dividing the water before them … That led them through the deep like a horse in the wilderness. (Is. 63:10–13)

Afterwards, we find a great cry in the face of terrible destruction:

Look down from heaven and see … Where is Your fervor, Your acts of might? (63:15)

Your holy cities became wilderness, Zion became a wilderness, Jerusalem a desolation. (64:9–10)

This cry is similar to Jeremiah's cry in his final prophecy (Jer. 32:16–25), and to the cries of the psalms of destruction.

Why, O God, have You abandoned us forever (Ps 74:1);

Arise, O God, champion Your cause (74:22);

How long, O Lord, will You be furious forever (79:5);

How long, O Lord, will You remain hidden forever (89:47);

O God of hosts, come back now, look down from heaven and see (80:15);

Shine Your face and we will be saved. (80:20)

The school of psalmists existed in Jerusalem from David's time until after the destruction of the Temple. David's followers, and Assaf and Ethan the Ezrahite, continued composing psalms through divine inspiration. Isaiah and his disciples took part in this lyrical composition through prophecy, and as David's psalms inspired psalmists after him, Isaiah's prophecies inspired his disciples to prophesy in his style and spirit.

Isaiah 65–66

The Struggle Against Foreign Worship (II)

T he final chapters (65 and 66) return to the struggle against Jews worshiping idols and adopting foreign cultic rituals: "a people that sacrifice in gardens...that sit on the graves...that eat swine's flesh," phenomena that became widespread in Judah in Manasseh's time. These phenomena were not completely purged from Judah and Jerusalem until the destruction, as Jeremiah's harsh prophecies testify (Jer. 7, 19).

Yet the opening of chapter 65 is surprising. God, as if in prayer, seeks out His people:

> I was ready to be sought by those who did not ask for Me, I was ready to be found by those who did not seek Me, I said, Here I am, here I am, to a nation that did not call out My name, I spread out My hands all day to a rebellious people, who walk a path that is not good, following their own thoughts. (Is. 65:1–2)

Can the nation still be considered a nation at this stage? From the north and the Judean lowlands, many were exiled as early as Hezekiah's time.

Among the remaining people of Judah, few still wanted to call out in God's name or even be considered part of God's nation.

Isaiah's answer is to focus on the remnant, the Lord's faithful servants:

> So will I do for My servants' sakes that I may not destroy them all … My chosen ones will inherit it, and My servants shall dwell there. (65:8–9)

The day will come when the Lord's servants will be differentiated from those who abandoned Him:

> Behold, My servants will eat, and you will go hungry. Behold, My servants will drink, and you will be parched. Behold, My servants will rejoice, and you will be ashamed. (65:13–14)

Then the world will be created anew, the heavens and the earth. Jerusalem will be a city of joy, without tears or anguish, and there will be wondrous longevity; even the sinner will reach the age of one hundred.

How will this miracle transpire? In the merit of those who maintain continuity. The nation is like an ancient tree whose older branches remain dry on the trunk, yet life is maintained within it, and new offshoots spring forth.

> For as the days of a tree shall the days of My people be … For they are the seed of the Lord's blessed, and their offspring with them. (65:23–24)

There is a precise parallel with the first messianic prophecy in Isaiah (11:1–9), and once again we see the unity of Isaiah's prophecies and those of his disciples:

> The wolf and the lamb shall feed together, and the lion shall eat straw like the ox, and dust shall be the serpent's food. They shall not hurt or destroy in all My holy mountain, says the Lord. (65:25)

REDEMPTION FOR THE REMNANT OF GOD'S SERVANTS

There is obviously no building on earth that can contain God's glory, for, as Solomon declares: "If the heavens – the highest heavens – cannot contain you, how will this house, which I have built?" (I Kings 8:27). Whether the house is standing or destroyed, the real question is whether the servants of the Lord "who tremble at His word" (66:5) are worthy of having God dwell among them in an earthly house, in Jerusalem.

According to one of the most intense chapters in the Bible, the answer is that which has been emphasized throughout the Book of Isaiah: that everything depends on people's attitude towards the destitute and the lowly. The sacrifices of cruel people are considered nothing but "the blood of swine" (66:3):

> Thus says the Lord: The heavens are My throne and the earth My footstool. Where is the house that you would build for Me?... For all those things has My hand made... But to this one will I look, to the poor and contrite of spirit, who tremble at My word. (66:1–2)

The ones worthy of standing in God's presence are the meek, the poor, and the humble, and God will harshly repay those who behave with arrogance and cruelty, just as He will repay those who sacrifice swine and eat "disgusting things and mice" (66:17).

But how is it possible to rebuild a living, healthy nation that aspires to stand before the Lord and be worthy of Him? The harsh, clear punishment on the future Day of Judgment will be accompanied by the triumph of those who are righteous and worthy. Yet this is not enough to rehabilitate a whole nation.

The prophetic solution (especially in chapter 11) lies in the ingathering of exiles. Here, in the final chapter of Isaiah, the prophet brings a particularly unusual description, of the surviving nations bringing back the survivors of Israel who were scattered among them, as a gift to God, using old and new methods of transportation. The prophet describes how God will even choose priests and Levites from among them:

> And they shall bring all your brothers out of all the nations for an offering to the Lord, upon horses, and in chariots, and wagons,

and upon mules and camels to My holy mountain Jerusalem, says the Lord. (66:19–20)

We have been privileged to witness the fulfillment of many of these prophecies of consolation with our own eyes, far more than the people of the Second Temple period saw, yet one particular vision is still greater than any familiar reality:

> For look, the darkness shall cover the earth, and deep shadow the nations – But the Lord shall shine upon you, and His glory will be seen upon you… Lift up your eyes and look around, all have gathered and come to you – Your children will come from afar. (60:2–4)

The nations will lead the sons and daughters of Zion back from all over the world as a gift for God, together with gold and silver for the altar; treasures will stream into the gates of Jerusalem day and night:

> For the nation and kingdom that will not serve you shall perish, those nations will be utterly destroyed… Bowing before you, shall come the children of those who tormented you; prostrate at the soles of your feet shall be all those who reviled you; and you shall be called "city of the Lord, Zion of the Holy One of Israel"… Your sun shall set no more, your moon no more withdraw; for the Lord shall be a light to you forever, and your days of mourning shall be ended. And your people, all of them righteous, shall possess the land for all time… I the Lord will speed it in due time. (60:12, 14, 20–22)

This prophecy implies that there will never be another destruction, and this is how Maimonides understood it (*Guide of the Perplexed*, II:29), but he interpreted these verses as being about the Messiah king and the notion that Israel's kingship will never again be revoked, even though the only messiah in this section is the prophet (61:1).

This prophecy certainly planted great hope in the hearts of suffering and grieving Jews, although it took two heavy tolls:

- In the days of the Second Temple, thousands of Jews lived in Jerusalem, certain that the Temple would never again be destroyed. Not because God dwelled in Zion (as they believed during the First Temple period), but because of God's promise in these prophecies. Without this belief, perhaps the Zealots would have feared rebelling against the Roman government; if they had not believed that there would never be another destruction, perhaps the destruction would never have taken place?

- Masses of Jews fully believe in the full redemption, but only in the *full* redemption. Even though more than six million Jews live in Israel, with an unprecedented ingathering of exiles, and a strong, independent Jewish state, not all are willing to accept this as the redemption, because our enemies do not yet submit to us.

The process of the current redemption began long ago; about two hundred years have passed since the days of Moses Montefiore. There were 480 years between the exodus from Egypt and the construction of the Temple (I Kings 6:1), and as Micah prophesied, "Like the time of your exodus from the land of Egypt I will show him wondrous deeds" (Mic. 7:15); this redemption, too, will be a long process, not one that takes place overnight, nor even over the course of a single generation.

The Prophetic "Songs of Songs"

During the deepest despair, in the darkest destruction, and after many prophetic declarations of "Wake up, wake up, arise, O Jerusalem" (Is. 51:17), and "Arise, shine, for your light has come" (60:1), a "bride" awakens, and for the first time, begins a song of marriage:

> I will rejoice, O, rejoice in the Lord, my soul will delight in My God, for He has clothed me in garments of salvation, in a cloak of righteousness He will cover me. (61:10)

Is one exclamation of a joyful – once despairing and abandoned - "bride," enough to counterbalance all that despair? It seems to have sufficed for the prophet, who then goes on to describe the bride and groom. The "groom," the Rock and Redeemer of Israel, stirs as well, and declares:

> For the sake of Zion I will not hold my peace, and for the sake of Jerusalem I will not be still, until her righteousness goes forth like radiance, and her salvation burns like a torch. (62:1)

The prophet then refers to their magnificent wedding, until their intimate encounter: "As the bridegroom rejoices over the bride, Your God will rejoice over you" (62:4–5).

The groom then grows protective over his bride:

> Upon your walls, O Jerusalem, I have set watchmen, all day and all night, they will never cease. (62:6)

Yet together with this ecstatic messianic vision, the prophet still urges his listeners:

> Those who mention the Lord – never be silent, and never let Him be silent, until He establishes and sets Jerusalem as glory in the land, as the Lord has sworn by His right hand and by the arm of His might. (62:6–8)

This bold prophecy shows the extent of the disparity between the prophetic echoes of Solomon's Song of Songs, and the bitter reality; this "Song of Songs" is sung during the depths of the destruction!

> Your holy cities have become a desert: Zion has become a desert, Jerusalem a desolation. Our holy Temple, our pride, where our fathers praised You, has been consumed by fire: And all that was dear to us is ruined. At such things will You restrain Yourself, O Lord; will You stand idly by and let us suffer so heavily? (64:9–11)

Intriguingly, a similar, wretched reality is hinted to in the bride's words in Solomon's Song of Songs:

> I open for my beloved – he has slipped away; gone, I had fainted for him as he spoke – I search for him, I cannot find him; I call out, but he does not answer. The guards find me, those who go around the town; they beat me, they wound me, they pull my scarf from me, those guardians of the walls. (Song. 5:6–7)

Isaiah's prophetic "Song of Songs" did not conceal the presence of lonely despair and suffering, and it was this combination of suffering interspersed with the promise of redemption that gave hope and strength to believers throughout history.

Appendices

Appendix 1

Hezekiah Failed to Sing – the Open and Closed *Mem*

T he Book of Isaiah is brimming with lyrical poetry.[1] It contains several poems in their entirety (in chapter 12 there is a song of redemption, in chapter 38, Hezekiah's sickbed prayer, and in chapters 63–64, pleas for salvation), and there are many verses which correspond to passages in the Book of Psalms. There are also fragments of poetry, disjointed lines strewn among obscure verses of prose, and the song that Hezekiah never sang because Jerusalem was in mourning after Sennacherib's army wrought havoc and destruction. Hezekiah's heavy payments to Assyria after his initial rebellion contributed to the atmosphere of frustration and despair, which prevented Judah from rejoicing at the miraculous withdrawal of the Assyrian army.

This tension is expressed in a Talmudic discussion of a verse found in the prophecy describing the salvation that Hezekiah's reign would bring: "Abundant authority, and endless peace, upon David's throne and kingdom, that it may be firmly established in justice and in

---

1. See Kaufmann, *The Religion of Israel*, vol. 3, 297–312.

equity now and evermore" (Is. 9:6). The Hebrew phrase for "abundant authority," *lemarbe hamisra*, contains an anomaly – the word *lemarbe* contains a final *mem*, which usually only occurs at the end of a word, instead of a regular *mem*.

> And the sages asked: Why is every *mem* in the middle of a word open, and this one is closed? [the final *mem* is shaped like a closed square, rather than the usual "open" shape]. And they answered: Hezekiah failed to sing [a song of thanksgiving] for the miracle of salvation – therefore it was closed! (Sanhedrin 94a)

This interpretation calls Hezekiah to account for failing to give thanks for the miracle that saved Jerusalem from the brink of destruction. The *mem* which should have been open, an expression of messianic abundance, was closed.

This unique typographical phenomenon is mirrored by another, opposite instance. In the Book of Nehemiah, a *mem* at the end of a word, which should be closed, is "open":

> I arrived in Jerusalem, and I was there for three days; I arose at night, I and a few men with me, and telling no one what my God had put into my mind to do for Jerusalem, and taking no other beast than the one on which I was riding, I went out by the Valley Gate, at night, towards the Jackals' Spring and the Dung Gate, and I surveyed the walls of Jerusalem that were breached, and its gates, consumed by fire. (Neh. 2:13–14)

"The walls of Jerusalem that were breached" appears thus: *beḥomot yerushalyim asher hem portzim*. Instead of הם, the word ends with a non-final *mem*, מה.

Nehemiah, a leader of the second return to Zion (roughly 250 years after Hezekiah reigned, 130 years after the destruction of the First Temple, and eighty years after the beginning of the rebuilding of the Second Temple), witnessed Jerusalem at its lowest point. Its walls were breached and broken, and its gates were burned and battered. Almost a century had passed since Cyrus' declaration that the people may return to the Land of Israel and rebuild the Temple. Yet Jerusalem was still mourning, ruined and deserted. It may have been nursing fresh wounds from more recent enemy attacks. Determined to rebuild Jerusalem along with Ezra, he launched a new era in Israel, when the nation established itself within its own borders once again. Despite the lack of complete autonomy, Nehemiah's efforts resulted in a sense of Jerusalem's return to its former glory. Before Nehemiah's arrival, the city was desolate, "And the city was vast and great, with few people within it, and no built houses" (Neh. 7:4). After Nehemiah rebuilt its walls, Jerusalem became a thriving, bustling, prosperous town. Verse 2:13 describes how the walls "were breached" (*hem portzim*) when he came to inspect them, a symbol of destruction and the loss of power. With stalwart faith, however, Nehemiah was able to restore the city despite the political, military, and social obstacles in his way, which had caused the earlier returnees to Zion to despair. With deep, undying belief, Nehemiah rehabilitated Jewish society in the Land of Israel. The open *mem* hints that Nehemiah's faith reopened Hezekiah's closed *mem*, allowing Jerusalem to receive the divine abundance that had been sealed away since Hezekiah's day.

This is suggested by Rabbenu Baḥya ibn Pekuda in his commentary on Genesis:

> Isaiah, of blessed memory, said: *lemarbe hamisra* ... "Of abundant authority and endless peace," and the *mem* is incorrectly closed, because a *mem* in the middle of a word is supposed to be open, but this is closed to hint that Israel's "abundant authority" is blocked during exile. And we found in [Nehemiah] that the *mem* is open at the end of a word, also incorrectly, in, "The walls of Jerusalem that were (*asher hem*) breached, and its gates, consumed with fire." And the Midrash says that this hints that when the walls of Jerusalem, which are now breached during exile, will be closed, then the abundant authority, which is now closed, will be opened. (Rabbenu Baḥya ibn Pekuda, Gen. 47)

Nehemiah was the harbinger of a new age in Israel, when there were no longer prophets and authority was transferred to the sages, the founders of the Oral Law. And at the same time as Nehemiah labored to restore each stone in the wall of Jerusalem, Ezra the Scribe, founder of the Great Assembly, grappled with each letter in the Torah, interpreting it and restoring it to its place of glory in the rebuilt city.

Appendix 2

A Comparison of Isaiah's and Micah the Morasthite's Visions of Redemption

I saiah's vision of redemption transcends earthly politics. Isaiah sketched out a dream of utopian reality, world peace, and cosmic harmony – a picture of heaven on earth. Was Isaiah convinced that Hezekiah would be the one to fulfill this dream? Did he believe that Hezekiah's revolution, the reinstitution of the Torah and the reunion of Israel and Judah, would elevate him to the role of the Messiah, who would lead the world to the utopian end of days? To gauge Isaiah's concept of the historical reality, he may be compared to one of his junior contemporaries, the prophet Micah.

Micah the Morasthite's prophetic style was similar to Isaiah's. Chapters 4–5 of the Book of Micah are devoted to the Messiah, and many commentators and scholars assert that the two prophets were members of the same school of thought, prophesying the same vision.

Micah the Morasthite's career spanned from Jotham's reign until Hezekiah's, during the same years as Isaiah and possibly shortly afterwards. He was active in the prophetic attempt to heal Judah's moral corruption. The sages mention that "Four prophets prophesied at the same time: Hosea, Isaiah, Amos, and Micah" (Pesaḥim 87a).

There are many similarities between Isaiah's and Micah's prophecies, especially their visions of the end of days and their descriptions of the Messiah. There is one striking difference that informs their prophecies, however: their backgrounds. Isaiah was a Jerusalemite of royal stock who grew up near the palace, and this may explain his despair at the earthly institution of kingship. Micah, in contrast, grew up in a rural setting, outside of Jerusalem. Far removed from the harsh realities of royal life, he may have found it easier to believe in the glory of the House of David in his own time.

A century later, the elders of Jerusalem gathered outside the Temple, listening to Jeremiah's predictions of Jerusalem's destruction (Jer. 26). The people and the priests wanted to punish the prophet for his harsh words, but the elders recalled a prophet who had walked the streets of Jerusalem, Micah the Morasthite, whose threats had been sharper and more biting even than Isaiah's: "Assuredly, because of you,[2] Zion shall be plowed as a field, and Jerusalem shall become heaps of ruins, and the Temple Mount, a shrine in the woods" (Mic. 3:9–12). Not only had Hezekiah spared Micah, but he had actually listened to his words, and taken action to improve.[3] Interestingly, the elders made no mention of the prophet Isaiah.

A comparison of Isaiah and Micah reveals differences in the words of two true prophets of God, although they prophesied around the same time, on the same subject. These differences result in a fundamental argument, stemming from one study house, about the nature of the Messiah.

---

2. Due to bribery, corruption, injustice, and exploitation of the weak; the same can be seen in Isaiah 1. These words of Micah's immediately precede his vision of the end of days (Mic. 4), which corresponds to Isaiah 2.
3. See the discussion of Shebna in the chapter "Micah vs. Isaiah: For and Against the Rebellion."

ISAIAH 2 AND MICAH 4

The striking similarities between the prophecies of Isaiah and Micah, and the subtle differences between them, can be illustrated through a comparison of Isaiah 2:2–5 and Micah 4:1–4:

Isaiah	Micah
And it shall come to pass at the end of days -	And it shall come to pass at the end of days -
Rightly will the House of the Lord be established upon the mountaintops,	The House of the Lord will be rightly established upon the mountaintops,
and exalted above the hills,	And exalted will it be above the hills,
And all nations will stream towards it;	And peoples will stream towards it;
and many peoples will go and say:	and many peoples will go and say:
Come, let us go up to the mountain of the Lord,	Come, let us go up to the mountain of the Lord,
to the House of the God of Jacob,	And to the House of the God of Jacob.
And He will show us of His ways and we shall walk in His paths,	And He will show us of His ways and we shall walk in His paths,
For the Torah will come from Zion, and the word of the Lord from Jerusalem;	For the Torah will come from Zion, and the word of the Lord from Jerusalem;
And He shall judge among the nations,	And He shall judge among many peoples,
and reproach many peoples,	And He shall reproach mighty, distant nations,
And they shall beat their swords into plowshares,	And they shall beat their swords into plowshares,
and their spears into pruning hooks,	and their spears into pruning hooks,
nation shall not lift sword against nation,	nation shall not lift sword against nation,
nor shall they train for war anymore.	nor shall they train them for war anymore.
	And each shall dwell under his grapevine and under his fig tree with no fear,
	For the mouth of the Lord has spoken;`
O House of Jacob, let us go and walk in the light of the Lord!	For all nations shall each walk in the name of its god, and we shall walk in the name of the Lord our God forever!

An additional phrase at the end of the passage in Micah: "For all nations...and we shall walk in the name of the Lord our God," seems to correspond to Isaiah's expression: "Let us go and walk in the light of the Lord," although Micah's pronouncement is more specific. Both phrases describe Israel's uniqueness among the nations, and may be interpreted as referring to the time before the end of days, or to the end of days itself.

However, the verse in Micah that precedes this phrase is entirely absent from the passage in Isaiah: "And each shall dwell under his grapevine and under his fig tree." Isaiah fixed his prophetic gaze on a utopian future, far removed from the political reality of his time. Micah, on the other hand, presented a vision of the Messianic Age that could be fulfilled in his own time, a grounded, tangible conception of a kingdom dwelling in peace and security. This had been the reality in Solomon's day:

> And Judah and Israel dwelt in security, each under his grapevine and under his fig tree from Dan until Beersheba all the days of Solomon. (I Kings 5:5)

This shows that Micah's messianic vision was presented as politically feasible, rather than as a transcendental, heaven-on-earth dream. Micah referred to the "first kingdom" (Mic. 4:1), the days of David and Solomon, as a model for the present. He yearned to return to the days when one king ruled over all of Israel, when the kingdom's borders were extended on all sides, and all the nations witnessed the greatness of Israel. This difference in the prophets' outlooks is reinforced in the next section of Isaiah. Isaiah alluded to Solomon's downfall, which was caused by his many acquisitions, "Silver and gold, and there is no end to his treasures; and his land is filled with horses, and there is no end to his chariots; and his land is filled with idolatry, they bow down to his own handiwork, to that which his own fingers have crafted" (Is. 2:7–8).

A MORTAL'S SWORD OR "A SWORD, NOT MORTAL": BETWEEN PASSIVITY AND ACTIVITY

Isaiah trusted that God's hand would intervene:

> Go, my people, enter your chambers and shut the door behind you – Wait just a moment, until the wrath passes! (Is. 26:20)

Similarly,

> Indeed, O people in Zion, dwellers of Jerusalem, you shall not have cause to weep – He will grant you His favor at the sound of your cry; He will respond as soon as He hears it. My Lord will provide for you meager bread and scant water. (30:19–20)

Isaiah did not believe in active struggle against the enemy; salvation would come from Heaven:

> For behold, the Lord shall come forth from His place to punish the dwellers of the earth for their iniquity. (26:21)

In addition,

> As a lion and the young lion growls over its prey… So the Lord of Hosts will descend to make war against the mount and the hill of Zion. Like hovering birds, even so will the Lord of Hosts shield Jerusalem, shielding and saving, protecting and rescuing…Then Assyria shall fall, not by the sword of man; a sword, not mortal, shall devour him. He shall flee before the sword…Declares the Lord, who has a fire in Zion, who has an oven in Jerusalem. (31:4–9)

In contrast, Micah urged Israel to take an active stance against Assyria. Instead of fortifications and walls, he called for war, for a battle deep in enemy territory:

> Writhe and scream, Fair Zion, like a woman in travail! For now you must leave the city and dwell in the field – And you will reach Babylon, there you shall be saved, there the Lord will redeem you from the hands of your foes. (Mic. 4:9–10)

Moreover, Micah's use of the metaphor of childbirth, urging Zion to labor and give birth, sharply contrasts with a similar depiction in Isaiah, who emphasized woman's helplessness:

> Like a woman about to give birth, writhing and crying out in her pains, so we are before you, O Lord, we were with child, we writhed – It is as though we had given birth to wind; we have won no victory on earth. (Is. 26:17–18)

This simile is followed by Isaiah's bid to take refuge and hide until God, the all-powerful, avenges the enemy, striking the "Leviathan" and the "Dragons of the sea" with "His great, cruel, mighty sword" (27:1). When Hezekiah turned to Isaiah in desperation following Sennacherib's threat, he used similar words evoking the helplessness of women:

> This day is a day of distress, of chastisement, and of disgrace. The babes have reached the birthstool, but the strength to give birth is lacking. (37:3)

It is possible that Hezekiah first shared Micah's attitude, and then turned to Isaiah once he found himself trapped.

While Micah described the victory of Israel alone, certainly not through an alliance with Egypt, his use of childbirth imagery, when compared to Isaiah's, and later, Hezekiah's, hints at the heated debate that raged in Hezekiah's time concerning Israel's role in the crisis.

This is what Micah advised that Judah should do if the nations gather against her:

> Indeed, many nations have assembled against you who think, "Let our eye obscenely gaze on Zion." But they do not know the design of the Lord, they do not divine His intent: He has gathered them like cut grain to the threshing floor. Up and thresh, Fair Zion! For I will give you horns of iron and provide you with hoofs of bronze, and you will crush the many peoples. You will devote their riches to the Lord, their wealth

to the Lord of all the earth. Now marshal your troops, city of troops. (Mic. 4:11–14)

The imagery in these verses links strongly to David, the founder of the "first kingdom." Threshing the enemy with horns of iron and hoofs of bronze recalls David's war against Ammon as depicted in Samuel:

> David mustered all the troops and marched on Rabbah, and he attacked it and captured it...He led out the people who lived there and set them to work with saws, iron threshing boards, and iron axes, or assigned them to brickmaking; David did this to all the towns of Ammon. Then David and all the troops returned to Jerusalem. (II Sam. 12:29–31)

The beginning of chapter 5 of Micah certainly alludes to David:

> And you, O Bethlehem of Ephrath, least among the thousands of Judah, from you one shall come forth to rule Israel for Me – One whose origin is from of old, from ancient times. (Mic. 5:1)

This verse clearly refers to "David the son of this Ephratite man from Bethlehem of Judah" (I Sam. 17:12), the youngest of Jesse's sons, who was nonetheless victorious over Goliath, "A man of war since his youth," (17:33). As a result, David was appointed "an officer of a thousand," (18:13) becoming the youngest commander in Saul's general staff, or in the words of Micah, "Least among the thousands of Judah." Micah anticipated that such a figure would arise from David's descendants and lead the people into a new age.

This formulation is parallel to Isaiah's famous prophecy of "an off-shoot shall issue forth from the stump of Jesse" (Is. 11:1), only Micah's emphasis was not upon the new king being "bright-eyed and handsome" (I Sam. 16:12), which symbolized his God-given spirit of wisdom and understanding, but rather on his success in war. As Abigail stated, "For My lord has fought the Lord's wars" (I Sam. 25:28), and as David himself testified, "The God who has vindicated me, and made peoples subject to me" (II Sam. 22:48).

However, David's song in chapter 22 of II Samuel refers to both stages of his life. The first part of the song (22:1–29) discusses how God did not allow him to fall into the snare of Saul when David was helpless, and the second (22:30–51) describes the period when David's military power became legendary, "With Your help I can attack a troop of soldiers." It is this period that Micah referred to when he bid Zion to "marshal your troops, city of troops" (Mic. 4:14). Rather than representing two different periods, perhaps this song outlines two different perspectives, as epitomized by Isaiah and Micah.

MICAH'S AND ISAIAH'S PRAYERS FOR PEACE

Isaiah's and Micah's prayers for peace also differed. Both prophets spoke of the eradication of evil before the establishment of God's sovereignty on earth and universal peace. Isaiah described how evil would be wiped out by God's hand: "Lo! The Sovereign Lord of Hosts will hew off the tree-crowns with an ax" (Is. 10:33); "Then Assyria shall fall, not by the sword of man; a sword, not mortal, shall devour him" (31:8), while the Messiah's glory would come from God's spirit being upon him, and not from his military abilities.

Micah, on the other hand, described how war would pave the way to peace:

> And this shall achieve peace – Should Assyria invade our land and tread upon our fortresses, we will set up over it seven shepherds, eight princes of men, who will shepherd Assyria's land with swords, the land of Nimrod in its gates. Thus he will deliver from Assyria, should it invade our land, and should it trample our borders. (Mic. 5:4–5)

There is a chiastic structure here, which discusses how Assyria will fall, with the result being identical to Isaiah's prophecy: "And this shall achieve peace." However, where Isaiah anticipated that Assyria would fall by "a sword not mortal," Micah described its defeat by human sword.

Isaiah's vision speaks of God defeating the enemy, and of the Messiah judging with God's spirit resting upon him. Micah, however, saddles military responsibility on the Messiah; he must lead his army over hill and dale, through mountains and valleys, day and night, and through fire and ice. He must overcome the enemy with calculated strategy, brave tactics, and fierce battles, with a mortal sword, the sword of "princes" and "shepherds," all in the name of God.

Micah's interpretation of Isaiah's famous vision of the wolf dwelling with the lamb is particularly surprising:

> The remnant of Jacob shall be in the midst of the many peoples, like dew from the Lord, like droplets on grass – Which do not look to any man, nor place their hope in mortals. The remnant of Jacob shall be among the nations, in the midst of the many peoples, like a lion among beasts of the wild, like a young lion among flocks of sheep, which tramples wherever it goes and rends, with none to deliver. Your hand shall prevail over your foes, and all your enemies shall be cut down! (Mic. 5:6–8)

Isaiah described a utopian vision: "The wolf shall dwell with the lamb, the leopard lie down with the kid…the calf, the beast of prey, and the fatling together… And the lion, like the ox, shall eat straw." Micah, on the other hand, spoke of a young lion stalking about the flock, trampling and consuming the sheep. Isaiah classically compared the nations to preying lions (for example Is. 5:29–30), while Israel is likened to God's helpless, dependent lamb. Micah used the same metaphor, but reversed its meanings; Judah was the predator, "Judah is a lion cub," and the nations of the world were his prey, "sheep to be eaten" (Ps. 44:12), "sheep for slaughter" (44:23), and there was "none to deliver!"

When Isaiah used the image of a lion roaring and saving Israel, the lion represented God, and not the Messiah:

> As a lion and the young lion growls over its prey and, when the shepherds gather in force against him, is not dismayed by their

cries nor cowed by their noise – So the Lord of Hosts will descend to make war against the mount and the hill of Zion. (Is. 31:4)

ISAIAH AND MICAH'S DISPUTE REFLECTED IN MEDIEVAL PHILOSOPHY

The two prophets' different perceptions of the Messiah and the redemption process developed into a fundamental argument which endures until today. Two notable medieval proponents in this dispute are Maimonides and Rabbi Abraham ben David of Provence (Ravad). Maimonides is a strong proponent of Micah's approach, and even quotes Micah's prophecies in his writings:

> The Messiah king will arise in the future and restore the Davidic Kingdom to its former state and original sovereignty. He will build the Sanctuary and gather the dispersed of Israel. All the laws will be reinstituted in his days as they had been in former years; sacrifices will be offered, and the Sabbatical years and Jubilee years will be observed fully as ordained by the Torah. Anyone who does not believe in him, or whoever does not look forward to his coming, denies not only the other prophets but the Torah and Moses our teacher. For the Torah attested to him, as it is said, "God, your God, will return your captivity." These words, explicitly stated in the Torah, include all such statements made by all the prophets….Do not think that the Messiah king will have to perform signs and wonders and bring about novel things in the world, or resurrect the dead, and other such things. It is not so. This is seen from the fact that Rabbi Akiva was a great sage, of the sages of the Mishna, and he was an armor-bearer of King Ben Koziba and said of him that he is the Messiah king. [R. Akiva] and all the wise men of his generation considered him to be the Messiah king until [Ben Koziba] was killed because of sins, and when he was killed they realized that he was not; but the sages had not asked him for any sign or wonder. The essence of all this is that this Torah [of ours], its statutes and its laws, are forever and all eternity, and nothing is to be added to them or diminished from them. (*Mishneh Torah*, Laws of Kings 11)

The Ravad counters Maimonides' argument:

> Didn't Ben Koziba say – I am the Messiah king, and the sages went to check him, if he could "scent the truth" or not. And because he could not – he was killed [by the enemy]. (Ravad ad loc., citing Sanhedrin 93b)

The expression "if he had the proper scent," corresponds to Isaiah's phrasing, "And he shall scent the truth by his reverence for the Lord ... thus he will judge the poor with equity" (11:3). Not only does the Ravad disagree with Maimonides' perception of Ben Koziba (Bar Kokhba) as the Messiah, but he is also opposed to his portrayal of the Messiah in general, for Ravad contends that if the person in question does not meet Isaiah's description, then he cannot be the Messiah. This also transpires from the dispute on the meaning of "and the wolf shall dwell with the lamb" (in Laws of Kings 12), as well as other places where Ravad disagrees with Maimonides' interpretation.[4]

THE INGATHERING OF EXILES OR THE MESSIAH: WHICH COMES FIRST?

If his prophecies follow chronological order, then Isaiah envisioned that an ingathering of exiles would *follow* God's appointment of the Messiah in Jerusalem:

> On that day, the stock of Jesse that has remained standing shall become a standard to peoples – Nations shall seek his counsel and his abode shall be honored. On that day, My Lord will apply His hand again to redeeming the remainder of His people from Assyria and from Egypt, Pathros, Nubia, Elam, Shinar, Hamath, and the coastlands. He will hold up a signal to the nations and

---

4. See Ravad's approach in chapter 6 of Laws of the Temple regarding the sanctity of the Temple Mount, which "in the future will change and become eternally sacred in God's glory forever." Maimonides defines the future Temple's sanctity as a return to the sanctity of the days of David and Solomon.

assemble the banished of Israel, and gather the dispersed of Judah from the four corners of the earth. (Is. 11:10–12)

Jeremiah's optimistic prophecies in Josiah's day (Jer. 3, 6, 31, 33), however, described the ingathering of the exiles, and only mentioned the regrowth of the Davidic dynasty at the end of chapter 33.

Ezekiel's prophecies (Ezek. 36–37) also began with a description of the ingathering of the exiles, and only then mention the branch of Ephraim, the branch of Judah, and their fusion into a single kingdom under one king: "My servant David," who will be "a prince over them forever" (37:24–25).

This indicates a dispute regarding the order of the redemption process; will the Messiah appear before the ingathering of the exiles, or will Israel's dispersed come back to their homeland before the Messiah's reign begins?

Maimonides (*Mishneh Torah*, Laws of Kings 11:1, 4) writes that the Messiah will gather Israel's dispersed once his kingdom becomes strong, in accordance with the order of Isaiah's prophecies. Nonetheless, he admits that the precise process of redemption is unknown, because: "These matters are undefined in the Prophets" (*Mishneh Torah*, Laws of Kings 12:2) and will only be clarified during the redemption itself.

In contrast, in the *Amida* prayer, the blessing of ingathering the exiles precedes the blessing for the restoration of justice, the calling of Israel's enemies into account, the blessing for the righteous, and the blessing for the rebuilding of Jerusalem. Only after these blessings, the blessing for "the offshoot of David" is recited; a passage which echoes the language of Jeremiah 33. Both the Talmud Bavli (Megilla 17b) and the Yerushalmi (Y. Berakhot 5a) explicitly state that the order of the blessings in the *Amida* prayer anticipates the stages of the redemption process.

The dispute reflects the differences between the prophets of Israel. According to Isaiah, God's kingship in the world is the most critical part of the revolution, and will ultimately lead to the resolution of all the world's problems, through justice, righteousness and the ingathering of the exiles. According to Jeremiah and Ezekiel, earthly leadership must operate within the confines of reality; the redemption process will begin with the ingathering of exiles, and culminate with the rise of a new king, of David's seed, upon the throne.

THE NATURE OF THE MESSIAH IN
THE PROPHETS AND SAGES

The prophets of Israel painted two different portraits of the Messiah king.

According to one opinion, the king will be God's instrument, channeling the divine will, but will not taking an active role in the redemption process. The prophet Zechariah declared, "And I Myself – declares the Lord – will be a wall of fire all around it" (Zech. 2:9). One of the sages interpreted this verse thus:

> R. Yitzḥak Napaḥa said...The Holy One, Blessed be He, said, I ignited a fire in Zion, as it says, "And a fire will be ignited in Zion, and consume its foundations" (Lam. 4:11), and in the future, I will rebuild it with fire." (Bava Kamma 60b)

According to this approach, the ingathering of exiles and the messianic wars will not be led by the Messiah; rather, like at the exodus from Egypt and the splitting of the sea, they will be led by a sword not mortal, "The Lord will fight for you, and you shall be silent" (Ex. 14:14).

Isaiah emphasized human insignificance as part of his criticism of earthly monarchy (Is. 2:7–11), and expressed his disappointment in humanity and human government in particular: "Cease to glorify man, who has but breath in his nostrils" (2:22). Accordingly, Isaiah's Messiah of chapter 11 has no significance as an individual; he is but a vessel for God's will. He will rule with justice derived not of his own common sense, not "by what his eyes behold," but through his "reverence for the Lord." In this spirit, the descriptions of drastic changes in animal nature may be read in a literal sense, as redemption is presented in supernatural terms. Moreover, this view illuminates Isaiah's warning against rebellion or surrender to foreign armies; human believers were to sit wait for God to strike the enemy with his "great, cruel, mighty sword" (26:20–27:1).

The other view of messianic kingship dictates that the king will have earthly, practical, political significance, although the king of Israel is unique among other world leaders according to the kabbalistic principle that he does not conquer and rule for his own glory, rather he represents the majesty of all Israel. The sages expressed this view in the Mishna (Sanhedrin 2), saying that the king may not leave his palace to join a funeral procession, even if a close family member has died. He is not an individual, but belongs to the people. Similarly, the sages dictate that a king may not sacrifice his honor, because honor and dignity are an integral part of majesty, which the wicked fear (Ketubbot 17a). In contrast, Torah scholars may suffer indignity, because God Himself descended in order to lead the Children of Israel out of Egypt, thereby sacrificing His honor.

The difference between the two approaches is tremendous. The first does not expect anything of human rule. When God decides to redeem the world, He will transform the natural order at its very core in order to achieve perfection. According to the second approach, however, the redemption process will maintain natural order, and humans will play a conscious role in fulfilling God's plan.

Surprisingly, the democratic system of government reflects the Isaian unwillingness to depend upon humanity and its shortcomings. This system prevents any individual (or royal dynasty) from seizing power for an extended period of time, subjects the ruler to constant scrutiny and criticism, and requires periodic replacement of the government in an attempt to reduce corruption.[5]

THE MESSIAH IN ISAIAH 11

Isaiah's vision in chapter 2 makes no mention of human rule, while chapter 11 opens with the prediction of "an offshoot shall issue forth from the stump of Jesse." Nonetheless, in both prophecies, earthly kingship is presented in a negative light, and the prophet places his hopes in heavenly rule. His vision of the end of days is comparable to the period of

5. See Yoel Bin-Nun, "A Conceptual Basis for a Democratic Regime according to the Torah," in *The Jewishness of Israel*, ed. Y. Stern and A. Ravitzky (Jerusalem: Israel Democracy Institute, 2007), 72–73 [Hebrew].

Solomon, when an ideal state was almost achieved, but the dream was thwarted as a result of Solomon's accumulation of wealth and horses, which led him astray. Chapter 11 expresses the hope that the utopian state will be reached as part of the redemption process.

The prophecy avoids referring to this "offshoot" as a king, and rather presents him as a "judge." This promotes a more ethically-based government than a monarchy, where the ruler is not a king in his own right but rather a judge, an instrument of God's majesty in the world. This ideal leadership is aptly expressed in the words of the judge Gideon, "I will not rule over you myself, nor shall my son rule over you; the Lord alone shall rule over you" (Judges 8:23).

The Davidic dynasty is, however, inherently different from a system of judges, as the former is based on a divine promise of eternal kingship. Isaiah's vision of the Messiah as a judge implies that the dynasty has no value in and of itself, but rather derives its power from above. He calls for an earthly leader who represents the King of the World, and who rules in the name of God.

Maimonides interprets Isaiah's vision in a real political sense, tellingly including his discussion of the Messianic Age in his Laws of Kings:

> One is not to presume that anything of the ways of the world will be set aside in the Messianic Age, nor that there will be any innovation in the order of creation; rather, the world will continue according to its norms. As for what is said in Isaiah, that "The wolf will dwell with the sheep and the leopard will lie down with the kid," this is an allegory and metaphor. It means that Israel shall dwell securely alongside the wicked heathens who are likened to wolves and leopards. (*Mishneh Torah*, Laws of Kings 12:1)

The Ravad challenges this view by bringing the verse from Leviticus: "I shall give the land respite from wild beasts" (26:6). In his opinion, this is proof that the end of days will bring about a change to the natural order, rather than maintaining the "ways of the world." This verse is the subject of a related argument between two tannaitic sages, R. Yehuda and R. Shimon:

R. Yehuda says, He shall remove [wild beasts] from the world;
R. Shimon says, He shall make them harmless, and R. Shimon
said: Which is greater praise for the Omnipresent – when there
are no perils, or when there are perils but they cause no harm?
When there are perils but they cause no harm, and He thus says
a Psalm for the Sabbath Day, in order to put an end to perils in
the world – to cause them to become harmless. (Sifra, *Parashat
Beḥukkotai* 1:2)

R. Yehuda interprets the text on a literal level; God's promise to remove
the wild beasts from the land means that He will eradicate them from
the world. This reading does not satisfy R. Shimon b. Yoḥai; he desires
the actual rectification of animal nature, and the eradication of evil
itself. He claims that God will change the nature of wild beasts so that
they will no longer be harmful. Evil will not truly be eradicated until it
is transformed into good.

The Ravad's views reflect R. Shimon's approach, while Maimonides follows R. Yehuda's reading. As we have seen, Maimonides and
Ravad were similarly divided with regard to Bar Kokhba:

Do not think that the Messiah king will have to perform signs and
wonders and bring about novel things in the world, or resurrect
the dead, and other such things. It is not so. This is seen from the
fact that Rabbi Akiva was a great sage, of the sages of the Mishna,
and he was an armor-bearer of King Ben Koziba and said of him
that he is the Messiah king. (*Mishneh Torah*, Laws of Kings, 11:3)

As mentioned earlier, the Ravad contests this: "Didn't Ben Koziba
say – I am the Messiah king, and the sages went to check him, if he
had 'the proper scent,' or not. And because he did not – he was killed
by enemies." The Ravad claims that Bar Kokhba did not meet Isaiah's
description of the Messiah because he did not have "the proper scent."
He was not able to "sense the truth through his reverence for God"
(Is. 11:3), therefore he could not have been the Messiah. Maimonides,
however, does not read Isaiah's prophecy in its literal sense, but rather
as a metaphor; in the Messianic Age, there will be no more wars. The

Ravad's philosophy is in line with Isaiah's anticipation of a cosmic revolution brought about by God's hand, "And the wolf shall [literally] dwell with the lamb."

Nevertheless, in our day, wild beasts pose little threat to humanity. In fact, countless laws have been instituted to protect the lions, tigers, bears, and wolves from human evil. Today, it is humans who pose the greatest threat to each other. Humans wreak destruction, violence, and devastation, while God's glory and truth seem very far away. It seems that the "ways of the world" really have been set aside.

The messianic vision of chapter 11 seems to be built upon the utopian prophecy of chapter 2, lending support to Maimonides' interpretation. From the parallels we have shown, the description of "the wolf shall dwell with the lamb" (11:6) corresponds to and develops the pacifist vision of: "And they shall beat their swords into plowshares, and their spears into pruning hooks, nation shall not lift sword against nation, nor shall they train for war anymore" (2:4). Isaiah's pronouncement that: "There shall be no evil committed, nor destruction, in all My holy mountain" (11:9), completes the vision of all nations streaming towards the mountain of God in chapter 2.

Thus Isaiah's prophecies anticipate an ideological and political revolution. Yet his vision seems far more distant and complex than the modern miracles of our day, such as the mapping and modification of the intricacies of the human genome, and of nature itself.

At the very end of his *Mishneh Torah*, Maimonides himself depicts the Messiah as a re-embodiment of David, a true and God-fearing leader, who will bring Israel and the world back to the golden era of Solomon:

> The sages and the prophets did not long for the Messianic Age so that they may rule over the whole world or dominate the heathens, nor to be exalted by the nations, nor in order that they may eat, drink and be merry; but only to be free for the Torah and its wisdom, without anyone to oppress and disturb them, so that they may merit the life of the World to Come ... In that era there will be neither famine nor war, neither envy nor strife, because good will emanate in abundance and all delightful things will be common as dust. The one preoccupation of the entire world

will be solely to know God. The Israelites, therefore, will be great sages and know the hidden matters, and they will attain knowledge of their Creator to the extent of human capacity, as it is said, "The earth shall be full with the knowledge of God as the waters cover the sea!" (Is. 11:9). (*Mishneh Torah*, Laws of Kings 12:4–5)

Timeline According to the Commonly Accepted Chronology

Year BCE	Judah	Israel	Assyria and Local Nations
750	The Days of Uzziah – Power and prosperity; the beginning of Isaiah's prophetic reproach and warning	Jeroboam son of Joash – Regional power; the prophecies of Amos and the beginning of Hosea	Assyria is weak; Aram is under Israelite rule; Judah's borders reach as far as Egypt
745	Continuing prosperity – Jotham begins ruling under his father as crown prince (?)	Jeroboam's death and the end of the Jehu dynasty; civil war in Gilead and Samaria	Tiglath-Pileser III of Assyria ascends the throne, begins his military campaigning
738	Uzziah's leprosy (?) – officers from Judah begin infiltrating Ephraimite borders	Menahem son of Gadi – Assyria demands a heavy fine, which is exacted from the people	A local alliance (possibly including Uzziah) gathers against Assyria in a futile effort to cut Assyria off in northern Aram

Year BCE	Judah	Israel	Assyria and Local Nations
734	The Days of Ahaz – Judah is under attack on every front (Rezin-Pekah and the Philistines); Isaiah confronts Ahaz in a prophetic attempt to influence his political decisions	Pekah and the Gileadites seize power in Samaria; Pekah rebels against Assyria and attacks Ahaz, reaching Jerusalem	Rezin of Aram seizes power in Damascus; forms an alliance with Pekah; conquers from the Gilead to Eilat
733	Ahaz in despair, refuses to listen to Isaiah; surrenders and pays tribute to the "savior," Assyria	The people oppose the leading of prisoners from Judah to Israel	Tiglath-Pileser conquers the Phoenician coast
732	Jerusalem becomes an Assyrian province; adopts Assyrian culture and religion	The beginning of exile – from the Gilead and the Galilee; Pekah is assassinated and Assyria rules	Damascus is conquered by Assyria and Rezin is assassinated; Tiglath-Pileser rules over Aram and Israel
727–726	Ahaz dies, Hezekiah reigns – God is worshiped once again	Alliance with Egypt in attempt to shake off Assyria's yoke	Tiglath-Pileser's death; hope that the empire will fall
724	Jerusalem is purified from Ahaz's abominations	Samaria is besieged for three years	Shalmaneser besieges Samaria
721	Samarians flee to Jerusalem; the city is expanded (?)	Destruction of Samaria; exile of 27,000 of its people	Shalmaneser dies; his successor Sargon exiles Samaria and brings people from Kut to settle in Samaria

Year BCE	Judah	Israel	Assyria and Local Nations
715	Passover is celebrated in Jerusalem together with the remaining Israelites after postponing celebrations by a month; Hezekiah is appointed king over a reunited Israel; the years of his reign are counted anew from this point	The "Kutim" continue worshiping at the Beit El temple; the remnant of the Israelite tribes flee to Jerusalem	Sargon's campaigns to Philistia (from 717 BCE); the Ashdod rebellion; a new capital is erected in Dur-Sharrukin in a pro-Babylonian spirit
713–711	Fear of the Tartan, which then subsides; Isaiah walks "naked and barefoot" in protest against joining the rebellion against Assyria		The Tartan is sent to halt the Ashdod rebellion; Sargon himself comes to destroy Ashdod following its repeated rebellion; the "Black Pharaohs" hand over the chief rebel
712	Hezekiah's illness – Isaiah prophesies his death, the king prays to God; God extends his life by 15 years and promises that Jerusalem will be saved; Merodach-Baladan's delegates are received warmly by Hezekiah after his recovery; Isaiah's prophetic wrath at Hezekiah's reception of the delegates		Merodach-Baladan leads Babylonia in a rebellion against Assyria (from 720 BCE)
710	Growing tension between Isaiah and Hezekiah		Sargon suppresses Babylonia and Merodach-Baladan escapes to Elam

Year BCE	Judah	Israel	Assyria and Local Nations
705–701	The fortification of Jerusalem and the building of Hezekiah's tunnel in anticipation of siege; Hezekiah accepts Isaiah and Micah's social criticism and makes changes in his government; Hezekiah joins the alliance against Assyria and sends delegates to Egypt		Sargon falls in battle, his body is never recovered – Assyria undergoes major changes with Sennacherib's ascent to power; religious reform, a return to Assyrian worship and relocation of the capital city back to Nineveh
701	Hezekiah surrenders to Sennacherib during the siege of Lachish; the Rabshakeh's delegation to Jerusalem; Hezekiah begs Isaiah to pray for the city; Jerusalem is miraculously saved		Sennacherib's campaign to Judah – the fall of Azeka, Lachish and the Shephelah; Taharqa's army fails to stop Assyria; the Assyrian army is struck by a plague and Jerusalem is saved; Sennacherib returns to Nineveh and boasts of his destruction of Lachish
697	Judah in mourning – no song of thanksgiving; Hezekiah dies and 12 year old Manasseh ascends the throne; return to Ahaz's policy: Jerusalem worships Assyrian gods		Sennacherib's conquest and humiliation of Babylonia (689 BCE); extensive building in Nineveh; Sennacherib's murder at the hand of his sons (681 BCE); Esarhaddon rises to power

The fonts used in this book are from the Arno family

Other books in the
Maggid Studies in Tanakh series:

Genesis: From Creation to Covenant
Zvi Grumet

Joshua: The Challenge of the Promised Land
Michael Hattin

Judges (forthcoming)
Michael Hattin

I Kings: Torn in Two
Alex Israel

II Kings: In a Whirlwind
Alex Israel

Jeremiah: The Fate of a Prophet
Binyamin Lau

Ezekiel: From Destruction to Restoration
Tova Ganzel

Jonah: The Reluctant Prophet
Erica Brown

Nahum, Habakkuk, and Zephaniah: Lights in the Valley
Yaakov Beasley

Haggai, Zechariah, and Malachi: Prophecy in an Age of Uncertainty
Hayyim Angel

Ruth: From Alienation to Monarchy
Yael Ziegler

Lamentations (forthcoming)
Yael Ziegler

Esther: Power, Fate, and Fragility in Exile
Erica Brown

Nehemiah: Statesman and Sage
Dov S. Zakheim

Maggid Books
The best of contemporary Jewish thought from
Koren Publishers Jerusalem Ltd.